Developing a Language

within the Key Stage 2 Curriculum

Developing a Leadership Role within the Key Stage 2 Curriculum

A Handbook for Students and Newly Qualified Teachers

Edited by

Mike Harrison

The Falmer Press

(A member of the Taylor & Francis Group)

London • Washington, D.C.

UK   The Falmer Press, 4 John Street, London WC1N 2ET
USA   The Falmer Press, Taylor & Francis Inc., 1900 Frost Road, Suite 101, Bristol, PA 19007

First published in 1995

A catalogue record for this book is available from the British Library

Library of Congress Cataloging-in-Publication Data are available on request

ISBN 0 7507 0424 1 cased
ISBN 0 7507 0425 x paper

Jacket design by Caroline Archer

Typeset in 10/12 pt Bembo by
Graphicraft Typesetters Ltd., Hong Kong.

Printed in Great Britain by Burgess Science Press, Basingstoke on paper which has a specified pH value on final paper manufacture of not less than 7.5 and is therefore 'acid free'.

Contents

Contents

Editor's Introduction

Since 1989 all initial teacher education courses in England and Wales have had to prepare primary teacher training students to be ready, when qualified, to take on the role of leading other teaching staff in a specialist subject area. In my experience, many students pay little heed to this element of their course, having talked to staff and headteachers in schools who say that taking on such responsibility is not a suitable role for those straight out of college. The main task of a new entrant to the profession is to perfect the basic classroom teaching skills of which only the foundations have been laid in their initial training. Recent evidence shows the attention which has to be paid to developing the newly qualified if they are to become successful teachers. *The New Teacher In School* (OFSTED, 1992) points out that 'a high proportion of unsatisfactory teachers experienced poor induction in their schools. Their professional needs had not been clearly identified by senior staff.' On this most of the profession agree. Yet these same students, when applying for teaching posts, specified I suspect by the very same headteachers, find they need to write CVs which show that they have the drive, ability and knowledge to lead and coordinate a subject in the primary curriculum — just in order to get an interview!

> School Teachers' Pay and Conditions Document 1988
>
> 11 (b) coordinating or managing the work of other teachers.
> (c) taking such part as may be required of him in the review, development and management of activities relating to the curriculum, organisation and pastoral functions of the school'

Such job descriptions can be daunting to read. Many headteachers, despite their knowledge of the priorities for teachers in their first few years of teaching, describe all the school's coordination roles equally in order to give the same emphasis to all subjects. Our profession is unique in this. There would be public concern if newly qualified accountants were routinely given the most difficult tax cases, junior doctors required to work alone with the patients with exotic complications and barristers the headline murder cases. Yet our newly qualified teachers are often given jobs in the less desirable schools and in those schools are often assigned to the classes left after the sitting tenants have had their pick. They are then asked to pick up the co-ordination areas which no-one else wants.

This book sets out to help students and newly qualified teachers to make sense of the roles they are asked to play and to develop techniques to begin a process which over a number of years will lead them to be able to take on managerial responsibility for the quality of work in specified areas of primary school life. In addition, it is recognized that these same teachers will find a need to increase their own subject knowledge and gain familiarity with the national curriculum definition of their subject. This book has been written so that by reading and working on its themes new teachers will be able to begin to establish clear policies for coordinating work amongst their colleagues in their schools.

Specialist writers who are primary practitioners have assembled the knowledge, skills and actions needed to be an effective curriculum leader in each of the subjects in the national curriculum. Newly qualified teachers and students preparing themselves for their first post, faced with the responsibility of leading these specialist areas, will find these chapters particularly useful.

The opening chapter is for all. It will help readers to begin thinking about the role of the coordinator and it will give guidance on how to become a strong influence in school.

References

OFSTED (1992) *The New Teacher in School*, London, OFSTED.
DFE (1988) School Teachers' Pay and Conditions London, HMSO.

Chapter 1

Developing the Skills to become an Effective Key Stage 2 Subject Coordinator

Mike Harrison

Effective curriculum coordinators have a significant opportunity to improve children's learning in their schools. The challenge of working with colleagues to produce an effective programme in any subject area is one which will contribute to personal development and enhance the image of the profession.

That primary teachers need support does not seem to be in doubt. The extent of the need for consultants and/or specialist support at Key Stage

> On learning that a curriculum development role (dealing with adults) is expected of you fear may be the predominant feeling. 'It may result in a temporary questioning of ability and suitability for leadership, throwing up all manner of doubts and insecurities.'
>
> Day *et al.* 1993: 26

2, however, is a matter for debate (Harrison, 1994a) and is likely to be so for the foreseeable future. Alexander, Rose and Woodhead in their 1992 report, *Curriculum Organisation and Classroom Practice in Primary Schools*, sought to stimulate a debate in primary schools about this role. They set out four roles that teachers might adopt.

- **The generalist** teaches most or all of the curriculum, probably specializing in an age–range rather than a subject and does not profess specialist subject knowledge for consultancy.
- **The generalist/consultant** combines a generalist role in part of the curriculum with cross-school coordination, advice and support in one or more subjects.
- **The semi-specialist** teaches his or her subject, but who also has a generalist or consultancy role.
- **The specialist** teaches his or her subject full time (as in the case of music in some primary schools).

(Alexander, Rose and Woodhead, 1992: para 146)

1

The second follow-up paper (OFSTED, 1994) to the three wise men report strengthened the definition of the generalist/consultant role described above, which is the one largely adopted by primary schools.

> In all but the smallest primary schools, headteachers are able to delegate the management of particular subjects to individual members of staff. . . . teachers who are subject managers for the whole school (coordinators is too limited a description) can be expected; a) to develop a clear view of the nature of their subject and its contribution to the wider curriculum of the school; b) to provide advice and documentation to help teachers teach the subject and interrelate its constituent elements; and (c) to play a major part in organising the teaching and the resources of the subjects so that statutory requirements are covered (para 37).

The key to quality in primary education lies in the skills of the class teacher (see, for example, Wragg's (1993) excellent report on the Leverhulme Primary Teaching Skills Project). Indeed, David McNamara (1994) argues that, 'at the heart of educational process lies the teacher', and all tasks other than imparting subject knowledge are merely a distraction for her. In Professor McNamara's *Classroom Pedagogy and Primary Practice*, a book of 145 pages arguing the primacy of teaching and teachers, no mention of curriculum coordination is made. Steve Harrison and Ken Theaker (1989) acknowledge that the role of the classteacher is at the very heart of British primary education. At its best, 'it concerns itself with the whole child . . . provides for secure relationships and covers all aspects of a child's development' (p. 5). However, the increasing complexity of the primary curriculum and society's expectations makes it difficult for the teacher to keep up to date. Within traditional subject areas there has been an explosion of knowledge and new fields such as science, technology, design, problem solving and health education – not to mention the uses of computers – are now considered entitlements for primary children. Furthermore, we now expect all children to succeed at these studies – not just the fortunate few who passed the 11+ (Harrison, 1994b). 'We have learned that we are no longer prepared to accept an education service in which only a minority prosper' (Barber, 1994).

All this has overwhelmed a teaching system largely unchanged since the inception of primary schools after the Second World War. For children to be

> **What you can do:**
> - articulate your feelings about your doubts;
> - accept that this is a challenge;
> - declare your need for a clear definition of what is expected of you;
> - allow yourself to be less than perfect.

inducted into some of this knowledge, without the use of specialist teachers, who, many of us believe, would damage the very nature of primary education, we need to exploit the talents of those within schools in a process of mutual support. As Harrison and Theaker point out, 'a great deal of enthusiasm and expertise in specific curriculum areas has been locked into individual classrooms. It is only when we share knowledge and skills that the true potential of the professional teacher is realised' (p. 5).

How can curriculum development (and by implication improvement in teaching) come about? It does not appear to be high on the list of ways in which headteachers spend their time. Blease and Lever (1992) examined the detailed diaries kept by twenty-five primary headteachers. They comment, 'None of the evidence supports the view that the headteacher fulfils the role of curriculum developer whilst the school is in session. There is little to suggest this takes place out of school either' (p. 193). By contrast however, Campbell and Neill (1994) show that by 1991 nearly nine out of every ten primary class teachers had such responsibility, and the average number of subjects each was between 1.5 and 2.2 (depending on the size of school). As a coordinator you are being asked, therefore, to join in a team, sharing your talents and expertise with your new teaching colleagues. You may see this as an exchange. As a new entrant to teaching you will find yourself continually asking questions. You will hear yourself asking daily about ordering stock, handling parents' evenings, the school's procedures, times, dates and practices. You **do** have something to offer in exchange – though you may not realize it. For example, your initial training in the use of computers possibly amounts to more than the training received by the rest of the staff put together. Your work in science or in methods to teach reading will possibly be far more up to date than many other teachers with whom you are working. The fact that you have recently been in as many as four different schools, examined their teaching and learning policies, have seen teachers' many different methods of organizing their classrooms, witnessed whole-school discipline practices and the ways in which children's special needs were met or the ways text-books are used. You **do** have a contribution to make. The discussions you had with your tutors and fellow students about their experiences will equip you to discuss educational issues with your new colleagues. This is, of course, not to deny that you still have much to learn and many skills still to develop, but the task before you is not impossible.

The jobs associated with being a subject coordinator are described in many ways. Webb's (1994) research shows that 'the amount and nature of the work fulfilled by coordinators varied enormously from school to school, and often between coordinators in the same school' (para 5.9). It may safely be assumed that there will be an even wider variation in the aspects of the role which a newly qualified member of the profession can or should play.

Here are two jobs as advertised in one week in the *Times Educational Supplement*:

> Required a newly qualified re-
> ception class teacher. Candidates
> should possess a sound philo-
> sophy of education based on a
> child-centred approach within a
> well-organised, aesthetically
> stimulating classroom structure.
> We seek an excellent teacher
> who can demonstrate an affinity
> with reception age children. Ex-
> perience in and enthusiasm for
> the following curriculum areas
> would be an advantage: English,
> Art and design, Music.

> Required for this expanding
> urban primary school, an enthu-
> siastic, flexible, well qualified
> teacher to promote technology
> and related areas throughout the
> school. You should have wide
> curricular interests including
> possibly games. Newly qualified
> . . . full-time permanent post at
> KS 2.

Such descriptions indicate expectations, give a clue to the range of responsibility and help applicants to get a feel for the environment in which they
would be working. They do not usually specify the way in which results may
be achieved. We argue that this has to be done by teachers working together
and agreeing on the basis for changes they want to make. Curriculum coordinators are the means for promoting and implementing these agreed changes
and monitoring their development. Webb found that some schools had set up
whole-school discussions to clarify the work, purposes and priorities of coordinators, and if they received non-contact time to decide how best it might
be used.

One way for newly qualified teachers (NQTs) to make sense of all this
is to look for the *givens* in their situation and then later consider the range of
choices with which one is left. To paraphrase a popular saying: we all need
the forbearance to put up with those things we cannot change, the skills to
alter for the good those things we can, and most importantly, the wisdom to
know the difference between the two.

The Givens

In his influential work *Management Teams: Why they Succeed or Fail*, Meridith
Belbin (1981) shows that a successful team needs people with specific skills,
knowledge, aptitudes, interests and personalities which interlock in order to
make a workable organization. You have to accept that part of what you are
given is the presence or absence of such ideally interlocking personalities. You
must also appreciate that the head, who, to newly qualified staff may appear
all knowing and all powerful, also has to suffer the same mix of personalities. He or she has probably inherited staff she would not have chosen her-
self. Those appointed ten years ago were selected to fit the situation of that

time. Now new skills and attitudes are needed, but not everyone can change so easily. Therefore, the first of the givens is the nature of your teacher colleagues. You have to work with them and appreciate that however enthusiastic you are about your proposals, coordination, like politics, is the art of the possible.

Teams of all sorts need leaders. Recent research has shown that the quality of the leadership of the head is probably the most important single factor in the effectiveness of the school (Mortimore *et al.*, 1988). Remember your headteacher (the second given) has chosen you and may have a great deal of hope pinned on your contribution to the school. He or she deserves your support and help and in turn you will deserve his or hers.

The third great area of givens is the particular culture of management which you will find in the school. What is expected of you as a coordinator will be better understood by thinking about whole-school issues than trying to fathom the import of words written on a job description, which really only serves any purpose in times of dispute. When the going gets tough the tough reach for their job descriptions! In *The Developing School* Peter Holly and Geoff Southworth (1989) discuss several whole-school concerns which will affect the work of subject coordinators. They show that teachers need to be receptive to a collaborative approach and to respect and acknowledge curriculum expertise from within their own ranks. Such an ethos goes hand-in-hand with an enabling and supportive structure where job descriptions are not highly prescriptive – leaving little room for individual enterprise and initiative. Ideally NQTs should see that their own job specifications show that the school has different expectations of a newly appointed coordinator than from one who has been in post for some time. To make any system work managerial responsibility and support for the coordination of the coordinators must be made explicit. Heads have to monitor their work as managers and offer guidance at critical times.

Time available for curriculum coordinators to do the paperwork will affect the degree of consultation possible and hence its quality. Time for coordinators to work alongside teachers in their classrooms will be necessary in order to change practice. Time to allow curriculum coordinators to see teaching and learning in parts of the school with which he or she is unfamiliar will be required for staff development. You may find headteachers agreeing with these sentiments but can still provide you with little or no non-contact time to allow you to do your work. In this case it will be necessary for you to

A study of the practice of Mathematics coordination in primary and middle schools investigated how time was created for these teachers to undertake their roles effectively.

'Time during the school day was usually made available . . . through headteacher, part-time or floating teacher cover. Other ways . . . included supply and peripatetic teacher cover, student teachers cover, exchange and doubling up of classes.'

Stow and Foxman (1988)

consider just how much personal time you need to devote to this role and how much to your task of providing for the children in your class. Campbell and Neill (1994) show that, above the directed time of thirty-three hours per week, teachers generally believe it is reasonable to spend an additional nine hours per week on professional tasks. However, this research of teachers' work from four differently selected cohorts of schools, each using different sampling methods shows that they appear to have been spending a total of fifty-two hours per week in 1991. Thus, conscious decisions about how long to spend on each aspect of your workload need to be taken before you can sensibly plan the extent of your coordination activity.

The school has to actively promote acceptance that the nature of this devolved responsibility implies emphasis upon managerial skill as well as upon curriculum expertise. Thus teachers selected to become curriculum coordinators will need to develop skills in areas such as the implementation of change, curriculum planning, evaluation and school development, in addition to attending subject based courses.

> **Activity 1**
> Consider each of these points as they may apply to your school. Discuss with your headteacher or in-school mentor the validity of these statements as indicators of the strength of an effective coordination system. How do such issues define what is expected of you?

Harrison and Gill (1992) set out to show that the degree to which any particular primary school has developed such policies may be indicated by:

- the nature of the decisions curriculum coordinators feel confident in making without recourse to the Head;
- the mechanisms by which the work of coordinators is monitored;
- the choice of particular teachers to be coordinators and the way they are managed;
- the strength of the systems in place to support coordinators (for example, class release time, training).
- whether coordinators are respected as models of good practice in their specialist areas;
- the ways in which coordinators are encouraged to learn personnel management skills from one another;
- the degree to which coordinators are able to work in harmony with the school's stated aims.

Making it Work for You

The importance of understanding and working with the culture of the school will recur again and again in the following chapters. Cultures are born and grow. 'Culture is the way we do things and relate to each other around here', (Fullan and Hargreaves, 1992). Thus the crucial factor in the development of an ethos is the people working in and around the school. You are now one of these people. Whether your influence is for good or ill, the strength of your sway will depend on the way you personally approach the task. Hence, whether

> **Activity 2**
> What defines the ethos of your school? Consider the ways colleagues relate to one another, the school's symbols and customs, the leadership styles and values on display. What does this tell you about the way to influence other teachers?

your school situation is ideal or not, by considering your actions carefully you can determine the most appropriate way to ensure progress.

Cross and Harrison (1994) suggest a strategy for this to begin to happen. Coordinators therefore need to persuade, cajole and affect the attitudes of staff toward the need for change; the focus of the change (the curricular area, or an aspect of it); and the change process itself. Change will never be achieved solely as the result of your plan, government legislation or incidental INSET. Change occurs only when teachers believe in the need for it, know where it is going, are committed to it and have some ownership of it.

Key personal skills which coordinators will therefore need to develop in order to promote curricular change include an ability:

- to act consistently;
- to maintain hope, belief and optimism;
- to want success (although not necessarily public approval);
- to be willing to take calculated risks and accept the consequences;
- to develop a capacity to accept, deal with and use conflict constructively;
- to learn to use a soft voice and low key manner;
- to develop self awareness;
- to cultivate a tolerance of ambiguity and complexity;
- to avoid viewing issues as simply black and white;
- to become an active listener.

adapted from Everard and Morris (1985)

Getting your Message Across

Some newly qualified teachers may find that their opportunities to influence colleagues are limited. Hence the method they use to get their message across may be just as important as the

> **Activity 3**
> Who are the leaders and opinion formers on your staff? How do they do it? Can you match any of their public behaviours with this list?

content itself. It may help to establish some guidelines for effective communication. The following list is based on the principles in Joan Dean's (1987) book *Managing the Primary School*.

- Teachers are more likely to be responsive to the advice of coordinators if addressed personally rather than anonymously in a staff meeting or by memo.
- Coordinators will need to learn that with teachers, just as with children, rousing the interest of the listener is necessary in order to get your message across.
- Information is more likely to be valued if it gives an advantage in power or status to the listener.
- No one likes to be seen as letting down the team or working group. Therefore, it is sometimes desirable for coordinators to present their information in such a way that it requires action upon which others will rely.
- Teachers charged with the responsibility of promoting curricular areas to their colleagues may find an advantage in choosing an appropriate messenger. The status of the source of the information is often seen to indicate its importance.
- The situation (surroundings, time of day, etc.) should be chosen carefully in order to predispose the listener to be receptive.

Meetings are the most common method that coordinators use in an attempt to get their message over, but they are not always a success. Just having a meeting is not enough. The prime consideration must be, 'What do you want to happen at the meeting?' This point is seldom addressed, for many meetings need never happen at all. You may need to call a meeting in order:

- *to communicate information;*

Subject coordinators will often need to give information to their colleagues, such as the dates and location of a local history and geography book exhibition, the list of computer programs bought by the PTA, and so on. Often this information can be given out in written form with only a brief explanation needed, possibly without having a meeting at all. The skill you will need to develop is to ensure that the information is read and acted upon. Wasting everyone's time for an hour, to compensate for your lack of foresight in not preparing a briefing sheet however, does not go down well with busy teachers.

- *to discuss issues publicly;*

If you want teachers to discuss issues, they need to have been properly prepared beforehand by being given the relevant information. You may need to arrange the seating in such a way that everyone can see each other in order to encourage participation. A brainstorming session recorded on tape can generate ideas or possible solutions.

The key to success for this type of meeting is to create an atmosphere which encourages staff to share ideas and perceptions. They will not do this if early statements (however unsuitable) are not accepted, at least as starting points for the generation of further ideas.

• *to make decisions together.*

If coordinators are organizing a meeting to reach a decision on a key topic it is vital that everyone is made aware that the meeting has this purpose. Time has to be allowed beforehand, such that small group meetings can already have aired some of the issues. Make sure teachers have had time to read and absorb printed material. Decide before the meeting if you intend to take a vote if necessary, or whether it would be more appropriate to continue the debate until a consensus is reached.

Coordinators will be more effective if they understand the difference between the various purposes of these staff meetings and realize what can go wrong. Coordinators need to consider a variety of strategies for organizing and chairing meetings. In *The Primary School Management Book*, David Playfoot, Martin Skelton and Geoff Southworth (1989), further useful information can be found on the conduct of effective meetings in school.

What You can Do Now

Find out how much work is going on in your subject area

Look at displays around the school. What do they tell you? For example do they show that Maths is seen as more than just sums in books? Can you see a variety of games and sports being played? Does children's artwork feature in assemblies? Do teachers talk about progression in technology skills at breaks or in staff meetings? Does the teaching of reading feature prominently in work labelled under another subject? Identify where teachers place IT in their curriculum planning forecasts. By considering such questions you may begin to develop a feel for the task ahead.

An impetus for change may come from:
– changes in staff;
– preparation for an inspection;
– perceived inconsistencies across the school;
– an OFSTED report;
– the influence of a respected advisory teacher;
– an INSET course;
– new resources available;
– new national curriculum orders;
– poor SAT or standardized test results;
– change in pupil roll;
– parents or governors comments.

Look further and ask questions

Listen if (and how) colleagues talk about work in your area. Will they talk to you about it? Talk to the headteacher to determine his or her attitude. Examine school documentation of all kinds. Has there been a recent inspection report (OFSTED or LEA)? What does this say about the quality of work in your subject area. Are there reference books in the school library in your subject? Find out whether there have been previous initiatives. How have colleagues responded to change in the past.

Find out about the latest advice

Make sure you have read the latest advice from SCAA and the most recent subject guidelines for OFSTED inspectors as set out in the Handbook. Make contact with a local adviser, advisory teacher, school, college or university where advice may be available. Take note of any courses which might help you or your colleagues. Enquire about any national association for teachers of your subject. Do they have a primary section? Do they have local meetings? How does the local community fit in? Are there people within your community with interest or expertise?

Keep a record of your activity

Start a portfolio where you keep:

- your notes;
- relevant documents;
- a diary

This will help you to show development and progress over time and to demonstrate your success.

Talk to the headteacher

- discover the head's thoughts and commitment to this area;
- determine its current priority within the school development plan;
- establish a professional dialogue between you and the head;
- register your interest and commitment;
- work out the next step;
- emphasize your priorities;
- formulate a rationale and targets for your work.

Subsequent to such a meeting, start to think in terms of a plan of action. Consider who can help us. How can we help ourselves?

Arrange to go into other teachers' classrooms to work with them, if possible

You will need to consider the reasons you will need to give teachers for your presence. Are you to be there as a critical friend, to focus on an area the teacher has identified, to discover the quality of the work in your area or to give you an idea of progression in children's skills across the school? Should you report what you find in other teachers' classrooms? Is this information for your headteacher, deputy, the governors, senior management team or for the class teacher only? Is the decision yours? Clarify

You may be able to create a climate for change by:
- showing off some aspect of good practice;
- inviting a speaker into school;
- displaying articles and reviews;
- running a workshop;
- asking a colleague to trial a new approach or recently published material;
- reporting back to colleagues on a course you have attended.

this in your own mind before you start. The very worst situation is one in which gossip about any particular teacher's practice should spread from such a activity. Up to now primary subject coordinators have often proved reluctant to direct colleagues and enforce ideas. Many teachers see their coordinating role restricted to writing paper policies and offering tips. Traditionally, primary teachers do not offer comment on colleagues' teaching styles, approach and lesson plans, or act as critical friends. A genuine whole-school commitment to improving standards of teaching performance would help acceptance of this role for all.

Ask to control and account for a small budget to support your area

You will then be able to buy and use resources without continual recourse to your head. Arrange to find a method of gaining agreement amongst the staff for the use of this money in your area. Record the results of any meetings (formal and informal) you have had to determine spending of this fund and include this record with an end-of-year account of what the money was spent on. Hand this in to the head even if he or she doesn't ask for (or want) it.

The willingness of your colleagues to accept your advice in part depends on their perception of your ability in the classroom. Teachers will also make judgements as to the value of the advice based on the coordinator's range of experience, ability to organize resources, knowledge of the subject and range of interpersonal skills.

Conclusion

Since the introduction of the national curriculum, teachers have made many changes. Unfortunately this has led to the idea that making change is always personally stressful, that it regularly leads to a blind alley and that it always results in wasted effort. We also have to recognize that externally imposed, centrally directed innovation has led to a disempowerment of the teaching profession. This has led in turn to concentration on the first two of Bredeson's (1988) three metaphors of leadership, survival and maintenance, at the expense of the third, vision. Teachers reaction to innovation overload has been some retrenchment and a wariness of more *good things*.

Despite everything, most teachers will accept change, especially if they believe it will benefit their children rather than merely enhance the reputation of the proponent. They want to maximize the effect of their efforts and teach as effectively as possible. They would like to see their work built upon in future classes.

If we accept that because of outside pressure teachers' horizons have been lowered, it follows that those who will be the most successful in the next few years will be the leaders who can raise the sights again of those with whom they work. For it is the attitude of the participants towards change which appears to be the most influential factor in its successful implementation.

Newly qualified teachers have the energy, enthusiasm and idealism to help schools maintain that vision and affect those attitudes. As Barber (1994) puts it

> the best teaching depends on an intoxicating mixture of pedagogical skills, love of learning and anger at the disadvantage so many young people suffer. If pedagogical skill is allowed to fade, teaching loses its charm. If love of learning dies, then curiosity among pupils dies too. If the fire of anger is extinguished, cynicism . . . emerges from the ashes. (p. 104)

Motivated by a vocation to do their very best for the children in their care, new entrants are every bit as capable of infecting their colleagues with enthusiasm and a willingness to develop teaching in their chosen subject area as their more experienced colleagues.

This is the essence of curriculum management.

References

ALEXANDER, R., ROSE, J. and WOODHEAD, C. (1992) *Curriculum Organisation and Classroom Practice in Primary Schools*, HMSO, London.

BARBER, M. (1994) 'Keep the new light burning brightly', *TES* 9 September.

BELBIN, R.M. (1981) *Management Teams: Why They Succeed or Fail*, Oxford, Bulterwoolt-Heinemann.

BLEASE, D. and LEVER, D. (1992) 'What do primary headteachers really do?', *Educational Studies*, **8** (2) pp. 185–99.

BREDESON, P.V. (1988) 'An analysis of the metaphorical perspectives of school principals', in BURDIN, J.L. (ed.) (1988) *School Leadership*, London, Sage.

CAMPBELL, R.J. and NEILL, S.R. (1994) *Primary Teachers at Work*, London, Routledge.

CROSS, A. and HARRISON, M. (1994) 'Successful curriculum change through co-ordination', in HARRISON, M. (ed.) *Beyond the Core Curriculum*, Plymouth, Northcote House.

DAY, C., HALL, C., GAMMAGE, P. and COLES, M. (1993) *Leadership and the Curriculum in the Primary School*, London, PCP.

DEAN, J. (1987) *Managing the Primary School*, Beckenham Kent, Croome Helme.

EVERARD, K.B. and MORRIS, G. (1985) *Effective School Management*, London, PCP.

FULLAN, M. and HARGREAVES, A. (1992) *What's Worth Fighting for in Your School?*, Buckingham, Open University Press.

HARRISON, M. (1994a) (ed.) Introduction to *Beyond the Core Curriculum*, Plymouth, Northcote House.

HARRISON, M. (1994b) 'Time to debunk the glorious past', *TES* 24 June.

HARRISON, M. and GILL, S. (1992) *Primary School Management*, London, Heinemann.

HARRISON, S. and THEAKER, K. (1989) *Curriculum Leadership and Coordination in the Primary School*, Whalley, Guild House Press.

HOLLY, P. and SOUTHWORTH, G. (1989) *The Developing School*, London, Falmer Press.

McNAMARA, D. (1994) *Classroom Pedagogy and Primary Practice*, London, Routledge.

MORTIMORE, P., SAMMONS, P., STOLL, L., LEWIS, D. and ECOB, R. (1988) *School Matters*, Froome, Open Books.

OFSTED (1994) *Primary Matters: A Discussion on Teaching and Learning in Primary Schools*, London, OFSTED.

PLAYFOOT, D., SKELTON, M. and SOUTHWORTH, G. (1989) *The Primary School Management Book*, London, Mary Glasgow Publishers, Ltd.

STOW, M. and FOXMAN, D. (1988) *Mathematics Coordination*, Windsor, NFER–NELSON.

WEBB, R. (1994) *After the Deluge: Changing Roles and Responsibilities in the Primary School*, London, ATL.

WRAGG, E.C. (1993) *Primary Teaching Skills*, London, Routledge.

Chapter 2

Developing a Key Stage 2 Policy for your Subject

Mike Harrison

This is often thought of as being the most daunting of tasks, the cause of many restless nights. It should not be so. The point of developing a whole school policy is that it is owned by the whole staff, describes what is actually happening on the ground and gives some indication of the school's direction with regard to your area.

A whole school policy can:

- publicly demonstrate the school's intentions in your subject;
- help make a case for funding;
- give information to governors, parents, inspectors;
- provide a framework for planning;
- aid coherence, continuity, progression and shape priorities, and;
- assist in achieving uniformity and consistency in school decision making.

It may also:

- help focus the minds of various decision making groups toward common aims;
- improve the effectiveness of meetings by helping us all to broadly share each other's understanding of the situation;
- help participants understand teaching and learning strategies employed by other staff;

> **Activity**
> Look at the school's policy statement for your own or another subject. Does the statement satisfy any or all of the purposes listed here? Could it be made to do so?

- help create a team spirit in making public the school's goals;
- offer a means of evaluation;
- help clarify functions and responsibilities of staff, and;
- help new staff settle in.

A Prototype Policy

The seven sections of the prototype policy presented here are offered to give you a skeleton on which to hang your own ideas and suggestions. Most areas will need discussion and agreement with staff to be meaningful but it is sometimes useful to have a starting document if only to give you something to knock down.

1. Introduction

1.1　This should be a general statement of the schools agreed intent in this area, which is suitable for teachers, school governors, the LEA and OFSTED inspectors.

It need to be based on national curriculum requirements and declare that every child should have access to learning in area X and that the school is dedicated to achievement in that area. The statement should reflect the school's ethos and overall aims.

> The school's aims in the English Curriculum consists of teaching children to read, to write accurately and neatly and to express themselves with fluency and confidence.

> Work in IT at Key Stage 2 will cover the five strands of capability namely: Communicating information, handling information, measurement and control, application and effects and modelling.

> In line with the document *History in the National Curriculum* (1991) we shall . . .

In my opinion this vital opening section must be drawn up jointly by the headteacher and coordinator and agreed by staff and governors before detailed work on guidelines can begin in earnest.

1.2　How the policy has been prepared or at what state it is in at present.

> After a year of study by the schools KS2 science working parties and discussion with other staff this document represents staff opinion and practice agreed at a special meeting held on the 23/3/95 and subsequently agreed by governors on 12/10/95.

1.3　At this point the contents of the rest of the document might be listed with page numbers.

2. Implementation

2.1　Experiences you intend, as a school, to give children through each Key Stage (or listed in other ways) in order to achieve the above should appear here. This may take the form of an interpretation of the NC programmes of study and attainment targets which takes into account the circumstances of your school. This section is not the scheme of work but the document does require sufficient detail to ensure continuity of approach and progression of work throughout the school.

2.2   The equipment and materials to which children will have access (are entitled to) by means of this policy.

> We use *Cambridge Maths* as our base book in the following ways:
> Year 3 Module 4
> Year 4 Module 5
>
> Every child will have experience of using a programmable robot and/or turtle linked to LOGO by the time they reach Year 4.
>
> We take children to the swimming baths for two terms in Year 3 – where they benefit from the instruction of qualified swimming teachers.

Curriculum maps, software maps and definite plans can help to ensure that the policy is adhered to rather than vague promises – however, such a stance is more easily assessed by inspectors.

2.3   This may be a suitable point to remind readers that gaining knowledge is not the only outcome of your teaching in this subject.

> We set out to help children to consider themselves as historians seeking evidence and evaluating what they have discovered.
>
> All children will be encouraged to develop positive attitudes towards work in music.
>
> Our curriculum is designed to promote confidence and enjoyment in using the mathematical skills they have learnt.

2.4   There is also a place for helping to gain agreement in the methods which will be used to promote learning in your subject area. If this can be done it may be recorded at this point in your policy document. This will help to remind everyone on what they agreed.

> Children will work individually, in groups and as a whole class in geography. This will ensure that . . .
>
> Each child will have the opportunity to change his or her library book each week.
>
> Children normally work in pairs at the computer under the guidance of their teacher.

Children working with programmable robots, such as the ROAMER, will normally be engaged in problem solving activities in groups outside the classroom or elsewhere.

2.5   Equal opportunities statement and any subject specific multicultural issues.

All children regardless of race, gender, ability and physical . . . will be given equal access to physical education.

In IT, Classroom management will take account of such issues, and classroom materials free from bias will be positively sought.

We respect the religious convention of all groups represented in the school and recognize the needs for flexibility in dress regulations including those for swimming and physical education.

2.6   The names and roles of persons responsible for overseeing or co-ordinating the implementation of the policy needs to be recorded here along with the various responsibilities of head and classteachers with regard to this.

2.7   Methods for monitoring the implementation of this policy.

Who is responsible for seeing that the agreed practices are being carried out in all classes? Who is to ensure children's entitlement? It may be covered above but still might need saying so here. How will this be done?

3. Schemes of Work

3.1   Whole school, or the Key Stage 2 scheme of work may be included here or as a separate document. This should fit in with everyone else's method of handling such matters.

3.2   Themes or topics to be handled may be listed here by year groups.
     This represents long-term planning from which individual teachers will create forward, medium and then short-term work plans. Whatever the method is in your school it is a good idea to state it here – then everyone knows where they stand.

3.3   The way IT will be used to support learning in your area.

Children will be introduced to the use of databases to support their work in Geography in Year 5.

Three different word processing packages are used to help children practice the process of writing. Each package has been chosen to give children access to more sophisticated features as they progress though the school.

3.4 Cross-curricular links

Every lesson is an English Lesson

and therefore . . .

3.5 A synopsis of work covered in the first year of the high school may be usefully included here.

4. *Assessment of and Recording of Pupils' Progress*

List here the purposes of assessment and uses to which records of children's achievement will be put.

4.1 Agreed methods of record keeping and times at which such assessments will be made.

> Teachers record of children's experiences are those kept in annotated forecast books.
>
> Children's work is recorded in their exercise books which are carefully stored to maintain a record of their progress in X.
>
> Example sheets of work in X are kept systematically throughout the year. A summative record is complied to pass to the next teacher.

This section should not be at variance with the school's assessment and recording policy and certainly not at odds with reality! It should state how, what, where and how often. It might even say why records are kept, and give the real purpose of plotting pupils' progress in your school.
How do you report progress to parents?
It may be desirable to demonstrate in the policy document what is meant by progression.

> As children progress they will be able to write stories with more complex themes, write in different styles and for different purposes, their handwriting will appear more mature.
>
> IT progression will be demonstrated by children carrying out more complex tasks, applying more advanced skills, becoming more independent and confident using IT and by using more sophisticated software.

4.2   The location of examples of children's work which exemplifies levels of attainment and progression between them might be stated here along with any other germane information.

5. Resources

5.1   A comprehensive list of equipment (with serial numbers if appropriate). Books in stock. Books in the library to support learning in this area. Software, posters, videos, working models, etc., available for teachers to use.

5.2   Deployment of resources.

Policy for who gets to use what when and how, where they are stored, any security features.

5.3   Future purchasing policy.

> The school development plan sets out an objective of complete re-newal of the maths scheme within four years.

> We are committed to replace all BBC computers with A4000s by September 1996.

> PE will be a priority area in 1995–96 and at that time . . .

5.4   Repair arrangements for equipment (with telephone numbers and necessary forms). Arrangements for safety checks on large PE apparatus.

5.5   List of appropriate television and radio broadcasts.

6. Staff Development

The successful implementation of the policy will probably need INSET, both school-based and using outside agencies. The policy document will appear more complete and credible if such arrangements are included here.

6.1   Targets for INSET may be a feature of your school and expressed here as a spur to achievement.

6.2   A list of recommended books for teachers' personal reading would be useful.

6.3   The job description or agreed targets for the curriculum coordinator might be published here.

6.4 Names and addresses of support agencies which may offer advice or materials for teaching in your subject area.

7. *Review/Evaluation of this Policy*

The headteacher and staff will need to review this policy to take account of changing circumstances. The date for its reconsideration may be stated here.

You might consider discussing with staff the inclusion of measures by which the success of the policy and its implementation may be judged. These may include teachers' and children's perceptions; children's work and other written evidence; SAT or standardized test results, a review of teachers' forecasts, parents' and governors' responses or classroom observation.

Chapter 3

Reading the Changes

Rita Ray

Context

The teaching of reading remains one of the most controversial areas of debate. Attainment in reading is fundamental to the learning process, not only in English but across the curriculum. The national curriculum has set out areas to be developed and assessed in reading, highlighting the basic skills and target levels that primary schools have always fostered. Teachers have definite ideas about the standards that need to be achieved in reading in order to facilitate attainment in English and in other subjects.

Most children have learned to read by the time they reach Year 3. For those who have not the gap becomes wider, not only in the skills of reading but in the acquisition of knowledge and understanding in other areas. The OFSTED *Report on English*, Key Stages 1,2,3 and 4, 1992–93 (hereafter referred to as *English 1992–3*) stated that work in English at Key Stage 2 should be improved '*as a matter of urgency*'. (p. 23, para. 47) So far as reading was concerned they found that:

> In 40 per cent of the lessons in Years 3–5, the generally good start made in Key Stage 1 was not maintained. More reliance was placed on commercial reading schemes and phonic skills were not developed. The result was that, in Years 3 and 4 particularly, some pupils became frustrated, and not enough progress was made. p. 7, para. 3.

The HMI report on reading at Key Stage 1 (1990) stated that where reading standards were good the coordinator has played an effective role in helping the school to achieve, by consulting and advising staff and helping to train non-teaching staff and parents. Where possible they worked alongside colleagues, but for many lack of non-contact time ruled out this kind of support. Clear, well formulated policies for reading were also strongly associated with good standards. This chapter aims to help the reader to address some of these issues and to begin to develop as an effective coordinator of reading.

The Role of the Reading Specialist at Key Stage 2

An obvious factor in successful subject leadership is good communication and the maintenance of open dialogue with colleagues about concerns and issues in reading. Most of all a subject specialist must quietly assert standards by presenting a good model and by putting into practice beliefs about what are the best and most effective ways for children to learn to read. It helps, too, to start with structured targets to match against outcomes when trying to evaluate effectiveness.

Starting Points

Make a plan identifying areas of change and desired outcomes for the long term (two years) and for the short term (six months). The plan will need to address the school's individual needs which may lie in some of the following areas:

- management and organization of reading at whole school level and/or class level;
- resources for reading;
- staff expertise in teaching reading;
- highlighting of awareness of reading in other subjects;
- monitoring and assessing reading;
- providing for special needs in reading.

In consultation with the head and a *critical friend* identify realistic goals, within the constraints of time, resourcing and teacher/pupil ratios. A critical friend is usually a colleague whose opinion you respect and whose comments can be taken on board without hard feelings. This might be your mentor or a colleague with whom you collaborate frequently.

What are the Central Skills and Strategies to be Developed in Key Stage 2?

By Key Stage 2, most children have mastered the basic mechanical skills of reading and need strategies for constructing meaning. Three main strategies that help to develop reading with understanding are listed below.

- Identifying main ideas – Seen by some as the essence of reading comprehension, identifying main ideas requires the reader to understand what has been read and make judgements about the importance of information.
- Making inferences – Children can benefit from strategies that promote

inference – such as building up skills of answering inference questions through discussion and guidance.

- Text inspection – As new words are met readers need to look back and ahead and use context to help them understand new information.

Children need training in these strategies and should learn to reflect on how they have read. – 'What did I learn? Were my predictions correct? Did everything make sense?'

As well as materials which foster these skills and strategies pupils should have plenty of good quality children's fiction to read for pleasure.

Communicating with Colleagues

We all like to feel valued as persons and as professionals. Sometimes it is hard to separate our worth as persons from our competence as professionals but working together will be easier if professional disagreements are not allowed to interfere with personal relationships. As subject specialist you can emphasize that no one, including you, can be expected to know everything. The professional approach is to identify gaps and to negotiate a plan of action. It is important to remind everyone of ongoing successes and achievements.

So, once armed with knowledge and information sources, how do you set about implementing change, especially if you are recently qualified and feel daunted by the task of approaching experienced teachers? Implementing change is a whole subject area in itself but is based on the kind of common sense knowledge that we can all access in dealing with other human beings. Most staff will be supportive but there are a few instances of teachers feeling deskilled and therefore threatened by demands that might be made by a new subject specialist. For example, what can be done if a long established member of staff does not see the teaching of reading as an important part of the Key Stage 2 timetable? Rather than tackling the individual problem directly, look at the way the whole school works together. Is there a consistent whole school policy for reading?

A whole school policy, backed up by practical, easy-to-manage routines for promoting and improving reading will make it difficult for one teacher to fall by the wayside. One unifying activity often practised by junior schools is *uninterrupted sustained silent reading* (USSR), or one of its variants. At a specified time, say 1.00pm–1.20pm, the whole school engages in silent reading. Those who cannot read well spend the time with books, looking at picture books or re-reading a familiar book. This concentration on reading ensures a regular, timetabled period in which every child gets the opportunity to spend a peaceful time with books. Doing it at the same time is an added bonus, especially in open plan schools.

Finally, new ideas will be more readily received if they are presented as accepted models of good practice rather than as your own personal preferences. Find a school that has a good example of the practice you would like to promote in your school and arrange a visit by members of your staff. Colleagues and advisers in your region or publishers' representatives may know of a school that has a novel way of storing and accessing central reading resources or an exciting way of organizing and displaying books that has motivated and improved reading in the school.

Updating Personal Knowledge and Expertise

Membership of an association such as the United Kingdom Reading Association (UKRA) will provide information on conferences and workshops as well as reports of recent practical research. The Centre for Reading at the University of Reading provides useful resource lists and books, such as the Cliff Moon Individualised Reading list, mentioned below. Get together with colleagues who are also subject specialists to discuss common strategies for updating expertise. Ensure that you have lists of courses offered by the LEA and other providers.

Staff Development

It is likely that you will be expected to lead staff training sessions in school. There are several ways of organizing staff development time, according to the purpose of the sessions. Here are some examples –

- to pass on information from conferences attended and to share any recent developments in reading that you have noted and summarized;
- to acquaint staff with new materials – either to have a preliminary demonstration by a publisher's representative before ordering materials or to allow staff to look at and organize new materials;
- to spend time on an identified INSET need, such as assessment of reading in the classroom. This may be run by the subject specialist or an appropriate visitor, such as an LEA adviser.

The English 1992–93 report stated that in more than 50 per cent of schools there were clearly identifiable INSET needs which were not being met – 'in particular, where reading was concerned, how to include the teaching of phonic skills in a broad approach to reading development.' (p. 18, para. 38)

Organizing Resources and Information

You can make a good practical start in your role as a specialist by updating the list of materials and, in consultation with colleagues, organizing these materials so that they can be used effectively and efficiently by all pupils and staff. For colleagues, staffroom and central resources need to be categorized and stored so that they are readily accessible and easily put back. For pupils the reading specialist's task is especially important since it involves the classification and storage of the major source of information – as well as pleasure – within the school.

The main requirements of book display are that it should be well categorized, accessible and attractive. It is important to maintain the display, keeping it tidy, focusing on different themes, genres and authors, and new books, so that it will always be fresh and stimulating.

Formal/informal Consultancy

You must be prepared to help and advise on an ongoing basis. However, when colleagues complain in the staff room that there are not enough comprehension materials, or stop the specialist on the corridor to ask what to do about a particular child, it does not mean that a solution has to be found on the spot. Comprehension materials can be ordered or, if the budget doesn't allow, organize some time to lead colleagues in finding or producing appropriate materials. The problems of particular children may be dealt with in the classroom or, in the case of severe problems, by referring the child on for more detailed testing. As with most areas of expertise it's knowing where to go for the answer that matters, rather than having all the knowledge at your fingertips.

Reporting to Governors

The subject specialist frequently has the responsibility of reporting back to governors concerning reading policy. Do not be daunted by the prospect. Governors are parents, councillors, representatives of the church and/or local community who, like you, have the best interests of the children at heart. That they might be interested in the way in which reading is taught is quite natural. They will not, of course, have had the training you have had, nor the day-to-day experience of working with children so they will be interested in what you have to say. As a newcomer to the profession a short statement about the way the policy was written, the checks made to see that it is implemented and the links with Key Stage 1 and 3 will be sufficient.

Forming a Working Group

The size of a working group depends on the number of staff members. As a rule there is a member of staff from each Key Stage if the specialist covers the whole school. The purpose of the working group is to discuss issues in reading, identify needs and make preliminary decisions before presenting policy, etc., to the whole staff. It saves time to work like this rather than starting a new topic from scratch in a large unprepared group. Much ground can be cleared quickly in well organized working groups. Before each working group meeting the members should have a briefing note which focuses on the issues to be discussed. During and after the meeting it is useful to take notes and record the action plan decided by the group, as well as any particular tasks taken on by group members. This will act as an aide memoire and provide material for the next briefing note. The main aim is to use colleagues' time efficiently and to feel that you are moving forward.

Compiling a Curriculum Document and Information Resource

This constitutes a major task for the specialist with the help of the working group. The reading policy forms part of this document. Although the school document is often referred to as *the reading policy*, the policy itself is simply a statement of the school's beliefs, rationale and aspirations in the area of reading. It is necessary to explain how this policy can be translated into action effectively throughout the school.

The curriculum document should be a working document. Members of staff should be able to refer to it for information about the school's resources and how to use them to the full. A useful way of organizing the document is to place the information in clear plastic envelopes in a ring binder. In this way information can be changed or updated and the contents list adjusted accordingly. An example list of contents for a curriculum document, with comments on each area, is suggested below:

Statement of rationale

The national curriculum document sets out the aims to be achieved in a Key Stage 2 reading programme and can inform the school's statement. The following is an example of a short statement of a school's aims for reading, derived from the *National Curriculum Programme of Study for Reading at Key Stage 2* (November 1994):

> We want our pupils to develop as enthusiastic, independent and reflective readers. They should be introduced to a wide range of literature, including poetry and plays, and have opportunities to read extensively for their own interest and pleasure. We want them to engage with a variety of non-fiction texts, including IT based reference materials, newspapers, encyclopedias, dictionaries and thesauruses, so that they will become confident, independent learners.

Methods of teaching reading used in school – including provision for special needs in reading. The main approaches to teaching reading:

- the *real* books approach, in which children learn to choose and share books and by an *apprenticeship* experience, gradually join in the reading and eventually become independent readers;

- the use of graded, commercially published reading schemes;
- the teaching of a phonics programme in which children learn to decode and build words by putting together the sounds of the letters.

NFER (National Foundation for Educational Research) and the English 1992–93 report found that in most schools there was a mixed approach to the teaching of reading. There was widespread use of reading schemes, as well as teaching of phonics and shared *real* books. In practice, teachers usually prefer a consistent reading programme backed up by phonic teaching and expanded by a choice of children's fiction. It should be borne in mind too that up to date schemes have many of the characteristics of good children's books. Children treat the scheme books as *real* books and frequently choose a book more than once rather than simply being anxious to move on through the scheme.

Management of reading

- organizing book area and information sources;
- group and individual reading;
- managing time to monitor reading.

Leaving aside the children who have reading problems, there are several ways to assess understanding in addition to hearing reading, which teachers tend to do less and in a different way once the child becomes fluent. Hearing reading becomes more like a reading conference between teacher and child involving discussion of content rather than correction of technical errors.

A provided format for a book report which makes sure that main points are included or the choice of two or three passages from the book to illustrate are enjoyable ways of checking understanding, especially if the child can choose to put these up on a notice board as a way to recommend (or not recommend) books to classmates.

Resources for reading

At Key Stage 2 most children have made a good start in reading and it is important to maintain a steady supply of children's fiction as well as a range of non-fiction books and information sources such as leaflets, special subject magazines, posters, packs and IT packages.

Many schools continue to use reading schemes at Key Stage 2 so there may be sets of readers with a phonic focus, such as *New Way*, materials which are suitable for group discussion and comprehension, such as *Ginn 360* and materials designed to fulfil special needs, such as *Wellington Square*.

One way to ensure the provision of good quality fiction at different levels is to order, or make up, book boxes. The boxes contain a selection of fiction sorted into different levels. For teachers who want to make up their own book selection the booklist *Individualised Reading*, compiled by B. Moon and C.

Moon (1986) (Reading and Language Information Centre, University of Reading), categorizes books into levels so that the reading and interest level can be matched to the child. The teacher can also feel confident that children can select a suitable book with some degree of free choice. Children may not always finish the book they select, but it is part of learning to choose. If books are a central, shared resource then teachers will need to agree upon a way of organizing, classifying and keeping track of the books. Some teachers like children to have free choice from books which have not been levelled. This entails extra work in monitoring progress and keeping a check on book displays and organization.

As well as boxes of fiction, some suppliers make up packs on particular subjects or themes – history, equal opportunities and so on. Most libraries used to make up topic boxes for loan but in some areas this service is now limited or has been cut. It is not so easy for teachers to judge the readability level of non-fiction books. These books are often written by subject specialists who are mainly concerned with conveying information. For children the task of taking in new information can be complicated by the kind of language structures they meet in some non-fiction texts. Non-fiction can be harder to read than fiction because:

- there is no narrative to lead the child;
- there are no fictional characters with whom to identify;
- the child has no clues to predict the content;
- the language structures may be unfamiliar.

What to look for in non-fiction texts:

- the information is clearly laid out and broken up by boxes, different print, question-and-answer format;
- text is supported by suitable images – pictures, charts, graphs and diagrams;
- the information is presented in a variety of suitable forms – for example, sometimes captioned pictures are the best format to explain a science process;
- key words highlighted and explained;
- in the case of lower Key Stage 2 or easy reading the information, where appropriate, is in narrative form.

Assessment and recording

- the school's method of recording and passing on records;
- reports to parents and others;
- list of tests used in school;
- national curriculum assessment.

You can study a range of record keeping systems, including the school's existing method, to find an efficient and manageable one. Record keeping should be kept as simple as possible. There are several recommended ways of keeping reading records which are worthy and valid in themselves but unrealistic when placed in the context of all the other records teachers have to keep. It is sufficient for everyday purposes to keep a book or file containing a list of names (which can be used with several pages), a space for the name of the book, noted errors to be worked on and comments by the teacher and child. Other test results, class and individual, can be kept in the same file for reference. The basic format of record keeping agreed on by the staff should be manageable and give the required information. Those who wish to can keep more detailed notes in addition to this basic format.

List the tests currently in use in the school, discard any out of date and inappropriate tests and order new ones. Most schools use a variety of tests for different purposes. *Norm referenced tests* such as the Young Test or the Salford Sentence Reading Test have been standardized on large and varied groups of children and are useful for monitoring standards as they give a *reading age*. The Young Test is a group test and can be given to a whole class; the Salford Sentence Test is administered to one child at a time. (The Salford Sentence Test is somewhat dated but is often used as it is difficult to find a test which serves the same purpose.)

Diagnostic tests, such as the Neale Analysis of Reading Ability (Revised version), are used to give individual profiles and show where a child's strengths and weaknesses lie. *Criterion referenced* tests are those in which a child is tested against a particular skill. National curriculum testing is criterion referenced – 'Pupils show understanding of a range of texts, selecting essential points and using inference and deduction where appropriate' – against which children are measured at Level 5, though most criterion referenced tests are more tightly constructed and measured than national curriculum assessment. In this kind of testing children are simply required to be able to do something. They are not assessed against other children as they are in norm referenced assessment.

In the context of national curriculum formative assessment and summative assessment have been highlighted. *Formative assessment* is carried out by the teacher in the classroom. In the case of reading it consists of ongoing monitoring of the child's progress, for example, hearing the child read, noting errors and growth points and using this information to plan the next steps of teaching. It is the specialist's job to make sure that staff are using the same kind of standards to assess children's reading.

Since the initiation of National Curriculum attempts have been made to standardize teacher assessment, especially through agreement trials in which teachers look at several pieces of work or observe a process and try to agree on standards. Further work is to take place in this area. For example, it is proposed that concise examples of the standards demanded by National Curriculum should be published so that teachers can draw on them. There will be guidance for headteachers on the key features of effective and manageable school approaches to promoting the consistency of teachers' own assessments.

Summative assessment means that assessments are summarized, especially at the end of a Key Stage, as in the assessments at the end of Key Stages 1, 2 and 3. *Miscue analysis and Informal Reading Inventories* give a picture of individual reading attainment and comprehension. These forms of assessment also accord well with the requirements of national curriculum. In Miscue Analysis children's reading errors are categorized and used in planning the pupils' teaching programme. The system may look complicated at first but teachers soon internalize the process and find themselves looking automatically for patterns in errors. Errors are categorized into syntactic (grammar), semantic (meaning) and graphophonic (letters/sounds).

The following, Figure 3.1, is an example of miscue analysis in the classroom from Arnold (1984: 61).

Informal reading inventories are reading passages on which miscue analysis is carried out, but which also have questions to test different kinds of comprehension, for example, *literal understanding* in which the answer can be

Figure 3.1: *Error analysis code and child's marked work*

MISCUE TYPE	ORIGINAL TEXT	ACTUAL RESPONSE	CODING SYMBOL
Non-response (refusal)	prairie	no attempt to say any part of word	prairie
Substitution	which crept between his toes	which kept between his toes	which ~~crept~~ between his toes (kept)
Omission	I feel like a grease-spot	I feel like grease-spot	I feel like ⓐ grease-spot
Insertion	and then found he couldn't stop	and then he found he couldn't stop	and then ∧(he) found he couldn't stop
Reversal	so tightly was he pinned down	so tightly he was pinned down	so tightly was⌐he pinned down
Self-correction	then the laughing turned	then he-the laughing turned	then ~~the~~(he) laughing turned
Hesitation	so wide that	Hesitates for some time then supplies word. Oblique stroke shows where hesitation occurs.	so wide/that
Repetition	Thomas tried to break the threads	Thomas tried to tried to break the threads	Thomas tried to break the threads

found in the text, and inferential understanding in which the clues to the answer are in the text. Teachers can prepare their own reading passages but it is easier to use those which have already been placed at a reading level and have appropriate questions. Such passages may be found in *Independence in Reading* by Don Holdaway and in *Making Sense of It* by Helen Arnold. Informal Reading Inventories can be time consuming for the teacher but no more so than most diagnostic tests. They need not be administered very often, nor to all pupils, but Informal Reading Inventories can be especially useful in pinpointing less obvious difficulties in order to plan programmes.

Children should contribute to their own assessment. They will feel that they have more insight into and control over their own development as readers if they have a say in their assessment. Although they may find it hard to express any difficulties they are experiencing, the act of consulting can be beneficial.

References and booklist

Use books and journals available in the staff room as well as other relevant material, such as reading scheme manuals.

Appendix

The appendix will contain more detailed explanations of methods, materials and resources used in school. For example:

- instructions for administering miscue analysis and informal reading inventories;
- how to organize a book week and a visit from an author;
- information on different ways of teaching and testing further reading skills.

Organizing Support for Children with Special Needs in Reading

The English 1992–93 report stated that at Key Stage 2 'a greater proportion of the teacher's time was devoted to the less able'. At the beginning of Year 6.75 per cent of those assessed were able to read widely on their own. There was a small proportion, approximately 1 in 20 children, who were hardly able to read at all. Most teachers were keenly aware of the slower readers, but in some schools there was uncertainty about meeting their needs. Statementing of children with problems means provision of support, provided that the statementing process goes smoothly. The Department for Education (DFE) Code of Practice for children with special educational needs explains how to set in motion a staged process of identifying needs and providing support. The DFE booklet (available in many libraries as well as from the DFE)

Figure 3.2: An informal prose inventory (Helen Arnold, 1984) from Independence in Reading, Holdaway, 1978: 114–5

An Informal Prose Inventory   **Level C (7–8 years)**

Name: **Age:**   **Date:**

Set: Do you like making things? This story will give you some ideas.

Fun with Paper Bags

Making a mask can be fun. Do it this way. Get a large paper bag and hold it in front of your face. Mark the places for your eyes, nose, and mouth. Lay the bag on a table, and cut holes the right shape. When it is finished the mask will fit right over your head.

Oral — IL: up to 4 errors.

Q1 What does the story suggest you use to make a mask? (L)
R1 *A large paper bag.*

Q2 How can you be sure that the eyes will be in the right place? (L)
R2 *Hold the bag in front of the face and mark the place for eyes, etc.*

Q3 Would people be able to see your ears? (1)
R3 *No. Paper bag right over head and no hole for ears.*

Silent:

What kind of mask will you make? Good ones are Indians, animals, flowers, and clowns. For Indians you will need feathers. For animals you will need fur or hair. Wool makes fine hair and whiskers. For flowers and clowns you will need bright colours. Use crayons or paint. A better way may be to paste on coloured paper or cloth.

Recall:

R4 Good masks are Indians, animals, flowers and clowns.
Q4 *What would be good masks to make?*

R5 For an Indian mask you will need feathers.
Q5 *What would you need for the Indian mask?*

R6 For animals you will need fur or hair.
Q6 *What would you need for making animal masks?*

R7 Wool makes fine hair and whiskers.
Q7 *What could you use to make the hair?*
What else could you make from wool?

R8 You need bright colours for flowers and clowns.
Q8 *What kind of colours are best for flowers and clowns?*

R9 Make bright colours with crayon, or paste on coloured paper.
Q9 *How would you make these bright colours?*

Q10 Suggest a completely new title. (1)
R10 *Open-ended. No words from original title.*

Comprehension — IL: 7 correct responses

Reaction: Which mask would you most like to make?

Imagery: What animal mask did you see in your mind as you were reading?

Creative thinking: What other mask would be suitable to make from a paper bag?

Figure 3.3: Test passage – level C (Helen Arnold, 1984) from Independence in Reading, Holdaway, 1978: 100–1

C   Fun with Paper Bags

Making a mask can be fun. Do it this way. Get a large paper bag and hold it in front of your face. Mark the places for your eyes, nose, and mouth. Lay the bag on a table, and cut holes the right shape. When it is finished the mask will fit right over your head.

What kind of mask will you make? Good ones are Indians, animals, flowers, and clowns. For Indians you will need feathers. For animals you will need fur or hair. Wool makes fine hair and whiskers. For flowers and clowns you will need bright colours. Use crayons or paint. A better way may be to paste on coloured paper or cloth.

Sub-test Level C
Consonant Knowledge
  scr sk squ thr soft c soft g
Central Method of Word Attack
  1. She dropped the cup on the fl - - -.
  2. Our baby can cr - - - a long way.
  3. The sleepy cat str - - - - - - in the sun.

explaining the Code of Practice to parents sets out the main points in a useful and quick to read format. It can also serve as a summary and reminder of the document for busy teachers. The reading specialist can work with the special needs coordinator to facilitate provision for those who have special needs in reading. Support of any kind must be handled sensitively as the child may feel singled out and lose confidence in the ability to perform alongside peers.

Providing texts for the struggling reader can prove difficult – 'There's not enough at one level' 'The books she can read are too babyish for her', are frequent comments by teachers. The teacher does not want to present too difficult a text yet cannot find enough suitable material which has the right reading level coupled with a junior age interest level. Often teachers retreat to a restrictive phonics-only approach in desperation. Certainly structure and consistency are crucial if the child is to build up competence but feeling comfortable with the material and being happy to be seen reading the book are important factors too.

One aspect of reading is the part it plays in social exchange and identification with the group. Children should be able to join in discussions (not just the formal teacher-led ones) about current favourites and will feel included through such activities as hearing the story on tape whilst looking at, not necessarily following, the book; sharing part of the story with teacher or other reading partner; reading more or less independently a carefully chosen passage to show that it is possible to access the book.

Ellay (1989) reports that the single most important activity for building knowledge and skills required for successful reading is reading aloud to children, though it is the child's active involvement in sharing the text that supports development. The foregoing elements can form part of an approach to reading which centres on daily consistent structure but includes the child in mainstream reading activities. This can also allay the frustration and subsequent behaviour difficulties often experienced by children who have reading problems.

How Can the Specialist Monitor Change and Evaluate Outcomes?

In order to improve something you must be clear about the existing state of things and able to identify areas of strength and weakness. Look at any recent reports in the school (HMI, OFSTED, LEA inspectors) and relate the reports' findings to your own observations and key points identified for development.

Evaluate outcomes against initial aims and long and short-term plans. Keep a short, weekly diary noting, for example, small achievements, changes in whole school approach or differences in the staff's way of working together. You may be surprised at the way achievements build up and at the improvements attained when looking back over the diary entries. Incorporate improvements and successful courses of action into the whole school plan for the following year.

References

ARNOLD, H. (1984) *Making Sense of It*, London, Hodder and Stoughton.

BOOKBINDER, G. (1976) *Salford Sentence Reading Test*, Sevenoaks, Hodder and Stoughton.

CATEN, V., GORMAN, T., FERNANDEZ, C., KIZPAL, A. and WHITE, J. (1992) *Teaching of Initial Literacy*, Slough, NFER.

DFE (1993) *Code of Practice on the Identification and Assessment of Special Educational Needs*, London, HMSO.

DFE (1995) *English in the National Curriculum*, London, HMSO.

ELLEY, W.B. (1989) 'Vocabulary acquisition from listening to stories', *Reading Research Quarterly* **24** (2) pp. 174–87.

HMI (1990) *The Teaching and Learning of Reading in Primary Schools*, London, DES.

HOLDAWAY, D. (1980) *Independence in Reading*, Scholastic.

MOON, B. and MOON, C. (1986) *Individualised Reading*, University of Reading, Reading and Language Information Centre.

New Way Readers (1987) Basingstoke, Macmillan Education Ltd.

OFSTED (1992–93) *Report on the Teaching of English, Key Stages 1, 2 and 3*, London, HMSO.

Reading 360 (1979) Aylesbury, Ginn and Co Ltd.

Wellington Square (1989) Basingstoke, Macmillan Education Ltd. (Now published by Thomas Nelson and Sons Ltd.)

YOUNG, D. (1980) *Group Reading Tests*, Sevenoaks, Hodder and Stoughton.

Chapter 4

Writing

Geoffrey R. Roberts

'Learning to write', according to Perera (1984, p. 207) 'entails mastering not only the physical forms of letters, spellings and punctuation, but also the structural and organizational patterns that characterize written language.' Acquiring this expertise will not have been completed by the time children arrive at Year 3. Throughout their junior school years and beyond children must learn and be taught to develop and apply these patterns of language in composing written texts. All too often teachers dwell upon spelling and basic punctuation but give insufficient attention to teaching children how to compose texts.

Anyone seeking to promote writing in a junior school must begin from the premise that writing is a complex activity comprising several subskills. Thus, in order to successfully teach children to write, teachers must have clearly in mind the ingredients and their relative importance in the activity that is encompassed within the general term, *writing*.

Before contemplating the various subskills of writing consideration must be given to what lies behind '*the structural and organizational patterns that characterize written language*'. Obviously, these patterns must be based upon what the writer has in mind to write. Hence, preceding each attempt to compose a written text, there must be a stimulus of some nature. It may be a story heard, a book read, an action undertaken, an event experienced or an interaction or its possibility with another person. From this stimulus thoughts will occur alongside which there will be some attempt at ordering those thoughts so that some degree of sense is made of the stimulus and its resultant thoughts. Frequently, this will result in the reproduction of those thoughts in their ordered sequence in the form of oral speech or, at later stages of development, in the form of written language. In the early years and well into the junior school children will produce an oral response before committing their thoughts to print.

Preparatory Activities to Initiate Thought

This basis for composing written texts suggests a number of important activities that will help to prepare children for writing through the exercise of their minds in response to stimuli of various kinds. These preparatory activities should not be seen in the same light as pre-reading activities; they are activities that must be developed as the abilities of the children develop throughout their years of schooling. They are activities of the mind which precede and percolate through every act of written communication.

These basic activities fall into three categories. It must not be assumed that they develop unaided, although there will be some natural development.

- Children must be encouraged to react to stimuli. As it cannot be taken for granted that all children make the most of the stimuli that they experience, teacher involvement is crucial.
- Children must be encouraged to develop thoughts about stimuli and this involves oral discussion.
- Children must be shown how to reflect upon stimuli in an ordered fashion: by hearing stories; by participating orally in the composition of stories, descriptions of things and events; by exercising the imagination to describe or foresee events, actions, wishes and feelings.

Thus, the bases of composing are reflection upon stimuli; discussion of activities; listening to stories and descriptions; storying both descriptively and imaginatively.

Parallel Activities

These activities give substance to the discussion, listening, storying and descriptions in the following ways:

- The promotion and encouragement of oral language. Oral competence develops through usage and through emulating adults, through language patterns picked up from stories read by the teacher and parents, and through an innate desire to wallow in the sounds and effects of speech.
- Development of handwriting skills leading to attempts to portray speech in writing. The enjoyment of manipulative powers over a pencil or pen form the basis of exploratory handwriting and inventive spelling. If children did not enjoy scribbling it is doubtful whether they would develop an ability in handwriting.

  The development of handwriting should not be regarded solely as a mechanical skill. Although the basis for writing should always be to communicate, nevertheless the teacher should not be inhibited from taking opportunities to demonstrate the mechanical aspects of letter formation and at the same time to instil spelling patterns. For example, when demonstrating the formation of letters the teacher should link that letter with an associated one, where possible one that is only finely distinguished in form from the target letter, e.g., *a*, *d* and placed in a word such as bad (the reason many children confuse b and d is that they seldom or infrequently see them together in a word), *h* and *n* and placed in a word such as hen.

Exploratory handwriting should remain a feature throughout Key Stages 1 and 2, less intensive naturally as the child develops a clear hand. Children should be encouraged to experiment with handwriting styles – increasing and decreasing the size of letters and experimenting with their form throughout their years in a primary school.

• Inventive spelling developing into innovative and experimental spelling, whereby children are encouraged to try to spell unfamiliar words and at the same time are trained to check their incursions into spelling so that reference to the dictionary becomes a habit rather than occasional occurrence.

In these ways handwriting, spelling and the composition of written texts are all integrated elements within the highly complex skill of producing written English. The complete list of elements is: activities and experience; thinking; the formulation or ordering of thoughts; the oral manifestation of this sequence of thoughts and ideas; their commitment to paper in the form of handwriting; spelling; composing of language patterns and their refinement into an appropriate style of written English. These elements are present on every occasion when a child at any stage of development is engaged in composing a written text. Some, such as handwriting and spelling, assume a decreasingly onerous role as the writer develops those skills, whereas others, such as the increasingly complex formation of ideas and language patterns, assume a greater and more exacting role.

Hence, in setting out a curriculum that encourages and assures development in writing, it must be ensured that at all stages there are continuing activities and a range of experiences provided that form the basic stimuli for writing. Second, the children must be encouraged and shown how to develop consciously a stream of thoughts which emanate from those activities and experiences through the medium of speech. Third, children must be shown how to and be given continuing help in transposing those thoughts and speech patterns into written form, through handwriting, spelling and through a second level system of language patterns which conform to the conventions of written prose or poetry – at its simplest the conversion of *I don't* to *I do not*, and at a more sophisticated level, *We've seen it and we don't agree* into *We studied the evidence and we find it unacceptable*. In other words, the conversion of language suited to particular situations into a form that can be understood universally.

The Application of the Basic Theory at Various Levels

Naturally, the various levels of ability in Years 3 to 6 will demand differing approaches. In the first place teachers of Year 3 will have to determine how much groundwork has been accomplished. They will have to ask the following questions:

- Has sufficient attention been given to the provision of stimuli in Years 1 and 2?
- What training have children had in the formulation of thoughts and ideas and how far have they been encouraged to express these thoughts and ideas orally?
- To what extent have children's powers to manipulate the implements of writing been exercised – what part has scribbling, drawing and the use of paint brushes played in their *everyday* schooling and how much experience of and guidance in exploratory writing and spelling have they had?
- How far have they progressed in transposing thoughts and speech into writing?

Experiences vary greatly from one infant school or class to another, not only in what the children do but in how much real help they have been given in understanding what they are doing. If the degree of real help is ignored one is in danger of starting from a false base. A child who has a clear notion of how to tell or retell a story is far in advance of the child who has no idea of how to go about it, as is a child who has been encouraged to try to spell and has had frequent opportunities of seeing the teacher write, and, of course, spell the words that are exercising that child at any particular moment. Learning is most effective when help or guidance is given at the point of execution of a task by the child. Timing is crucial and half an hour after the task has been completed may be as ineffective as leaving the correction and teaching until the following day. (Hence, the need for supernumerary help in the classroom in order to achieve immediacy of help, guidance, instruction and learning.) Thus, the teacher in Year 3 has to be prepared to cover ground normally covered in Year 2 and even, in some case, in Year 1.

Moreover, in many ways the work of Year 3 will follow the same pattern as that in Year 2. There must still be the provision of activities and experiences followed by the exercise of speech emanating from them together with attempts to transpose the thoughts and speech into texts. Differences will be in the emphasis given to the various elements of writing. Increasing attention will be given to spelling, and in particular to the conscious learning of various common spelling patterns. This is not to suggest a formality in the presentation of spelling patterns but to advocate an increasing emphasis in pointing out and ensuring the noticing of common patterns and the associating of them with their sound forms.

In this work teachers will begin to delineate boundaries within words so that children who have encountered, *come* and *fort* will have some basis for identifying *comfortable*, especially if they have encountered previously words such as *likeable* or *eatable*. This aspect of teaching can be done by drawing comparisons between similar elements in words when or immediately after a child has attempted to write an unfamiliar word. This approach, however, will only be truly effective if teachers keep notes of the words encountered in this way and, on subsequent occasions return to these words with the child in order to ensure reinforcement of learning. Learning is seldom immediate; it can be accomplished only with repeated efforts. If only this maxim was more rigorously followed, much inconsequential teaching would disappear from classrooms.

Just as the teaching of spelling will become oriented towards the study of letter strings within words so there will be a move simultaneously to look more closely at word formations and patterns of language. Children will be encouraged to describe orally in more appropriate ways the experiences or actions in which they have been engaged or which they have witnessed. Sometimes the emphasis will be on more explicit detailed descriptions; at others, the emphasis will be on clarity or vividness. The use of appropriate adjectives will be an important part of their speech in these oral expositions, and in transposing these oral statements into writing. There will be continuing attempts throughout Years 3 to 6 to convert natural speech patterns into appropriate written language structures.

Much of this work in the transforming of spoken into written language will also encompass training in thinking about actions and experiences, and there will be a conscious effort to show children how to expand a thought or an idea. For example, a child may fall on an icy playground and the idea of the fall can be expanded to express feelings of falling, the consequences of falling and the precautions that may be taken to avoid falling. Hence, a simple action and its associated word – fall – can be expanded into a series of thoughts which can be portrayed in language, spoken first and subsequently transposed into written form. Such an exercise in the organization of thoughts and their concomitant language is the basis of training a child to compose texts. Furthermore, if children follow up such an exercise by reading what they or the teacher has written this activity will take the form of reflection upon what they have learned; they will see the activity come to fruition and they will begin to adopt it as an habitual activity in thinking about actions and experiences; gradually, they will come to appreciate their own powers for developing themes, whether they be descriptive or imaginative. Nothing could illustrate better to children the need to think about, round and through problems in order to achieve a satisfactory statement in writing. Furthermore, through these activities teachers will be able to instil a flexibility in approaches by children to writing which will eventually get them away from a stereotyped repetition of their experiences.

Naturally, underpinning all this teaching will be the literature that is read to and by the children every day of their school lives in Years 3 to 6. From this they will acquire a feeling for a variety of language structures which will eventually emerge as part of their own language. But again it must be stressed that this process of language acquisition will be greatly enhanced if a proactive approach is adopted to reading so that children reflect upon what is read and how it is expressed. Poems are an excellent source for experiencing the sensitive usages of language, and folk tales allow great scope for the imaginative use of language.

Some teachers have a flair for teaching children to write poetry, but all have the ability to help children to appreciate poetry and poetic expressions. The effective use of words, phrases and language patterns of various lengths encountered in poetic texts can be noted and discussed. In this way children will be encouraged to experiment with segments of language other than narrative to express their feelings and reactions to a variety of stimuli. This approach is particularly appropriate in Years 3 and 4, while in Years 5 and 6 it will provide a starting point for composing writing which approximates ever more closely to poetry in the full sense of the word.

Such an approach points yet again to the inter-relationship between reading, discussion and writing and emphasizes the need for teachers to encourage reflection upon what is said and written. Also it suggests a gradual progression from reading poetry or listening to it in Year 3 through an increasingly intensive reflection upon the elements of poetic writing to actual attempts to reproduce poetry of various kinds.

Some Technical Considerations in Developing Writing

Kroll (1981) reminds teachers that young children's writing relies heavily upon their oral speech patterns and only at the approximate age of 9 years does it begin to differentiate clearly from their speech. Furthermore, it is at approximately the same age that Calkins (1980) found children beginning to be aware of audience, while Birnbaum (1981) found that 9-year-olds were more concerned to produce a 'neat, error-free end product' than to reshape and revise the actual text. These researches show the age of 9 to be somewhat of a watershed in the development of writing. Nevertheless, as Perera notes, these developments cannot be attributed solely to maturation, implying that developments can be enhanced by pertinent teaching.

This teaching can best be done through a workshop or masterclass arrangement whereby what the child writes is discussed and critically appraised by teacher and child together and with the teacher demonstrating the outcomes emerging from such appraisal. This form of teaching is most suited to fostering an emerging awareness of the language patterns appropriate for use in written texts and for creating an awareness of the demands of an audience together with a willingness to redraft what has been written.

There is an additional pedagogical approach based on the group composition of a text. This can best be accomplished with a reasonably large group of children with the use of an overhead projector. The spoken contributions of members of the group can be written up and subsequently altered by the teacher to achieve a more acceptable written structure. The amount and degree of alteration will, of course, depend upon the age of the children, but this type of work should certainly begin before the age of 7 or 8 and continue well into the junior school. Indeed, it can be used most effectively in a more highly critical sense in Year 6 and especially with more able children, where increasing refinements could be expected.

Microcomputers can also be used as a tool in composing text. Words and ideas can be registered, reordered and tried in a variety of sequences so that children may experiment with the composition of a text without the chore of rewriting. This lends itself to group work with several children cooperating to produce a more polished text and as such is a training in the refinement of ideas leading to new structural and organizational patterns of language. However, it must be remembered that computers cannot provide the kinaesthetic aid to learning that is provided by handwriting in learning to spell words and to visualize more intensely the language patterns of written English.

However, it is not only through workshops and masterclass writing sessions that children's awareness of the demands and constraints of writing can be aroused. There are other approaches that can be taken simultaneously by teachers who must, of course, be aware themselves of the various developmental aspects of writing.

Developmental Aspects of Writing

The development of children's writing is a complex subject and continual references to Perera (1984) section 5.3 will help teachers to be aware of developments in clause, phrase and sentence structure as children progress through the junior school years. But knowing what to look for is not enough; it is necessary for teachers to see that the children are made aware of these structures in the books that they read. For example, the change from the use of third person narrative in the early years of the junior school to the use of the first person, roughly at the age of 9 (Harpin, W. (1976)) would be promoted substantially by encountering the use of the first person in the narratives that are read in both private and teacher-led reading sessions. Similarly the adoption of complex, as opposed to compound sentences, where an increasing use of subordinate clauses emerges between the ages of 8 and 10 (Perera, 1984: 231) will be enhanced through pointed references to complex sentences in works of literature.

Furthermore, as Perera (1984: 240+) shows writing instructions – how to play a game, make a cake, carry out an experiment – forces writers to use a greater variety of language patterns and 'to exploit all the linguistic resources they have at their command'. Naturally, these increase with age and not too much can be expected before the age of 9 or thereabouts.

For a text to qualify for the status of discourse – a cohesive piece of writing that hangs together in presenting a theme or idea – tenses must agree and cohesive grammatical devices must be used such as reference back, substitution of a word such as a pronoun for a longer construction, ellipsis where part of a sentence is left out to avoid repetition (I would like to play football but I am not able . . .) and the use of connective words such as *then, if, however, consequently*, etc. (see Crystal, 1992). The resulting variety in sentence patterns that contribute to discourse can only be expected to emerge through experience of reading other texts and consciously and subconsciously trying to emulate more experienced writers. Hence, not only must children be introduced to samples of more sophisticated patterns of discourse but they must be imbued with a desire to recreate them in their own writing. This explains the importance of teacher feedback in which children's work is remarked upon and through which encouragement is given for the child to experiment with new language patterns. (Discourse connections are best explained in Perera (1984) and Crystal, 1992).

Children naturally adopt a personal style of narrative when they begin to write. It is a style in which names of people and the personal pronouns play a significant part. However, the demands of reportage and scientific description require an impersonal style involving the use of the passive voice and the avoidance where possible the use of personal pronouns, as in:

> *Some water and flour were mixed and passed to another child, who placed the dough in the oven* (impersonal), as opposed to
> *I mixed some water and flour and handed it to Jean, who placed the dough in the oven* (personal).

Young children do not find the writing of impersonal narrative easy when reporting generalized activities, but that does not mean that efforts should not begin in the upper juniors to introduce children to this form of writing. However, it will entail their introduction to books which are written in an impersonal style. Furthermore, writing in this style should begin with descriptions of events or activities in which the writer was not involved as this will reduce the temptation to lapse into the personal.

General Approaches in Teaching Children to Write

Throughout the junior school years teachers will be concerned to help children to improve and refine their written texts. In Year 3 they will need to continue the move away from any over-reliance upon the production of loosely coordinated clauses as the basis of writing towards a more easy reliance upon sentence patterns. This will come about as a consequence of teachers inserting and explaining the use of capital letters, full stops and, to some extent commas, in the work produced by the children. It will also be enhanced by the concentration of the children's writing on the expression of feeling or on intense reactions to experiences, activities and events, which they will be expected to express in very short texts, often containing only one complete sentence. This will concentrate the mind and avoid lapses into desperately dragging out a series of ineffectual statements. Teachers can discretely enhance children's reactions in oral discussions preceding writing thereby incurring greater intensity of feeling in the actual writing.

This intensity of feeling will lead to the development of more imaginative writing and to increasingly vivid powers of description, especially if accompanied by searches for new forms of expression – individual words at first and subsequently phrases, clauses and sentences. Here teachers would wish to encourage children to turn to literature for stimulation and sources of word usage. Much of the children's writing should be planned with the use of children's literature as a source in mind. Such stories as the naughtiness of Goldilocks in straying into the forest and 'house-breaking' or the audacity of Peter Rabbit can be starting points for raising children's reactions to stories.

With the discovery of new words the question of spelling will arise. This is an ideal way in which to approach spelling. New words discovered in the pursuit of interest and linked with intensity of feeling will undoubtedly be more memorable to a child than words presented out of context. Thus the writing workshop should also be a spelling workshop, when words needed and used by the writer are committed to memory, preferably in comparison with a previously learnt word which has some parts in common with the new word. Learning through comparison and association is more potent than learning an item in isolation. Again, as with writing and punctuation, the teacher's task is to show children how to look at words and how to draw comparisons between words using the boundaries within words to note the spelling patterns of English. Word families, as suggested in the national curriculum, are an excellent source for reference and use in making comparisons.

Teachers may wish to consider the following as causes of weakness in spelling:

- an insufficient store of the basic spelling patterns which occur in numerous English words;
- an inability to call up what has been learned and apply it;
- a lack of understanding that words have constituent parts of varying length – letters, blends, syllables and predictable strings of letters;
- an unfamiliarity with the serial probability of which letters follow and precede other letters.

Teachers may wish also to reflect upon what constitutes a viable background for good spelling:

- attention to words that have meaning and importance for each child;
- facilities for comparing words which have some elements in common;
- having been taught a method of learning to spell words, such as the finger tracing – vocalization method used by Fernald (1943);
- installation of a foolproof method of checking that words have been learned thoroughly (see Roberts, 1989);
- instilling a disposition in children to identify words which cause difficulty, where letters are doubled before adding a suffix, where double consonants do or do not appear in words (occasion, occur, occurring), or where the pronunciation of a word does not clearly indicate the correct letter to use (sep*a*rate, defin*i*te);
- the creation of a desire to spell correctly through emphasis on achievement rather than failure in spelling.

In their reading children will not only encounter a growing range of sentence patterns, they will also experience superb openings and endings to stories as well as the main substance of the stories. (The opening to the *Iron Man* and the ending to *Mrs Frisby and the Rats of NIMH* are excellent examples). These, if referred to frequently by teachers will implant the idea of beginnings which stimulate interest and endings which satisfy. From these children can be encouraged to think of openings and endings to their own stories. At first only some children will grasp what is needed and realize what they can do about it. Many children in Years 3 and 4 will find it easier to find a reasonable opening to their stories than to find endings of any note. Nevertheless, they will have begun the slow process of learning how to structure their writing.

Eventually, it will be feasible in Years 5 and 6 to introduce the idea of a simple story frame and one suggested by Stein and Trabasso (1982, p. 9) springs to mind. Using a workshop approach the teacher leads a small group (it is possible but less effective with a large group) through a series of steps having decided upon the topic, for instance, 'A storm over the Atlantic'. The first step is to *set the scene*: 'Captain Miller of British Airways flew on the Manchester to New York route. He was based in Manchester.' Next identify an *initiating event* thus: 'On one trip, halfway across the Atlantic, he saw a huge/vivid electric storm directly in front of him.' This requires a *response*: 'The dangers of these storms were well-known and Captain Miller realized that he must change course.' Next, the *action* taken as part of that response: 'He took a new course', and the *consequence* of this action/response was: 'This took him further south than he intended and he began to realize that he was running out of petrol.' The *result* or *reaction* would be: 'His only chance was to head for the Azores.' This was done as a group exercise by a student during a primary school practice, and it led to further attempts by the children to compose stories under the headings of the story frame: Setting, Initiating Event, Response and Action, Consequence, Reaction. Obviously the children's ability and experiences will determine how far this can be taken but it is something that should be approached in the upper junior school and teachers will wish to compare notes on its application.

Working to a story frame is a useful device but it would be restricting to overuse it. Rather it can be most effectively used as a pointer to the children in their writing and as a corrective when they are failing to produce well structured texts. Children must experience a fair amount of freedom to develop their ability to compose. For a substantial part of their time in the junior school this will fall into what Bereiter and Scardamalia (1985) have termed *knowledge telling*. This is best explained by a 12-year-old quoted in Bereiter and Scardamalia's book (1987):

> I have a whole bunch of ideas and write them down until my supply of ideas is exhausted. Then I might try to think of more ideas up to the point when you can't get any more ideas that are worth putting down on paper and then I would end it. (p. 10)

This type of writing, depending upon the emergence of sequential thoughts, is perhaps best developed after the experience of the initial stimulus by the compilation of pertinent words following group discussion and a buzz session in which children participate, thinking up words connected with that stimulus. Obviously, the writing that follows from this type of activity is simply a matter of stringing together ideas virtually as they arise.

However, the aim of the story frame approach is to introduce an increasing degree of craftsmanship into the composition of a text, helping to instil an ability to reform the ideas created by the stimulus and any word search or buzz session that follows into a text which has shape and balance. Buzz sessions, word searches and writing of the *knowledge telling* kind are invaluable in provoking thought and helping to eliminate inhibitions about writing. The story frame approach helps to constrain the uninhibited reproduction of those ideas in printed form. Therefore both devices have their uses.

Furthermore, the use of the story frame approach can be seen as an instrument leading gradually and eventually to a more sophisticated form of writing called *knowledge transforming* by Bereiter and Scardamalia and best described by this quotation by Aldous Huxley:

> Generally, I write everything many times over. All my thoughts are second thoughts. And I correct each page a great deal, or rewrite it several times as I go along . . . Things come to me in driblets, and when the driblets come I have to work hard to make them into something coherent. (Huxley, 1963, p. 197)

For this type of writing to emerge it is necessary to train children to plan, draft and revise both their thoughts and their transcripts as required by the national curriculum. This is a form of reflection parallel to the training they receive in reflecting upon what they read in order to improve their comprehension of texts. Only through guidance and practice will children learn to transform their knowledge and their ideas into a form which in turn makes the reader or audience reflect upon what is written rather than to merely note a sequence of ideas. Transformed knowledge is knowledge or thought reformulated to give a particular slant to the message or to meet the needs of a particular audience. This form of writing will only emerge with the adoption by the writer of new strategies, ones that follow on from previously acquired strategies (knowledge telling) but which are radically different and require specific and prolonged training.

Much the same can be said about impersonal non-narrative writing. This in its simplest form usually refers to descriptions of scientific or technological experiments, games or constructional activities and requires the use of language that is more economical, direct and terse than imaginative, personal narrative. At its more advanced stage impersonal, non-narrative writing is concerned with explanations, propositions and arguments. Writing such as this falls within the category of transforming knowledge.

Naturally, most of the impersonal writing that is done in the junior school will be of the less involved descriptive type. To promote this concise type of writing it is necessary to set tasks with which the children are already familiar. For example, compiling instructions on how to play a game, make a sandwich, repair a puncture or describe a school activity or experiment all require the children to transform the knowledge they already possess into a succinct and eventually impersonal style. This process may sound very simple to adults but, like other forms of writing, it needs to be taught. Children need to be shown how to order their statements, how to omit irrelevant details and use short direct sentences. Children have a tendency at first, to over-use coordinating conjunctions such as *and*. As exemplars of impersonal writing teachers may wish to produce workcards showing how they would describe an activity or an experiment, or they may provide sequencing cards containing all the relevant pieces of text which the children then have to arrange in an appropriate form. But the main practice will come in actually writing descriptions which are altered appropriately by the teacher, immediately after the children have written them, if possible – again using a workshop approach to teaching children to write – where the responses of teachers are seen as contributing to the composition of a text rather than as the correction of mistakes.

A Teaching Cycle

A.N. Whitehead described what he saw as a cyclic process of learning which comprised three stages: romance (motivation), precision and generalization. The first stage covered involvement in the topic; the second stage was where the learner acquired the precise knowledge or tools with which to address the topic; the new knowledge or skill was used for general purposes. These stages were seen not as sequential happenings but as revolving intertwining processes, each fortifying the other.

This cyclic pattern can be applied equally to teaching children to write. First there are activities which are consequent upon the stimulus and which precede the preparation for writing. Like the stimulus, they are motivational and take the form of further reading or relevant activity, discussion and the identification of global goals (Perera, 1984). At the second stage group or individual activities will include word searches, buzz sessions and the compilation of a word and phrase bank that relates closely to the topic. This is a stage at which the teacher can give subtle guidance in the selection of words and phrases and the setting of more specific goals, and can thereby foster discrimination in the young writers. At the third stage the children will put together the material they have collected and transcribe it into a viable text. As this proceeds the cycle will be reactivated where and when necessary with further efforts to stimulate and motivate the children, further guidance by the teacher and discussion with other pupils including reading what has so far been written, followed by a continuation of the writing. By following this cycle teachers will leave little to chance and will find themselves able to make vital contributions while the writing is in progress, and they will not simply have to rely on the nebulous inactivity of waiting until the writing is completed before making much of an impact on what is written.

A Suggested Development Plan for English

This plan reflects the requirements of the national curriculum and ensures the development of children's writing skills in the primary school.

Year 3   Simple sentences, speech directly transcribed. Presence of capital letters and full stops with the appropriate use of question marks. An increasing accuracy in spelling more commonly used words.

Year 4   Complex sentences being used more frequently. The exploration of more varied openings and the development of more satisfactory ways of ending stories. Descriptive and informative writing beginning to develop. Pauses indicated by commas. The use of speech marks. A concerted effort to tackle polysyllabic words.

Year 5   Language patterns more appropriate to written English: clause and phrase structure more varied and an increasing use of subordinate clauses. Developments in discourse – global and local coherence – narrative less repetitive. Growing ability to develop ideas within a theme. In spelling, evidence of an awareness of serial probability in the sequencing of letters and an increasing familiarity with letter strings and the structure of polysyllabic words. Handwriting developing as a distinctive style and a growing ability to write more quickly but clearly and neatly.

Year 6 Writing has its own distinctive structures and organization is more firmly established. Personal writing shows greater intensity of feeling with the use of a wider vocabulary. Impersonal descriptive and informative writing showing economy and exactness of language while at the same time showing an adept use of subordinate clauses. The development of punctuation to accord with the more complex forms of language. Greater facility in attempting to spell unfamiliar words, and evidence of and understanding that the spelling system rather than the sound system of English embodies meaning.

Discussion Points

- Is there a school policy of relating as nearly as possible the children's writing to their experiences both in and out of school, including experiences through literature?
- Is there a balance between personal and impersonal writing? Are both aspects of writing taught?
- What decisions are taken to ensure continuity between infant and junior classes?
- Is sufficient attention given to linking the children's reading with their writing?
- Is spelling linked with writing and is it regarded as an exploratory activity which involves word study and increasing familiarity with serial probability in the spelling of words?
- What steps are taken to ensure thoroughness in learning to spell? Is learning sufficiently reinforced by recall and recapitulation?
- Is experimentation and development of handwriting encouraged throughout the junior school?
- Is punctuation taught as an aspect of meaning?
- What steps are taken to enhance the progression in mid-juniors from writing based largely upon speech patterns to writing bearing its own distinct forms of organization and structure?
- Is the teaching of children to write seen as a workshop/masterclass type of activity on the part of the teacher?
- Is there a developmental plan for English in the school?

Useful Sources of Information

It would seem futile to attempt to name any particular English text books or workbooks, because of the plethora of adequate examples on the market and the fact that new ones are appearing every year. Perhaps it would be more useful to suggest some guidelines for the choice of books.

Teachers should look for books or schemes of work that cover the various aspects of English and which engage the children in activities that promote their reading, writing and spelling skills. The books should be written specifically for children, they should not also serve as a plan of work for the teacher. Too many books published in the past have been helpful in guiding teachers with indirect suggestions of work to be done but have failed hopelessly to satisfy the demands and requirements of the children. The questions and guidelines set should be clear to children who should be directed to some further reading, planning or enquiry. Also there should be scope for children to use their reading, reflective and reorganizing skills in planning and proffering answers to questions set. Where possible exemplars of good answers should be given so that children should be able to learn from the text instead of merely being tested by it.

Ideas for writing can be obtained from the following books:
BURGESS, C. (1989) *English Skills Series*, Huddersfield Schofield and Sims.

The Bright Ideas Books from Scholastic especially the one on Writing.
FORWARD, B. (1987) *All Kinds of Writing, Books 1 and 2*, Cambridge, Cambridge University Press.
GRAVES, D.H. (1983) *Writing: Teachers and Children at Work*, London, Heinemann.
MCCALL, P. and PALMER, S. (1986) *Presenting Poetry, Books 1–4*, Edinburgh, Oliver and Boyd.

and an old but invaluable book:
LANGDON, M. (1961) *Let the Children Write*, London: Longman, which suggests an interesting and effective method of getting children to write imaginatively and poetically with intense feeling.

Useful ideas for activities that can form the basis for writing:
JONES, A.V. (1988) *Things for Children to Make and Do*, London, Human Horizon Series.
MONAGHAN, H. and UNDERWOOD, K. (1988) *Early Explorations*, Bedford, Bedfordshire Education Service.

and for Y3:
EMBLEM, V. and SCHMITZ, H. (1992) *Learning Through Story*, Leamington Spa, Scholastic.

Three important source books about the English language are:
CARTER, R. (ed.) (1990) *Knowledge about Language*, London, Hodder and Stoughton.
CRYSTAL, D. (1992) *Rediscover Grammar*, Harlow, Longman.
PERERA, K. (1984) *Children's Writing and Reading*, Oxford, Blackwell.

Two books that deal with various aspects of teaching English to young children:
ROBERTS, G.R. (1989) *Teaching Children to Read and Write*, Oxford, Blackwell.
ROBERTS, G.R. (1994) *Learning to Teach Reading*, Hemel Hempstead, Simon and Schuster.

A book dealing specifically with the development of writing beyond the early stages:

BEREITER, C. and SCARDAMALIA, M. (1987) *The Psychology of Written Composition*, Hillsdale, NJ, Lawrence Erlbaum.

and a book on spelling:

REASON, R. and BOOTE, R. (1994) *Helping Children with Reading and Spelling*, London, Routledge.

References

BEREITER, C. and SCARDAMALIA, M. (1987) *The Psychology of Written Composition*, Hillsdale, NJ, Lawrence Erlbaum.

BIRNBAUM, J.C. (1981) *A study of reading and writing behaviours of selected 4th grade and 7th grade students*, D.Ed.thesis, Rutgers University of New Jersey.

CALKINS, L.M. (1980) 'Children learn the writer's craft', *Language Arts*, **57**, pp. 207–13.

CRYSTAL, D. (1992) *Rediscover Grammar*, Harlow, Longman.

FERNALD, G.M. (1943) *Remedial Techniques in Basic School Subjects*, New York, Megraw Hill.

HARPIN, W. (1976) *The Second R*, London, Allen & Unwin.

HUGHES, T. (1968) *The Iron Man*, London, Faber & Faber.

HUXLEY, A. (1963) *Writers at Work: The Paris Review Interviews*, Second series, New York.

KROLL, B.M. (1981) 'Developmental relationships between speaking and writing', in Kroll, B.M. and Vann, R.J. (eds.) *Exploring Speaking-Writing Relationships: Connections and Contrasts*, Urbana, IL, NCTE.

O'BRIEN, R.C. (1972) *Mrs Frisby and the Rats of NIMH*, London, Gollancz.

PERERA, K. (1984) *Children's Writing and Reading: Analysing Classroom Language*, Oxford, Blackwell.

ROBERTS, G.R. (1989) *Teaching Children to Read and Write*, Oxford, Blackwell.

ROBERTS, G.R. (1994) *Learning to Teach Reading*, Hemel Hempstead, Simon and Schuster.

STEIN, N.L. and TRABASSO, T. (1982) 'What's in a story: an approach to comprehension and instruction', in Glaser, R. (ed.) *Advances in Instructional Psychology*, **vol. 2**, pp. 213–67 Hillsdale, NJ, Lawrence Erlbaum.

WHITEHEAD, A.N. (1955) *The Aims of Education*, London, Benn.

Chapter 5

Working Towards Becoming the Mathematics Coordinator

Mike Harrison

The Importance of Coordinating Mathematics Teaching

The evolution of mathematics curriculum developments including the national curriculum and formal assessment has called increasingly for school-based and school-focused support for primary teachers. The mathematics coordinator's role has consequently emerged as one means of providing this support and utilizing teachers' particular strengths. As a newly qualified teacher (NQT) working towards such a position your main task in this regard over the next few years will be to equip yourself with relevant knowledge and skills in order to give your colleagues this support. This will involve you becoming increasingly credible as a consultant, improving your own teaching, interpersonal and presentation skills, acquiring knowledge and demonstrating positive attitudes towards the teaching and learning of mathematics.

To begin with let us consider why we spend so much time teaching mathematics in primary schools. After language work, mathematics takes the lion's share of the timetable of all primary classes. The non-statutory Guidance to Mathematics in the National Curriculum emphasizes that 'Mathematics is taught not only because it is useful but because it should be a source of delight and wonder, offering pupils intellectual excitement and an appreciation of its essential creativity' (NCC (1991)).

After all mathematics is:

- a powerful means of communication – to represent, to explain and to predict;
- an increasingly powerful tool in many commercial and industrial environments;
- a discipline which, with others, can contribute to the development of logical thinking skills;
- also worthy of study for its intrinsic interest, beauty and enjoyment.

Do all your colleagues appreciate that this is the case? Are there ways in which you can, over time, set up attractive teaching displays to emphasize these features? Make no mistake about it, there is a very strong selling job that you have to do to bring about positive attitudes towards mathematics teaching in your school, if it is like most others.

Mathematics teaching is often characteristically different from activities in other subject areas. Not for nothing is it often called the *silent subject* (Duncan, 1992). The way work in mathematics is assessed also differs from other primary outcomes. A child's story is seldom marked WRONG!; instead suggestions are made as to improvements in clarity, handwriting style, use of punctuation, the incorporation of adjectives, etc. In PE children are encouraged to improve the way they move, jump, throw a ball or swim – it is rare for the result of an activity to be marked with a big red cross. Yet in some classes that is exactly the (sole) result for a child from an hour's work in mathematics.

As the Cockcroft report demonstrated 'Mathematics is both difficult to teach and difficult to learn' (DES, 1982) and the insecurity which many primary school teachers may feel can only be deepened by the periodic attacks on mathematics teaching mounted by the press. Yet successful mathematics has to do with confidence. Women sometimes hold the view that mathematics is a male domain, perhaps promoted by teachers' expectations that boys will find it easy while girls will be less likely to succeed. Other beliefs include that mathematics teaching places an emphasis on speed, with the associated false expectation that mathematicians find answers almost instantly; still others have vivid memories of failure (Davies, 1990).

Fear of failing at mathematics is an attitude which prevails amongst many of the adult population including teachers. The approach adopted by teachers continues to have a profound effect upon pupils' attitudes to mathematics. Research shows that negative attitudes often persist into adulthood. One of the most important gifts you can bring your school, therefore, is to help teachers to appreciate the worth of teaching mathematics. Just including a statement such as, 'pupils should enjoy mathematics' as part of the aims for teaching mathematics in school is scarcely enough. Historically mathematics has aroused considerable anxiety amongst learners and greater scrutiny from parents and the world of work than have most other subject areas. Every effort must be made to ensure that *all* teachers are aware that their own enthusiasm, interest and enjoyment of mathematics and how it is presented impacts upon pupils. Clearly this is a crucial part of the coordinator's role.

Knowing what we are doing – and why – can help us all to work together to common purpose and avoid allowing children to develop negative attitudes. The following pages contain boxes of lists of aims which represent the outcome of several hours of staff meetings at one school (Stewart, 1995). A collection of aims are useless on their own. They will be of value only if there is corporate and committed ownership. Therefore, they cannot be merely lifted from one school to another. However, as a newly qualified teacher, you need a starting point to begin discussions, and faithfully reporting some ideas from elsewhere in order to begin the process of writing an agreed policy or to start discussions is a valid strategy.

It is not just the *what* and the *why* and *when*, it is also the *way* mathematics is taught which has a great bearing on the view your pupils will develop of mathematics as a subject. As a newly qualified teacher you will need to consider just how much influence you could or should bring to bear in this matter with more experienced colleagues. You might well feel it is best approached from the point of view that you, as a newcomer to the profession would value an open discussion between senior colleagues of how mathematics teaching can achieve some of the aims on which you all agree. This will then not be seen as a threat nor an inappropriate suggestion from someone perceived as not having the experience to offer suggestions – but part of the service your school needs to offer to you.

A starting point for such discussion may be to use the inspection handbook (OFSTED, 1994) which gives inspectors guidance.

AIMS of teaching mathematics: Attitudes and personal qualities. We aim that children should:
- enjoy mathematics;
- enjoy a sense of achievement;
- have a positive attitude to mathematics;
- gain confidence and flexibility of mind when facing new problems;
- be able to challenge ambiguity in text, media etc.;
- become persistent, even when things go wrong;
- grow to be creative and imaginative – able to determine own methods and pose own questions;
- develop good work habits;
- understand the part which mathematics plays in the world;
- undertake sustained periods of mathematical study.

where teaching is good appropriate opportunities are offered, and a range of approaches managed and differentiated for individual pupils to:

> develop and consolidate knowledge, skills and understanding across all attainment targets;
> develop links between attainment targets;
> solve unfamiliar problems and investigate mathematics itself.

OFSTED go on to re-emphasize Cockcroft's oft quoted plea for a mixture of methods.

> At all levels the range of teaching approaches should include exposition, discussion, practical work, consolidation and practice, problem solving and investigations. A sequence of carefully planned activities must be

provided by teachers to ensure that basic skills are developed and used to the highest level of which each pupil is capable (part IX: 29).

It is perfectly acceptable to tell your colleagues that your head will need to have an opinion on the degree to which this is being achieved and part of your role through discussion is to provide him or her with the evidence.

The Role of the Mathematics Coordinator

As with all job descriptions local needs will determine the exact duties a mathematics coordinator will be asked to perform and quite obviously the expectations made of a NQT will be different from those made of a more experienced teacher. However some duties may possibly involve you in:

- auditing, marshalling, ordering and taking care of the school's mathematics equipment and books in common use;
- monitoring of school's mathematics policy and updating this where necessary;
- keeping up to date with best practice in mathematics teaching and the national and local Curriculums;
- attending courses provided by your LEA or Higher Education Institute (HEI);
- occasionally talking about the school's mathematics teaching to visitors, governors or advisers;
- arranging staff INSET or focused discussions on agreed practices.

Whether or not you are expected to do all or any of these in your first year (or whether no specific demands are made on you) you may wish to start working towards some of these on a small scale so that you gain the experience for when they do become a requirement.

This is not quite as easy as A–B–C but the following sections are designed to give you some assistance in carrying out elements of your job description.

> Aims of Teaching Mathematics
> Social Skills
> We aim that children should be able to:
> cooperate with others
> (sharing materials and ideas);
> work as a member and leader of a team;
> respect different views.

Assisting in the Management of a Key Stage 2 Mathematics Policy

In Chapter 2 a case was made for the benefits of having a school policy. We might take a few of these statements and use them as criteria against which to judge the policy document you will have inherited.

- Are the school's intentions in mathematics made clear by this document? Do teachers know what to expect when they receive a new class? Do parents know what you are trying to do in teaching mathematics to children of different ages and abilities?
- Does the policy document have any funding implications and are these built into the budget? Such items as the replacement of broken equipment or lost books should be accounted for and a regular re-appraisal of mathematics schemes should be built in.
- Is the document written in language(s) accessible to give information to governors, parents, inspectors?
- Do members of staff find the document useful as a framework for planning? Which parts are the most useful?
- Are teachers' understanding of coherence, continuity, progression in mathematics teaching helped by the policy? Does it shape teachers' classroom priorities?
- Does it assist in achieving uniformity and consistency in school decision making in the opinion of the senior management team?
- Have teachers been helped to understand the teaching and learning strategies employed by other staff?
- Does the document help create a team spirit in making public the school's goals for children's achievements in mathematics?
- Do teachers think it offers a means of evaluation of the quality of provision of mathematics teaching in the school?
- Does it help clarify functions and responsibilities of staff?
- Did it help new staff (including you) to settle in?

> AIMS of teaching mathematics: Study Skills
> We aim that children should learn to:
> - read and comprehend mathematics books and use appropriate reference skills;
> - plan independent work, be organized, logical and systematic;
> - retrieve, use and return appropriate resources.

A school policy is useful if teachers refer to it in their daily planning. By asking around and keeping your ear to the ground you may form an opinion as to whether the current mathematics policy does any or all of these things. The school's development plan will tell you when/if the document is next to be revised and your opinions might well be best kept to yourself until nearer this time. What you may find, however, is that the policy document needs servicing – do all staff have copies, are they in use, have members of staff who have taken up appointments since its inception had the opportunity to discuss its implications, are staff doing what they said they would do? Within these questions lies your role in the management of the policy.

Being watchful of Consistency from Class to Class

Close observation of teachers classroom practice may alert you to some continuity issues which need attention. For example, the use of language such as *oblong* and *rectangle* in shape work and the way time is taught in analogue or digital format are both needed in school, but care needs to be taken to present these in ways that will not confuse children moving from class to class. Here are some common areas where continuity issues may arise:

- teaching style – the balance between practical work and consolidation of skills;
- use of appropriate structural apparatus;
- balance between number work and maths topics;
- the use of calculators;
- access to practical equipment;
- types of books used (both text and exercise);
- shared recording systems;
- the setting out of sums (position of signs, etc).

> Aims for Teaching mathematics
> Manipulate Skills
> We aim that children should be able to:
> - make appropriate and accurate drawings;
> - work to appropriate degrees of accuracy;
> - write clearly, recording in statements, clearly and systematically;
> - use symbols and terminology logically;
> - use instruments such as ruler, compass, scales, calculator etc.

In two-form entry schools or where the classes are vertically grouped, is the experience of children in parallel classes roughly equivalent or likely to be so by the end of the year? Do teachers of such classes regularly talk about the mathematics curriculum, plan collaboratively and support each other (by sharing homemade worksheets, for example).

Many of these problems will be resolved where a common published mathematics scheme has been adopted. A common methodology and language will be in place and teachers will use this guidance. Schools which use a combination of published schemes and those which rely on banks of home produced materials will need coordinators to be more watchful in this regard.

Continuity and Progression over the Junior Years

Over the four years of Key Stage 2 the national curriculum defines a block of knowledge to be mastered but, unlike earlier when levels were specified within the programme of study and statements of attainment labelled, there could now be a tendency for teachers to feel that they need to start from scratch in each topic area unless progress is clearly specified and monitored for each class. For example, *handling data* includes under section b: 'collect and represent discrete data appropriately using graphs and diagrams, including block graphs, pictograms and line graphs; interpret a wider range of graphs and diagrams that represent data, including pie charts, using a computer where appropriate' . . . Previously teachers had each statement within such a list labelled as suitable for specific ages and an order of progress defined. One could therefore assume that work at Level 3 was being done in the lower juniors and SoAs for Levels 4 and 5 in the upper classes. Now that this labelling has disappeared the intervention of a coordinator is even more important.

If children are to use the time allocated to mathematics to best advantage, there will have to be some agreement that certain aspects within the Key Stage 2 programme of study are tackled in some classes and built upon later in the school. In some schools successful progress has been achieved by setting mathematics groups so that for at least some of their junior years children are taught in like ability bands. The way this has been achieved in one Manchester primary school is set out below.

Creating four sets from 120 Year 5 and 6 children spread across 3 ability levels		
Set 1	24 children	working at level 5
Set 2	34 children	working at level 4
Set 3	36 children	working at level 4
Set 4	16 children	working at level 3

In addition, for part of the year the school's head and a floating teacher are able to create a fifth group allowing for even greater differentiation by task. This is not only the province of the two-form entry junior school. It is possible to set across two year groups in the smaller school and achieve similar results if we think about *levelness* rather than simply year group.

Defining AT1

When the latest version of the mathematics national curriculum was being devised, serious consideration was given to incorporating AT1 into the other attainment targets. *Using and applying Mathematics* certainly makes no sense unless carried out in the context of number, shape, data handling or measuring. It's retention as an attainment target of its own was overwhelmingly supported by respondents to the consultation, who believed that only in this way would it retain its emphasis in the minds of teachers. Thus we are required to give children in Key Stage 2 opportunities to use and apply mathematics in practical tasks in real-life problems and in mathematics itself; to take increasing responsibility for organizing and extending tasks; to devise and refine their own ways of recording; and to ask questions and follow alternative suggestions to support the development of reasoning. This implies that such objectives feature in the minds of teachers when they devise activities and supervise the tasks for children to do. Your eventual aim as a coordinator must be to see that this is so, but for now just consider how much work in AT1 is going on in your school and how successful the outcomes are. If you find that things are not ideal then work perfected in your own classroom may come to define AT1 in the minds of colleagues.

Example task: Find the closest estimate to the number of lentils/grains of rice in a coffee jar provided by the teacher.

Attainment Target	Intentions for children	action of teacher
AT1–2. Making and monitoring decisions to solve problems	a. select and use appropriate mathematics and materials;	provide both suitable and unsuitable equipment for the task and sometimes let children choose badly;
	b. try different mathematical approaches; identify and obtain information needed to carry out the work;	provide calculators to encourage a wider range of mathematical approaches and access to work of previous groups given similar (but different) problems;
	c. develop their own mathematical strategies and look for ways to overcome difficulties;	by intervention show that you value persistence;
	d. check results and consider whether they are reasonable.	ask group to publish and defend their conclusions against those of their peers.

In similar vein you will be able to develop children's mathematical language and other forms of communication to help them understand and use the language of number, shape, measures, simple probability and relationships; use diagrams, graphs and simple algebraic symbols and present the results of investigations.

Using and applying also involves teaching children how to reason mathematically, investigating general statements – there are more red cars than yellow cars, head circumference is one-third of reach, you can join four unifix cubes in six different ways. They can be taught to search for patterns in their results and then make general statements of their own explaining their reasoning.

Such work in your own room will assist other teachers to understand the value of open ended problem solving, and if well executed, they may emulate you.

Encouraging the Use of IT in Mathematics

Teaching mathematics through the use of computers and other IT devices and using mathematical IT experiences to enhance children's competence and confidence in IT are both valid interpretations of this aspect of the role.

Databases are frequently used to show children (and adults) the power of the computer. The speed at which micros can make calculations, sort data, and provide graphic capabilities to show the results are all impressive. Whichever package your school has, you will be able to obtain specimen files. Use these at home. Find out what analyses are possible – how to print out a list or a pie chart; delete or replace a file; print out an individual record. Can you analyse a subset of data (boys/British moths) only? Do the publishers suggest ways in which your class could use the program? The oft heard criticism of graphs work in primary classrooms in the past has been the disproportionate amount of time children spend constructing the chart compared to the mathematical thought it prompted. The interpretation of pie charts and graphs has been particularly poor. With the use of IT that ratio can be reversed as the time-consuming aspects of drawing graphs is simply and swiftly handled leaving pupils time to consider such matters as which is the best sort of graph to use; what will we expect; how shall we explain our results?

Drill and Practice programs are often scathingly attacked as the unacceptable face of computer use. You

AIMS of teaching mathematics
Mathematical Process Skills
sort, match, discriminate, classify; look for patterns and relationships; analyze a problem; simplify difficult tasks – select suitable strategy;
apply appropriate techniques;
make and test a hypothesis;
generalise, prove and disprove; reason, enquire;
apply combinations of mathematical skills and techniques;
estimate and approximate and develop a feel for number (at 'homeness');
recall, apply, interpret, mathematical knowledge;
make logical deductions from given mathematical data;
select appropriate data, interpret results; decide when it is sensible to use a calculator – and how to use it sensibly!
Carry out mental calculations; appreciate the relationships between concepts;
understand the need for standardization (e.g., in measurement);
recognize and use spatial relationships in two and three dimensions;
understand mathematical principles;

might argue however, that in mathematics such programs often support specific learning objectives, generally give instant reward, they have appeal to some pupils, the work can allow for differentiation (the rest of the class being occupied with other matters) and spread the practice of certain skills across a number of media. Such software is occasionally used as an electronic blackboard demonstrating a method to obtain the right answer in an attractive and often tuneful manner. The question you will need to answer is whether this is the best use of an expensive and scarce resource.

As Judith Judd (1991) points out in *Children, Computers and the National Curriculum*, 'It is more important for children to become skilled in general purpose computer applications than to spend time practising spelling tests. Skilled exploitation of a spreadsheet, graphics package or desktop publishing programme . . . can improve personal productivity dramatically and is also transferable between topics . . .'

A variation of this is the use of software to create a series of unique drill and practice workcards tailored to stress specific number bonds, number sequences, operations or combinations of these. Such a programme for the A3000 series is *Maths Card*, which many teachers would view as a boon for computation work, as it does not occupy the computer for more than the time it takes for the teacher to set up the parameters and print out the result, leaving the machine itself for more creative work. It could be that some teachers may need to be persuaded to use the computer in ways which extend children's skills in using their imaginations by composing written texts, creating graphics, generating and solving problems, devising programs and investigating data. Ways in which this might be achieved might form a discussion point between you and the IT coordinator.

Those of us who react negatively to the idea that children can be taught by computers are more enthusiastic about the concept of children themselves teaching computers routines and procedures. This is the concept behind LOGO. *LOGO* and *turtle graphics* are widely spoken of as important elements in work in IT in primary classrooms. Many references to such work are contained in the national curriculum (mathematics, technology, science) and teachers who have worked with children in this area report enthusiastically on the benefits for children both in their development of cognition, their confidence and, by the mode of working, their ability to cooperate in problem solving situations.

In her acclaimed book *Children Using Computers*, Anita Straker (1989) points out that there are three related but different aspects of the use of LOGO with young children that make it worthwhile:

- it can encourage discovery learning;
- it can help children to develop mathematical concepts;
- it can provide insight into the power of programming.

Some teachers consider this work better undertaken with a programmable robot such as PIP or ROAMER and you may wish to consider the purchase of such items to add to the stock of mathematics equipment under your control.

Forging Mathematics Links across the Curriculum

There are many ways in which mathematics can act as a servant to enhance understanding in other areas of the curriculum. In geography, for example, coordinates, time, direction, distance and speed are all useful for explaining concepts in this area. Greek mathematicians and their ideas may be studied in history and the creation of time-lines fundamental to its understanding. Islamic art is intrinsically mathematical, and science is a natural bedfellow with mathematics, relying on linear, area, volume, and temperature measures and often graphing the results.

> AIMS of teaching Mathematics
> *Communication Skills*
> We aim that children should be able to: explain, discuss, describe and listen; communicate with clear expression and fluency; record findings by means of real objects and diagrams and present them to others using tabular, graphical forms applying suitable scaling and labelling of axes; interpret and critically analyze mathematical information (e.g., statistics in the media for example).

Gaining a Budget and Recommending Mathematics Equipment

Being responsible for spending a budget means that you will then be able to buy and use resources without continual recourse to your head. You will need to arrange to find a method of gaining agreement amongst the staff for the use of this money. Record the results of any meetings (formal and informal) you have had to determine spending this fund and include this record with an end-of-year account of how the money was spent. There are many brochures regularly sent to school from suppliers of maths equipment. If your school has no universal system for storing these brochures then create a file, to which all staff should have access, for those which contain maths equipment.

Helping to Choose a Mathematics Scheme

Teaching mathematics is demanding and many primary teachers express the need for expert, day-to-day support which they feel a commercial scheme can provide. Such a scheme provides materials which have been tried out on a large sample of children, is generally more attractive and colourful than that which can be easily produced by teachers alone, often captures children's interests and gives the impression that individual activities build together into long-term solid learning.

Most schools therefore adopt a scheme for the major part of the mathematics course work throughout Key Stage 2 and much discussion goes into its choice, for it is a major investment of both money and teacher's effort to understand and operate the scheme and will, of course, affect the mathematical life of hundreds of children. Periodically schools consider adding to or replacing the scheme and the decision for this will be taken at the highest level. At this time, depending on seniority, the mathematics coordinator will play a role and you would be wise to have some thoughts to place before the head, the staff or the governors if such a purchase is imminent.

You might wish to put together some ideas which would help others to come to an agreement based on criteria which you might develop under these headings:

The school

What is the job you want a mathematics scheme to do? Are the school's needs as expressed in the aims, the emphases given to different topics within the national curriculum, the teaching methods generally employed and the assessment needs clear enough to establish some criteria against which to make judgments?

The scheme

Can you distinguish between schemes in terms of their organization of material, the balance between new work and consolidation, the presentation including print style and language used, suitability of pictures, amount of work on a page, whether it consists of workbooks, textbooks, cards, games, etc.? Does the scheme help you identify supplementary material such as video tape, computer programmes and teachers' manuals? What are the demands on the teacher and classroom? Is the scheme easy to use? What equipment does it require?

The People

'The successful use of a mathematics scheme essentially requires a sympathetic match between the people who create it and those who use it. If the aspirations of one are out of line with the beliefs and capabilities of the other, the materials are unlikely to be used successfully' (Harling and Roberts, 1988, p. 16). Thus some knowledge about the way in which the scheme came into being (as a result of INSET, for example), or whether it originated in another country may be useful information. The beliefs of those who will use it must also be a consideration and the differences between these taken into account. A scheme which appears condescending and dictatorial to one teacher may be a lifeline to another. What about the children? A judgement will have to be made about the suitability of material for the particular group of children – those in your school. If the books within the scheme do not make it easier for children to develop insights into the connection between mathematics and their everyday lives, it will have failed.

In their book *Primary Mathematics Schemes*, Paul Harling and Tessa Roberts (1988) have produced a full set of criteria for examining mathematics schemes under seven headings.

Characteristics, design and construction
Aim, objectives and scope of the scheme
The scheme in relation to teachers
The scheme in relation to children
Language
Assessment and record keeping
Supplementary questions for the individual teacher or school

To these you should add manageability of the delivery of the national curriculum.

Improving the Assessment of Children's Progress in Mathematics

Many teachers see the formalization of assessment and the keeping of records of children's progress as a mammoth burden and the use of results by the government to create league tables as anti-educational and as a threat to schools in areas of disadvantage. It is not recommended therefore that an NQT should seek to win friends and influence colleagues by promoting this topic. However, the fact remains that judgments of each child's attainment in mathematics based on the best fit to given level descriptors are required at the end of Key Stage 2, and that primary teachers already make much use of assessment to inform their teaching in many ways. Help in finding ways to bring these two together would save time, effort and stress. Whether you or the assessment coordinator are the most qualified to do it may be debated, but working together you will gain from their professional knowledge.

As with a number of features in this chapter you may well be best advised to start with your own practice. You could use your own mathematics mark book or pupil records for your class and consider each of these questions.

- Does this record of mathematics reflect what an individual pupil knows and can do?
- How useful is this record in identifying where an individual pupil is and has been? (for gaining insights into how the pupil is learning)
- How useful is this record for planning future action? (ensuring progression)

- How useful is this record for the next class teacher? (ensuring continuity)
- To what extent does this record presuppose a fixed sequence for learning mathematical concepts?
- How much of a burden does maintaining this record place upon me?
- By how much have children changed since I recorded this?
- Is this a record of what has been taught or what has been achieved?
- What purposes of assessment are served, or not served, by these records?
- What modifications will you make a result of this analysis?

You may wish to talk to your assessment coordinator about your findings. He or she would be able to assure you as to whether you were in step with other staff.

Whatever conclusions you reach about your own recording system and that used by others, remember your main task is to impart knowledge and skills to children, not to serve purely bureaucratic needs or other people's political purposes. That is not to say that assessment is not important. Teachers have always assessed children's progress in mathematics and other subjects, evaluated their own activities and recorded and reported to parents in the best interests of children. You need to keep on trying to improve upon the methods you use. What you don't have to feel bad about is that you cannot accurately know the inner workings of the mind of all 35 of your class, while delivering nine aspects of someone else's curriculum (conceived by a committee). We are not staffed to the same degree as say Scandinavian Primary schools (or our own secondary ones for that matter). Our public and fee paying schools make a great play that their small classes of generally highly motivated pupils allow teachers to give attention to individual pupils needs. For all teachers to be able to do the same thing all will need similar conditions.

Judging and Improving your own Effectiveness

Feedback is the breakfast of the gods, and just as you will aim to grow in confidence to give feedback to teachers on their mathematics teaching, you need to arrange to get some feedback yourself in this area of your work. One way in which you cannot be ignored is to send a report to the head listing your achievements in this role over the past six months and setting out the gains you expect to make over the next. Wanted or not, this should elicit some response and has the added bonus that you cannot be accused in years to come of not doing the right thing if you give the head every opportunity to express an opinion and give you guidance on your work in this role. Much of your success will depend upon the support you receive from the senior management team in broadening your experience both of mathematics teaching and in management.

All the staff need to have a clear understanding about the role curriculum coordinators are expected to play within a team of professionals. A collaborative atmosphere can only be maintained where changes introduced are consistently seen to benefit children throughout the school rather than merely to advantage the reputation of the initiator. Teachers who are receptive to a collaborative approach grow to respect and acknowledge curriculum expertise from within their own ranks. Developing the strength of your own mathematics teaching is therefore obviously important. Teachers will also make judgements as to the value of the advice based on the your range of experience, ability to organize resources, knowledge of mathematics and range of interpersonal skills (Holly and Southworth, 1989).

In order to allow for growth in the areas outlined above, you will need some latitude in the way you interpret your role. In schools where job descriptions are highly prescriptive, there is little room for individual enterprise and initiative. You will also need time. Time available for you to do the paperwork will affect the degree of consultation possible and hence its quality. Time for you to work alongside teachers in their classrooms will be necessary in order to change practice. You will need time to see teaching and learning in parts of the school with which you are unfamiliar for your own development. Stow and Foxman (1988) showed ways in which time was made in some schools to allow mathematics coordinators to do the task. Some are 'through headteacher, part-time or floating teacher cover. Other ways in which release from class teaching was arranged included supply and peripatetic teacher cover, student teacher cover, exchange of classes or doubling up of classes'. (p. 57)

As the needs of schools change new demands will be made of you, but even the longest march has to begin with the first step. By making moves promoted by ideas in this chapter you will, in turn, provide support for colleagues within the school and help coordinate children's first steps in learning mathematics.

References

DAVIES, J. (1990) *Working with Colleagues: Supporting Primary Mathematics*, Milton Keynes, Centre for Mathematics Education at The Open University.

DES (1982) *Mathematics Counts*, report of the Cockcroft committee, London, HMSO.

DUNCAN, A. (1992) *What Primary Teachers Should Know about Maths*, London, Hodder & Stoughton.

JUDD, J. (1991) *Children, Computers and the National Curriculum*, Coventry, NCET.

HARLING, P. and ROBERTS, T. (1988) *Primary Mathematics Schemes*, London, Hodder & Stoughton.

HOLLY, P. and SOUTHWORTH, G. (1989) *The Developing School*, London, Falmer Press.

NCC (1991) *Mathematics in the National Curriculum*, HMSO, London.

OFSTED (1994) *Handbook for the Inspection of Schools*, London, HMSO.

SCAA (1994) *The National Curriculum Orders*, London, HMSO.

STEWART, B. (1995) 'Directions in mathematics: The coordinator effect' in Davies, J. (ed.) *Developing a Curriculum Leadership Role in Key Stage 1*, London, Falmer Press.

STOW, M. and FOXMAN, D. (1988) *Mathematics Coordination*, Windsor, NFER-NELSON.

STRAKER, A. (1989) *Children Using Computers*, Oxford, Blackwell.

Acknowledgments

The computer programme referred to is *Maths Card* published by Creative Curriculum Software, 5 Clover Hill Road, Saville Park, Halifax, HX1 2YG.

Roamer is a programmable floor turtle used independently from the computer. It is manufactured by Valiant Technology plc., Myrthe House, 69 Salcott Rd, London SWll 9DQ.

Chapter 6

Coordinating Science at Key Stage 2

Alan Cross and Dave Byrne

Introduction

In this chapter we recognize that much of what is said will also apply to Key Stage 1 (5–7 years). It is, therefore, essential that coordinators working at Key Stage 2 make themselves aware of work at Key Stage 1 and earlier so that they can promote progression within science. Our focus will be upon those things which are most pertinent to the management and implementation of science in the later primary years. Emphasis is placed upon questions relating to the delivery of a science curriculum which ensures that continuity and progression is achieved across and between the phases of primary education and which is consistent with a balanced and rigorous approach to the whole curriculum. This progression, built firmly on Key Stage 1, is we feel, the essence of education at Key Stage 2.

Science education in primary schools has undergone quite dramatic changes in the 1980s and 1990s. It has developed from a subject at the periphery of the primary curriculum to its place alongside the other core subjects of English and mathematics. It is now compulsory throughout the primary years. There have been and remain enormous pressures placed upon primary schools and the teachers within them, to introduce, manage and develop this challenging area of the curriculum, for some detail see HMI 1992; HMI 1993.

This chapter is written principally for students and newly qualified teachers (NQTs) preparing to take on the role of science coordinator. It is expected that all those involved in promoting science as part of primary education will find it interesting and helpful.

The Place of Science in the National Curriculum

Visiting several primary schools or reading the freely available OFSTED reports will soon reveal considerable difference in the quality of teaching of science from classroom to classroom and school to school. During the year of its introduction as part of the national curriculum (1989) science became the focus of curriculum planning in many primary schools. Since then its core status has been somewhat eroded by pressure from other subjects, removal of SC1 (science attainment target one) from formal assessment and more recently removal of science SATs (Standard Assessment Tasks) at Key Stage 1.

Tension within the subject was increased by the Dearing Report (SCAA, 1993) which recommended that science at Key Stage 2 should be taught for 72 hours per year. This represents a mere 2.0 hours per week, as compared to 3.5 hours per week for mathematics and over 5 hours for English. Any erosion in time allocation may lower the status of science (ASE, 1994) especially when viewed as part of an overcrowded curriculum (Campbell, 1994).

Despite this background of change and confusion, science in primary education remains a considerable success story of the National Curriculum (ASE, 1993). It is now compulsory from the age of 5 to 16 and is part of the curriculum activities of most nurseries. Department of Education initiatives such as the GEST funded twenty-day courses and the earlier educational support grants have provided a pool of primary teachers who have received, in some cases, quite significant training. From 1995 all entrants to teacher education courses will require at least one GCSE pass in a science subject and from 1996 teacher education courses will be required to provide 150 hours of science, an increase of 50 per cent on the current requirements.

The future challenge for primary education is to introduce and manage the complexity of this still new curriculum area. Schools must learn from each other by adopting examples of good practice where they exist. Student teachers and NQTs approaching the subject may be somewhat daunted by this complex picture. However, with change occurring rapidly, NQTs may be as qualified as experienced colleagues to deal with issues arising from the latest curricular reform. Schools need enthusiastic coordinators for science who can clearly see the achievement of all children as the overall goal and who are prepared to work with colleagues, utilizing their experience and strengths to promote science.

Learning Primary Science – Recent Research

It is our contention that we must build on the already significant progress of science in primary education. We had a basis in the 1960s of sound science going on in isolated schools and classes. We moved in the 1970s and 1980s through initiatives emphasizing the science process which reassured many primary teachers in their belief that they could contribute to children's learning in science. During the 1980s and 1990s there has been increased emphasis on content knowledge. There appears to be in the 1990s an acceptance that a balance between the two is desirable. We would support this, but add that we need knowledge in these areas:

- implementation knowledge (planning, organization, recording and assessing);

- personal scientific knowledge process of and content;
- knowledge of the way in which children achieve scientific knowledge and understanding.

This is, of course, a considerable task for those with a heavy teaching schedule (typically full time in primary schools). We offer the following example of these areas of professional knowledge related to a common science activity dealing with insulation.

Activity – Insulation of Ice Lollies – knowledge useful to a teacher

process knowledge	– ideas about measurement and recording
	– notions about fair testing and variables
	– developing an hypothesis
scientific knowledge and understanding (content)	– solids, liquids and gases
	– insulation, materials
knowledge of children's scientific learning	– that informal ideas tend to stick, i.e. children often think that coldness is something rather than simply the absence of heat, that young children often think that the insulating material is producing heat!
	– how we might use children's alternative ideas to move them toward scientifically accepted ideas
implementation knowledge	– that different groups might trial different materials and report back to the whole group
	– that careful teacher questioning may direct attention

There is a small but growing body of research which examines primary teacher's understanding of scientific principles (PSTS Project, 1993). Such investigation clearly reveals that primary teachers require considerable support and input in order to raise their confidence in science teaching.

There are also interesting questions being asked about children's conclusions in scientific investigations. There is evidence that while children may do science practically, they may not always reach any kind of conclusion based upon evidence from their experiments. Phipps (1994) suggests that children will often come to intuitive conclusions which may be wholly unsubstantiated. He suggests that the most important part of a science investigation is its conclusion and that this is an area often underemphasized in primary school science.

Developing the Role of Specialist or Coordinator

The effectiveness of the coordinator for science in each primary school is a very significant factor (HMI, 1991) in the subjects' development. In order that the coordinator is influential it is important that he or she should have the backing of the headteacher. The coordinator needs to devote time to informing the head of progress.

Science at Key Stage 2 has considerable breadth in its programmes of study. It is safe to assume that some teachers will find this breadth a considerable challenge (Wragg, Bennett and Carre, 1989). They will naturally look to the coordinator for guidance and assistance. The coordinator should therefore do three things in relation to content knowledge. Namely:

* seek to further your own personal scientific knowledge;
* gather around yourself sufficient materials to support that personal knowledge and that of colleagues;
* seek to develop ways of communicating this and other subject related knowledge in a non-threatening and supportive professional manner which is focused directly on improving the teaching of science to the children in the school.

Developing the Science Policy

The science policy must be linked to the school development plan and will be a strong ally in your role as coordinator. It will provide a focus for everyone involved in the school's curriculum. It will guide you in the classroom, offer a framework for your work as coordinator, assist colleagues who are co-ordinators of other areas, as well as informing parents and governors. It also gives a means of evaluating the effectiveness of the curriculum. The science policy should adopt the style of other similar documents in school. It should be as short as possible, be well presented and be subject to constant review and improvement. Any such document should be written in close collaboration with colleagues. Often a series of staff meetings will be used to write a policy. In some schools a small subcommittee will meet to construct a proposal either in detail or as a framework. You must consult the headteacher or deputy headteacher to discover how this has proceeded in the past and how you will give teachers opportunity to effect the evolution and shape of the science policy and give them a sense of ownership and commitment to the policy without over burdening them with too many long staff meetings. It is important that policy is driven by teachers and yourself, starting from where you are and developing your practice.

School policy documentation varies from school-to-school. Commonly there is a short statement of policy, one or two sides of A4, followed or accompanied by a file which deals section by section with the following:

- the organization of science within the curriculum (including the national curriculum), broad based themes and science topics;
- teaching styles;
- the importance of AT1 and suggestions for its development;
- resources for teachers and classroom resources – catalogue or list, siting, access;
- suggestions about how children might record their science activities;
- advice on progression, continuity, differentiation, record keeping and assessment;
- provision for special needs;
- cross-curricular themes and dimensions;
- multicultural education;
- personal, social and health education;
- multilingual education;
- environmental education;
- economic and business education;
- information technology;
- numeracy and literacy;
- problem solving;
- transition from class-to-class and from phase-to-phase (Key Stages 1 and 3);
- parental involvement (SHIPS project, Solomon and Lee, 1991);
- relationship of science with the whole curriculum;
- health and safety (ASE 1990 *Be Safe*!);
- how you will evaluate teaching and learning of science in the school.

It is important that an annual review of the policy takes place; this might be conducted by you in relation to your monitoring and evaluative role. An annual report to the head on the extent of implementation of the policy and perhaps bi-annually to staff may be sufficient.

Job Description

There are a number of issues to establish. You will need to clarify these with the head and colleagues. The extent to which you are seen as a specialist scientist and/or coordinator is important.

The policy will need a statement of the school's understanding of science and its place in the curriculum. Your job description might include the following:

- coordinating policy development and writing of policy;
- making sure science is represented and accounted for in other policies, such as special needs, assessment, mathematics;
- monitoring and coordinating staff development;

- ordering and managing resources;
- providing advice and support;
- ensuring that science is well represented and catered for in curriculum planning (including time allocation);
- leading the selection of materials and resources;
- monitoring and evaluating the subject within the school.

Developing Short, Medium and Long-Term Plans

In order to deal with the above you will require some kind of action plan. A sound basis for this will be a series of short-term, medium and long-term plans for the subject. You will need to talk to the head so that these might tie in with the school's overall five-year development plan. Long-term goals may relate to objectives set out in the policy statement for example to ensure equality of provision for all, to ensure that SC1 is emphasized. Medium-term goals may be achieved in a year and may include writing a draft policy, reviewing equipment in the upper and lower junior science cupboard, improving the planning to fit in with other curricular areas, monitoring assessment procedures and developing record keeping.

Planning

An important part of your role will be to support colleagues' curriculum planning. Do they feel comfortable with their level of science subject knowledge? You might offer assistance through discussion or you might make available publications such as *Forces* (NCC, 1992) or Jennings (1994). You might encourage colleagues to attend local courses and events run by the Association for Science Education, the LEA or local university.

Science will need to fit into the overall curriculum plans which are made for each year within the Key Stage. These plans or programmes of study should address themselves to breadth and continuity within the subject across the Key Stage. Over the four junior years children return to the strands of science and within SC1 regularly. As science coordinator you will need to be involved in any whole-phase or whole-school planning of the curriculum. You might inform yourself prior to this by conducting an audit of coverage.

At one level you must avoid several classes trying to do electricity at the same time with limited resources. At another level you might wish to see SC1 develop over the years. You will also need to be involved with medium-term planning in which teachers take the overall year or Key Stage plans and put them into a form which gives a forecast over half a term or a term. These plans should interpret the overall science objectives stated in school science policy and should seek to articulate progression over a number of weeks. The final stage for most teachers is weekly activity plans. At this stage the teachers are planning activities and should be focusing on differentiation. Schools and teachers will have different approaches but must address these areas. Very much related here are issues of classroom organization and teaching style. School policy on teaching style would be very useful. The teaching of science would be an important consideration in any such policy. Each stage of planning has its challenges and in science this is compounded by the subject's breadth, the importance of the subject and the lack of confidence of many teachers.

Teachers and Teaching

Teachers are concerned on a day-to-day basis with all the complexities of the classroom including teaching and learning. Try to determine the extent of practical work, who takes the lead, teacher or children? What is meant by group work? Do children go outside the classroom? If so, why? Can the children use measuring instruments? How are science sessions concluded? What sort of scientific vocabulary is used by teachers? How comfortable are they with AT1? Is science taught as a separate subject? Always? Part of the time? Can children talk about their work? How do they report their science? These are all questions to be answered by observing, talking to colleagues and children. They may feature in staff meetings.

Initially it will be important to demonstrate your own credibility (avoid any suggestion that you teach science perfectly, rather, you are like your colleagues, developing your teaching and taking this process seriously) but also to be taking a real interest in the work of colleagues. Assemblies and display around the school are good ways of showing what you are up to in your classroom science. Teachers will also have expectations about you in your role as science coordinator so make sure that you deal with teachers positively. If all the magnets are dead, avoid shrugging your shoulders, make a realistic promise and keep it. You don't want colleagues to rely on you totally, but you do want them to see you as a resource.

Look for opportunities to gain access to other classrooms. This, of course, can be formally negotiated with the head, but as this will normally require you to be released from your classroom, you must have a clear objective in mind, for example, to examine AT1 in action or to look for signs of progression throughout the school. All the better if this relates to stated policy, your action plan or the schools development plan.

Steps to Achieve Continuity, Progression and Differentiation

There are three important words here, planning, planning and planning! While there is much to this truism, plans must include a foundation of the teacher's knowledge of the subject, how it might be taught and knowledge of individual children. Assessment, which is dealt with later in more detail, will feed everything that is said here; without constantly updated knowledge about the children's attainment, progression may be seriously inhibited.

It might be suggested that progression in scientific learning is the product we seek from teaching. It would appear that there are some circumstances where learning is more likely than others. Ideas can sometimes be presented in a specific order (e.g., teaching the concept of density in floating and sinking) whereas at other times reinforcement is required. We draw here from the constructivist movement within science education which argues that children bring to the classroom their own views about science which need to be challenged by their education at all stages.

Progression must be planned. The first essential is some knowledge of the children and the science. Progression might then be planned in the process of science (SC1) and in the content (SC2,3,4). For example, we might identify a strand from SC1 *obtaining evidence* and focus our attention for assessment and teaching on this area. Thus, we might expect that we could recognize and plan for progression. One approach, having identified this strand, would be to plan one or two activities where the teacher would determine or elicit what the children know, understand and can do. The children can be involved – get them to talk about what they understand, draw concept maps and annotated pictures, discuss their ideas. This information would then lead to a number of sessions where you might seek to teach and develop theses ideas. The children should be given opportunity to challenge their misconceptions, to explore ideas in new situations, to share their learning. The final sessions might seek to determine what the children have learnt through its application.

Assessment as a Tool For Development of Science

Assessment is a powerful tool for the coordinator as it requires teachers to observe and listen to children doing science, to think about scientific words carefully and, crucially, to act on the information they collect. Assessment is therefore important in the teaching process, it also provides a vehicle and a need for teacher INSET.

First teachers must be clear about scientific terminology in any criteria they are to apply. As we have already suggested there is a broad scientific programme of study at Key Stage 2 including a challenging amount of science. Teachers of Key Stage 2 must make themselves aware of what the children know and can do so that they can further children's understanding.

The National Curriculum (SCAA, 1995) defines level descriptors to indicate children's achievement for teachers. For example, the Level descriptor for SC1 – Experimental and Investigative Science, Level 3 reads:

Pupils make simple predictions where appropriate and suggest how ideas can be tested. They make relevant observations and use simple apparatus to make measurements. They recognize when a test is unfair and plan a fair test, with some help. They provide simple, reasoned explanations for observations and measurements.

We are asked to consider which descriptor best fits a child's performance. In making a judgment it is important that we clearly understand the criteria to which reference is made. In this case it is essential to have a clear understanding of terms such as *predict, test, observe* and *fair test.* Level descriptor SC4 – Physical Processes, Level 1 reads: 'Pupils observe and describe simple events such as the movement of familiar things, pushes and pulls or changes. They recognize that phenomena, such as light, come from a variety of sources' (SCAA, 1995).

This example from Level 1 demands understanding from the teacher. *Pushes, pulls, changes* and *light sources* are mentioned. The statement refers to *phenomena,* this might include *sound, heat, vibration,* etc. How much knowledge is required of the teacher to assess Level 1?

Record Keeping

Records of children's experience and achievement in science must inform the teacher, the school, the parent and the child. Which of these you consider the most important will govern some of your decisions about records. We see the partnership of teacher, parent and child as essential. A system of records has been devised by professional teachers to inform the partners and promote the objectives of the science curriculum.

The school science policy will require reference to record keeping. You will need to record experiences; these records should be based on the Programme of Study (some schools copy the teacher's planning sheets and highlight work actually covered). This will require care in science because of the subjects' breadth of content and the subjects' core status. Science AT1 is a good example as the programme of study is divided into three subheadings (SCAA, 1995):

- planning experimental work;
- obtaining evidence;
- considering evidence.

You will also require some record of achievement which gives you information about which level descriptor best describes the child's achievement, when the assessment was made and whether achievement was uniform across the whole of the level descriptor. This detail about children's achievement will be important to teachers and is invariably valued by parents.

SC1 Level 3 (SCAA, 1995) pupils respond to suggestions, put forward their own ideas and, where appropriate, make simple predictions. They make relevant observations and measure quantities, such as length or mass, using a range of simple equipment. With some help they carry out a fair test, recognizing and explaining why it is fair. They record their observations in a variety of ways. They provide explanations for observations and, where they occur, for simple patterns in recorded measurements. They say what they have found out from their work.

Each level descriptor contains some considerable detail, it will be possible on some occasions to treat the descriptor as one statement (particularly when it is clear that the child has achieved everything). It will become more complex in the cases where a child patently has not achieved parts of the statement.

Children can be involved in their own record keeping. Numerous examples exist of records which might be made by children (Harris, 1994). Teachers ask children to record (in some form) almost all the science that the children conduct. It would be sensible to develop and use this capability which all children have. Teachers who have done this report positive spinoffs within and beyond the curriculum.

Resources

You can do a lot with a little in science; all sorts of science can be conducted with vary basic equipment. Materials and equipment can often be recycled or reused as science equipment. While this approach has much to commend it, it must not result in science as part of primary education being delivered on the cheap. Primary schools need good stocks of high quality measuring and observation equipment. Hand lenses should be widely available and of the highest quality you can afford (made with glass lenses). They should be complemented by binocular microscopes, two-way viewers, minispectors, magnispectors, etc. Observation and measurement are the bedrock of scientific investigation. In your school children should be able to measure, length, mass, volume, time, temperature, light, PH. Equipment should be sufficient for the schools needs and as easily accessible as possible. You must accept some loss and breakage each year. There is a comprehensive list of equipment at the end of this chapter.

It is important that children have immediate access to basic science equipment. As coordinator you must make sure that each class has basic equipment and that when topics, such as electricity are being studied, that sufficient resources are available. You must have some catalogue and organization of resources. You may be allocated funds by the head or be asked to bid for them. In either case you must be well informed about what the school has, what the school needs and what is available on the market. It is sensible to attend courses, conferences and exhibitions and write to suppliers and publishers for details.

If you are buying teachers' books or materials be careful in your choice, consider:

- relevance to the national curriculum?
- how elements match your curriculum?
- the place of AT1 in the materials?
- resources required?
- are progression and differentiation promoted?
- does the material cater for children with special needs?
- does the material deal in a balanced way with gender and cultural diversity?
- is assessment and record keeping part of the material?
- are cross-curricular links stressed?
- are the materials, activities safe?

Be sure that all teachers have access to *Be Safe!* (ASE, 1990)

Staff Development

Teachers will need assistance in all the above areas. It is a challenge to all teachers acting as coordinators. If you are new to the role you might make it a medium term goal, so that you can seek advice and assistance. Include staff development as part of the medium or long-term plan. You will need to provide assistance at a professional level, such as the teaching and learning (including assessment and record keeping) as well as background scientific knowledge. The latter might in the first instance be based around the science topics or elements of the programme of study which colleagues have agreed to over. In larger schools there may be more opportunity for colleagues to support one another. In smaller schools the support is just as important, perhaps even more so! Support may be found in a cluster of primary schools, at a local high school, at LEA level, in the local ASE branch, at the local college or university or a combination of these. Staff need to have good reference books available, a list is provided at the end his chapter. A published scheme may provide necessary support to colleagues.

You may wish to reconsider this section when you have read the later one on monitoring and evaluation. It is important that staff development in the long term is driven by the staff themselves. The teacher who admits to you that he or she is concerned about gender balance or about SC1 or 'how questions are used by the teacher' is giving you a precious insight into his or her professional life. A good starting point is to establish what the situation is at present in the classroom. This might mean the two of you examining the children's work, the teacher keeping a log of science session, the teacher making an audio recording of lessons or you doing a focused observation of a lesson.

Parental Involvement

Parents are very knowledgable about their children and are often keen to know more about what they are doing in school. Here we distinguish between informing and involving parents. The following ideas will seek to inform parents. As science coordinator you might organize open afternoons, science weeks, science evenings, etc. where parents can observe children at work and perhaps have a go at some activities. These sessions usually have lots of positive spinoffs and give you an opportunity to raise the profile of the subject and tell parents about the science you are doing. Often coordinators will write a short guide or handbook for parents which will inform them about science in school and about activities which parents can do at home with their children. You might also recommend visits in the locality, visits to the local library, television programmes, etc. A term newsletter from the coordinator, the teacher or headteacher might inform parents of current science work in school and again might offer ideas for home. As interest grows, parents may wish to be more involved, so you might look to projects, challenges, fund raising, developing resources and supporting classroom activity as ways in which parents might be involved.

Monitoring and Evaluation

This is perhaps the latest and most challenging aspect of the role of science coordinator, especially at Key Stage 2 because of the length of the Key Stage and the breadth of the programme of study. You are asked to monitor the outcomes and the delivery of four years of education. Of course, this is a function of senior management but it is possible that after several years of experience, responsibility for this may be delegated to you by the head. Like assessment, it is a powerful tool and will enable you to be more effective. Colleagues cannot deny your role, particularly if it is included in your job description. The important thing here is to communicate to them that the only purpose of this process is the improvement of the children's achievement and as such is a mechanism for you to tailor your support for and management of science in the school. As a student teacher, NQT or even teacher with experience, it can be daunting to realize that you are being asked to monitor colleagues. You will find this easier when you have already established your role as supportive coordinator. You want colleagues to accept you for what you are, an interested colleague who is there to help. A good way to break the ice is to admit how you feel while stressing the purpose of the activity. Also you might stress that your colleague, as coordinator of at least one other area, will be doing the same to you!

Ideally, as you become more experienced and more confident, the head may be able to give you time with colleagues either outside or inside their classroom. Both are valuable and you ought to make a case for at least a biannual visit to each classroom on top of visits you ought to make informally each half-term. Try to focus on the positive, a teacher success, a new topic, a scheme, part of the National Curriculum or a new resource and use this to start a professional dialogue. You might then ask the teacher to identify an area where he or she wishes to develop practice. The response of the teacher to such a question is usually very revealing. If he or she is not forthcoming, try to move the focus on to the children – special needs, differentiation, etc. When an issue is identified you can begin an element of staff development which is likely to be successful as it has been identified by the teacher and shows a strong interest in finding a solution.

It is important that you go about this systematically, that you keep a record and that you have opportunity to report your findings to colleagues and to the head. You may have to choose words very carefully! Sources of information will include:

- informal discussion with colleagues;
- more formal biannual review;
- displays and assemblies;
- children's behaviour in science and their work;
- time allocation;
- teachers' planning;
- results of teacher assessment;
- is assessment used to feed the planning process?;
- teachers use of IT well for science.

A diary might be a good way to start. You will need to constantly move from the anecdotal to some sort of evaluation of what you have seen. Beware of simplistic conclusions. Solutions in the classroom are rarely simple. Be aware that children's behaviour generally and classroom management are usually tied up with the solution to any challenge!

An annual review should examine aspects of the process of teaching and aspects of the pupils' achievement. Collect evidence about each so that you have as full a picture as is reasonable. A review might include:

- How clear a picture have you got?
- How do standards compare with previous years?
- Are all children receiving their full entitlement?
- What amount of science is going on? is this enough? less or more than in the past?
- How is SC1 fairing?
- Is the scientific curriculum featured in school documentation and school policies?
- How has your role been facilitated?

Preparing for a School Inspection

The words above on monitoring and evaluation are timely as you consider your role as coordinator in any inspection. You will eventually be expected to have an overview of what is happening in school, but in your first year it is accepted that your view will, of necessity, be limited. You will find that inspectors are looking for what they call a *thinking school*. By this they mean a proactive school which asks questions about its performance and actively seeks to deal with weaknesses. Therefore you might consider that they are looking for *thinking* coordinators, again by this they mean active, questioning coordinators who are engaged with the task of improving standards in the school. Remember, they don't expect you to solve all the problems yourself. They do expect you to be reasonably informed and to have a plan! You are expected to use every opportunity to build up a picture of how the school is performing, to be in dialogue with the head about how things will develop and to use every opportunity to make constructive steps. With regard to science their main interests, are:

- standards of achievement;
- quality of learning;
- quality of teaching;
- assessment, recording and reporting;
- curriculum and its organization and planning;
- management of the subject;
- the effective use of teaching and support staff;
- learning resources;
- accommodation.

You might use these as headings as you review the state of science in the school. You must draw your evidence from as many sources as possible and weigh it carefully. Determine areas requiring immediate attention and others to be tackled in the longer term. All of this should be discussed with the head so that your ideas tie in with those of other aspects of school management. Make sure that you have a look at the Inspection Handbook (OFSTED, 1993) and within it the overall framework and reference to science and subject coordinators.

Conclusion

Be a Team Member

Construct your own informal action plan and put it to the head who will give you the benefit of experience and the wider view of school policy. Show that you can take initiative but that you value advice. Quite understandably a primary headteacher like to know what is happening in his or her school! In fact, it will assist you in the long term and add to the credibility of your work if you keep the head and staff involved. Keep yourself up to date in and out of school.

Be Scientific

A scientific approach may help you in your role as coordinator. Science is about questions and uncertainty. It is about seeking answers to the questions of humans. It tries to be systematic but usually has to accept practicalities. Scientists tend to do a lot of observing, in your case this will involve listening, watching and reviewing evidence. Science recognizes that systems (like schools) are complex with many variables which can change in its nature. The role requires objectivity but sympathy with real life in classrooms. It requires observation and recording, investigation, conclusions and action based on what you learn.

Be Realistic

Don't try to do everything at once, don't suggest to colleagues that you will have everything done quickly. Plan for the long term but try to get some things moving in the coming term so that you see some fruits for your efforts. It is important that colleagues see you in this role. Be clear in your own mind about your role. You are there to assist and coordinate but not to do things for everyone!

References

ASSOCIATION FOR SCIENCE EDUCATION (1990) *Be Safe!*, Hatfield, ASE.

ASSOCIATION FOR SCIENCE EDUCATION (1994) *Science as Part of the Whole Curriculum*, Hatfield, ASE.

CAMPBELL, J. (1994) 'Managing the primary curriculum: The issue of time allocation', *Education 3–13*, **22** (1), Harlow, Longman.

HARRIS, J. (1994) *My National Curriculum Record of Achievement*, Derby, Primary Associations Limited.

HMI (1991) *Science in Key Stages 1 and 3: A Report by HM Inspectorate on the First Year*, 1989–90, HMSO.

HMI (1992) *Science in Key Stages 1, 2 and 3: A Report by HM Inspectorate on the Second Year*, 1990–91, HMSO.

HMI (1993) *Science in Key Stages 1, 2 and 3: Third Year*, 1991–92, HMSO.

NATIONAL CURRICULUM COUNCIL (1992) *Forces*, York, NCC.

OFSTED (1993) *Handbook of the Inspection of Schools*, London, HMSO.

PHIPPS. R. (1994) 'Data handling in scientific investigations in the primary school: Some findings and implications of a research project', *Education 3–13*, **22** (2) June, Longman.

Primary School Teachers and Science Project (1993) *Understanding the Earth's Place in the Universe*, Oxford, Association for Science Education.

SCAA (1993) *The National Curriculum and its Assessment: Final Report* (The Dearing Report), London, SCAA.

SCAA (1995) *Science in the National Curriculum*, London, HMSO.

Solomon, J. and Lee, J. (1991) *School Home Investigations in Primary Science, The SHIPS Project*, Hatfield, Association for Science Education.

Wragg, E.C., Bennett, N. and Carre, C.G. (1989) *Primary Teachers and the National Curriculum*, Research Papers in Education, England and Wales.

Useful Readings

Jennings, T. (1994) *Primary Science in the National Curriculum*, Oxford, Oxford University Press.

Sherrington, R. (ed.) *Primary Science Teacher's Handbook*, Hemel Hempstead, ASE/ Simon and Schuster.

Chapter 7

Getting IT Together in Key Stage 2

Mike Harrison

Introduction

This chapter is written for students and newly qualified teachers (NQTs) who wish to be influential in promoting children's learning by the use of computers. Of all the areas of the curriculum, in formation technology (IT) is probably the one most suitable for students and NQT to coordinate in primary schools. The teachers with whom you will be working will welcome your advice and help and will be unlikely to criticize you if things go wrong; you will be surprised just how much basic knowledge you have absorbed during your training. Your qualifications for this role will be substantial. Many students have developed through their Initial Teacher Education (ITE) courses a level of understanding in the way computers can support high quality learning in the classroom far beyond that which most classroom teachers have had the time to do. With the implementation of the national curriculum and formal assessment, many Key Stage 2 teachers have had to learn new material and develop new techniques which have absorbed a great deal of their attention. Therefore, many teachers may have been unable to exploit fully the potential of IT in their classrooms. In addition, many teachers appointed as IT co-ordinators have carried this responsibility alongside another major area of the curriculum, so help may not always have been forthcoming in the way needed to encourage teachers to use computers to the full.

This is not to say that you do not have a lot to learn. As we shall see, to work effectively as a co-ordinator you will have to gain an understanding of the school's needs and its methods for the implementation of the whole curriculum; develop the skills necessary to influence older and more experienced members of staff and be prepared to give the time to be on hand to solve the problems of others and eventually pose problems

> *Research facts*
> Students who have not enjoyed learning can be encouraged by the use of IT.
>
> IT can present information in new ways which help students to understand, assimilate and use it more readily.

for others to solve. This will take time and you will find that some aspects of this work suit you more than others. Nonetheless, by studying the advice given here, along with the first chapter in this book, you will go a long way towards being recognized as not only a beginning teacher in your school but also as a respected resource of information and skills.

The Role of the IT Coordinator

The purpose of coordinating IT is to foster the achievement of high standards for the children in the school though good quality teaching and learning. It could be useful to ask your colleagues to help you, a newcomer to the profession, to define what this means. Imagine that the team of teachers were charged with making judgments about the standards of children's achievement in IT in a school. What would they use as a yardstick? You could start by suggesting criteria such as these which I have modified from NCET/NAACE (1993).

> Where teaching involving the use of IT is good, progression, pace, challenge, clarity of purpose, differentiation and full participation are all features of the IT agenda. The use of IT is suitable and enhances learning found in other aspects of children's work. The organisation of children's access to desktop computers and issues of equal opportunity are taken into account in classroom management and appropriate records of both children's experience and achievements are kept. The teaching features regular monitoring of children's work on the computer and includes sensitive intervention. Pupils are encouraged to reach the highest levels of accomplishment. In a school with good standards of achievement, most pupils use equipment and software competently and confidently to perform a range of tasks in a variety of curriculum contexts appropriate for their age and abilities. Where learning with or about IT is good, pupils respond with enthusiasm and commitment to the challenge of the task. They are able to use IT appropriately in a wide range of situations, applying skills developed in other contexts. The opportunity which IT affords for trial and experimentation is used systematically to improve outcomes.

It could also be a useful exercise to agree between yourselves what you would judge as unsatisfactory.

> Teaching with IT is unsatisfactory where work in IT is not connected to other learning tasks. Pupils may be asked to perform irrelevant or mundane tasks or be expected to use IT with insufficient guidance. Computer use is considered as a reward or as a means of occupying pupils. Where standards of IT use are unsatisfactory there is evidence

of considerable variation in achievement between pupils, subjects, classes and modes of use. Where children's learning is unsatisfactory, they are unable to apply IT skills and methods learnt in one context to new situations. They use IT in inappropriate ways, concentration is short lived and the computer may be viewed as a toy rather than a tool. Experimentation is random and undirected in the hope of finding a better result.

Using such ideal models, or other points for discussion you may be able to develop with your colleagues a vision of where you would like teaching and learning with IT over the years to end up. How does this translate into practical tasks for you to do?

Talking to IT coordinators, teachers, headteachers and inspectors, students find that the most common expectations of the IT coordinator are that he or she will:

- maintain and manage the school's IT policy (including its creation where necessary);
- review the provision and care for resources, both hardware and software;
- demonstrate good practice in the use of IT in their own classroom and elsewhere;
- arrange the provision of technical support;
- give staff advice on software;
- attend relevant INSET courses and keep up to date with developments in other ways;
- promote, foster (and possibly implement) staff training in IT;
- disseminate IT information throughout the school;
- review IT practice throughout the school;
- liaise with IT support staff and advisors; and,
- review regularly his/her own role and effectiveness.

> Re-read the list of tasks expected of the IT coordinator.
> Which of these do you feel confident to begin to tackle? Which are more suited to teachers later in their careers?
> Your headteacher is probably thinking the same way!

Let us examine some of these task areas and offer some starting points for you to develop.

Managing the School's IT Policy

Whether the school has a written document or not there will be a *de facto* policy relating the use of IT in your school. Even if you should find that teachers are entirely free to choose whether or not to use IT at all, that children use computers only to play games as a reward for good behaviour, or that the school's IT practice consists of typing up children's already written stories – that amounts to a policy! If senior management are content for such use to be made of this resource then they will not mind it being documented in a formal written policy to be given to governors, new teachers and students, inspectors and advisers. If, however, these happen to be undesired practices, then your effort in pulling staff together to agree to more appropriate uses of computers in order to tell the outside world (who pay for these resources) the uses to which they are put will probably be welcomed and supported.

If a policy document exists then you have a starting point to compare practice and policy and an anchor to hold onto if the going gets rough. If not, or if the policy bears no relation to reality then sooner or later you will need to begin the process of working with teachers to create one which does. Writing a policy document and scheme of work is often thought of as being the most daunting of tasks. It should not be so. You are in many ways the best member of staff to carry out such a task. You will probably be seen as someone who genuinely needs the help of other teachers to compile such a document – someone without an axe to grind; someone who is entitled to ask naive questions (which may be seen by teachers as a threat, if asked by the headteacher). After all, the point of a whole school policy for IT is that it is owned by the whole staff, describes what is actually happening on the ground and gives some indication of the direction the school is going with regard to the use of computers and other IT apparatus (see Deveraux, 1991). If in its construction teachers become a little more aware about what other teachers are doing in IT, which computer skills are being developed in each part of the school, which programmes are being used, then a more coherent approach may well evolve without you having to do very much at all. A clearer understanding of a progression in IT skills may grow amongst staff through open discussion and more or less appropriate uses of the school's computers can be debated without you ever having to declare your hand. A whole school policy for IT can:

> *Research facts*
> Using a computer to produce a successful piece of writing can motivate students to acquire basic literacy skills.
>
> IT allows students to reflect upon what they have written and to change it easily.

- publicly demonstrate the school's intentions for children's learning with IT;
- help make a case for funding;
- give information on IT to governors, parents and inspectors;
- provide a framework for individual teacher's planning;
- aid coherence, continuity, progression and shape priorities;

- assist in achieving uniformity and consistency in school
decision making by helping to
focus the minds of various
decision making groups such
as governors, the senior management team, other subject
coordinators, toward com-
mon aims.

> *Research facts*
> IT removes the chore of pro-
> cessing data manually and frees
> pupils to concentrate on its inter-
> pretation and use.
>
> IT has the flexibility to meet the
> individual needs and abilities of
> each student.

The process of its development may:

- help participants understand teaching and learning strategies with IT
employed by other staff;
- help create a team spirit in making public the school's goals;
- offer a means of evaluation of the IT work being planned;
- help clarify functions and responsibilities of staff, and;
- help new staff (including you) to settle in.

Hardware Issues

Primary schools will have been buying computers over the past ten years
under the influence of government departments (who offered schools 50 per
cent discounts on certain makes); LEAs who attempted to create homogenous
provision of machines across all primary schools in the county in order to
simplify software purchase, training and technical issues; and the individual
preferences of headteachers and previous coordinators. The constraints of
money, technical know-how and security issues will also have contributed to
the particular pattern of provision you will find in your school. It is unlikely
that you will be the sole decider about any possible future purchases but you
will want to present an opinion to show that you are on top of the job you
have been given.

You will be best advised to help whoever will take the final decision by
setting out the important factors as you see them.

You might list them as:

- how this new machine fits into the current pattern of provision (Is
there an up-to-date list of the exact specifications of the computers in
school?);
- whether any of the proposed purchases are about to be technically
superseded by superior machines and what this might imply;
- how available is educational software generally for proposed computers and particularly whether you will need to purchase programmes

specifically for new machines or will they run software currently used elsewhere in the school;
- whether additional training will be necessary for staff to use any new type of machine and where such training can be purchased;
- how the prices compares across the model ranges. Are the facilities worth the additional cash over the lower priced models?

There is no need, unless asked, to recommend one specific purchase – if you make an honest attempt to detail the relevant criteria and involve the teachers who would be most likely to have access to the new machine, you can leave the final decision to those who hold the reins of power and can argue the case for this or that particular computer with various bodies.

An option you might like to put before the senior management team is to purchase a number of small handheld *palmtop computers* in preference to the larger desktop ones we are used to. The portability of these computers, the versatility of their in-built software and usage, along with the fact that they can be easily linked to larger machines for transfer of data make them a choice to be considered, especially if your school has already reached the stage of having one desktop machine per classroom (see NCET, 1994, Cross and Birch, 1994).

An area in which you may eventually be asked to make recommendations or decisions is the purchase of peripheral hardware such as CD-ROM drives and printers. Under government backed schemes a number of primary schools are beginning to take advantage of powerful methods of storing information. ROM stands for Read Only Memory and when stored on a compact disc, CD-ROM gets its name. Such vast quantities of information can be stored on one disc that a whole encyclopedia, even with moving pictures and sounds as illustrations, can be stored. Every edition of the *Times* over a year, or complicated national timetables such as that for the British Rail Network are sold in this form and combined with a programme to handle the information these make a powerful contribution to any school's collection of computer hardware. On a simpler level, the storage of thousands of clip art files which children can access and use in their own art work or as part of their writing in *Pendown* or *Phases* may be a useful addition to your school's resources.

However powerful the computer and whether or nor enhanced by CD-ROM images, the quality of the presented product depends on the capacity of the printer. Although schools do not always appreciate it at first, the more they can spend on a printer the better. Here is an area where gentle influence and persuasion will enhance your reputation.

Most primary schools will have a number of dot matrix printers which, as rough and ready methods

> *Research facts*
> Programs which use digitized speech can help pupils to read and spell.
>
> IT offers potential for effective group working.

of obtaining a hard copy of children's LOGO designs, drafts of written work and outlines of artwork, are satisfactory workhorses. Dot matrix printers have a number of pinheads (typically 9, 16 or 24) which form themselves into letters or other shapes and strike a ribbon leaving an impression of the shape on the paper beneath. Some printers have ribbons with differing strips of colour and can produce a coloured effect by this means. Some programmes such as *Folio* can instruct the pinheads to strike the ribbon two or three times to give a darker impression but at best the end result looks jagged around the edges of printing.

To obtain a higher quality of output many schools have chosen to purchase at least one ink-jet printer. They use this for work which they will put on display or for other special purposes. Ink-jet printers squirt black or coloured ink onto paper and give a finer definition of around 150–300 dpi (dots per inch) which is a very noticeable increase in quality. Newer, more expensive models are even capable of 720 dpi which they claim to be of nearly photographic quality.

Such printers cost a little more than the dot matrix printers and the ink-jet cartridges are expensive to replace (typically around £30 each). The other option is to consider buying a laser printer (around 600 dpi). The high price and running costs have prevented these from being popular in primary schools. They are considerably heavier than other types of printer which also makes them far less portable. Whichever type and make of printer you have, or change to, you will need to install a printer driver to match. This piece of software translates the screen you wish to copy into a language which your printer can understand in order to reproduce the text or graphics you wish to print.

Software Issues

Whereas the headteacher may want you to give him or her advice on the purchase of hardware, the first expectation of teachers is that their IT coordinator should know all about the software packages currently in school. New to the post, you will need to build up a knowledge of the school's stock of programs. Some of this can be done by collating information already available about regularly used programs. A simple index box will suit your purpose. However, it will be the pile of unmarked discs and lost manuals separated from their discs which will cause any newcomer to the job to despair in the first few weeks.

First, don't panic.
If the school has been able to manage with such chaos over a number of years then a few more months won't matter. Recruit any sympathetic teachers to help you find out just what you do have in the school

and how useful it is. Buy some labels and use them to identify discs. Distribute two or three discs at a time to your colleagues and ask them to write on the labels in felt pen (biros may damage the discs). Negotiate a deadline for each little task or you may be hindered rather than helped in this exercise. In this way you will start to make sense of the multiple versions, damaged discs and pirate copies which no doubt will be present in the pile. Destroy any copyright material which you suspect to be pirate copies. You do not want the first money you manage to obtain to go on the payment of fines for breach of copyright.

Second, attempt to match the discs with their booklets.
The accompanying documentation which publishers supply with their software will vary in quality, quantity and type. It is a rare booklet that is of no use to anyone – unless, of course, it is separated from its disc. You should ensure that packages returned to you do still have the documentation.

Third keep a record of what you have found.
Use your index file. You will then be on your way to organizing the resources such that they will be of use to people. At first you may wish just to record these and catalogue them alphabetically. Later as you will have seen some of the software in action, you may choose to create a catalogue in terms of age suitability.

You will discover that some of the discs you find will be master copies. These should not be used by the children. Make backup copies of these and lock the originals away securely. Be assured that the first time you decide that it will not matter if you use the master copy for once – it will!

The organization of access to software is a perennial problem for co-ordinators. You may come up with ingenious solutions but in the main you have three basic choices:

- Keep disks and associated documentation centrally. Give a copy of the list of programs to each teacher. When any class teacher wants to use a particular disc, book it out to them. Keep backup copies in a separate place in order to be prepared for accidental damage to discs.
- Make multiple copies of popular programs so that each teacher can have his or her own. You will need to consider whether to make copies of the handbook where allowed, for each teacher.
- Issue discs to the most suitable class or department keeping a note of who has what. The locations of the discs will have to be issued to all teachers by means of a general list. Frequent checks will need to be

made of the discs and documentation. *Remember, never give anyone a copy of a master disc.*

The system you choose will need to account for the types of computer in your school, the convenience of a location for central storage, the popularity of certain programs and whether you have site licence or single copy software. What is most important however is the quality of information teachers have to hand about the software available.

> *Research facts*
> Difficult ideas are made more understandable when information technology makes them visible.
>
> Computers can reduce the risk of failure at school.

It is hoped that your school will have purchased software which includes much of this in the accompanying documentation. Whether this is the case or not, it will prove a worthwhile investment to buy folders for each of your main programs into which are put both the disc and accompanying booklet with examples of use by teachers in your school. Clear plastic foolscap folders with zip openings are best for this job in order that contents are visible. The graphs children have drawn using data handling packages, fancy lettering used in stories children might have written, a teacher's jotting on the work children did as a result of adventure program, are all examples of items teachers would find useful to be included in such envelopes. This is merely an extension of the pooling of topic worksheets which goes on in many schools, but by creating browsable packages you may make a contribution to a change in some teachers' use of IT.

As you develop your role you may wish to be more proactive in the way you distribute software to various classes. The cycle presented in Figure 7.1 represents a transition between controlling factors in the distribution of software. Free choice in the use of software may be your most appropriate strategy. Newly qualified teachers may, quite naturally, find it difficult to assert that teacher X cannot use package Y with his or her class, even if there are excellent reasons for this decision. In addition, if the use of computers is somewhat spasmodic in your school, putting obstacles in the way of staff is clearly not the way in which to promote increased usage and to persuade teachers that using IT in their teaching will be painless and beneficial for their children.

It may be possible, however to persuade teacher X that package Z more closely fits his or her needs. Thus we move to the situation where software is assigned to different areas of the school, in the hope that this will contribute to a progression in skill development – more sophisticated software with more facilities being provided to older children. The final move in the diagram is to where such skills take the centre stage and teachers use aspects of different software to enhance this learning. The diagram implies that once such a move has been established and teachers used to planning children's IT work in this way then moving back to free choice may again be most appropriate.

Figure 7.1: *A model for distributing software*

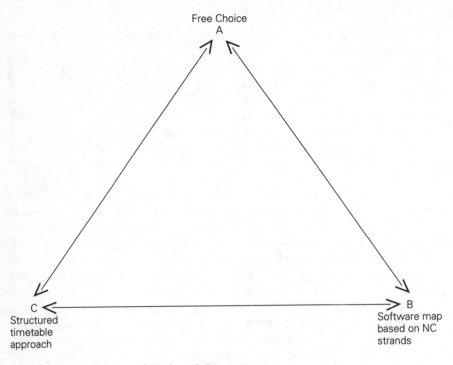

Free Choice
A

C
Structured
timetable
approach

B
Software map
based on NC
strands

The Provision of Technical Support

The IT coordinator is unique in the demands made upon him or her for technical support and know-how. It is indeed rare for the maths coordinator to become involved in repairing maths equipment, or the geography co-ordinator to be called out of his or her class in an emergency to mend the globe. Yet time after time those with responsibility for IT seem to be expected to know what to do when Y2 has put a biscuit in the disc drive, provide an instant solution when the caretaker has dropped the discs in the fish tank or Johnny's LOGO pattern will not print. At an early stage you will need to decide how to handle these requests. More than one co-ordinator has been asked to leave his or her class to see to a computer, connect to a turtle, solve a

One IT coordinator was sent a note first thing on Monday morning. This requested that she leave her classroom urgently to come and switch on another teacher's computer in a different part of the building. It was needed in that lesson. On her arrival the classteacher told her that water had dripped into the machine all weekend from a leaky roof. As it might be dangerous the teacher thought it would be better if the coordinator did it!

disc problem. What will *you* do? My advice would be to send a polite but helpful message back but refuse to leave your children unattended. Normal lesson preparation includes making sure that the equipment needed, be it paper, paint, PE apparatus or floor turtles, are present and in working order. Teachers may need to be encouraged to think well in advance in order that the time at which you may be needed for consultation and even emergency action will be one where you may be free to give assistance.

There is, of course, a case for having someone on the staff who has taken the time and trouble to learn to cope with some of the technical matters which can get in the way of using computers efficiently. That someone is you. When repairs are needed, it may be necessary for you to understand and describe the problem and put the system back together on its return to school. Manuals and guidebooks should be read and important matters highlighted, so that the attention of other readers will be attracted to essential information.

Where I draw the line, however, is whenever a screwdriver is needed. Unless you are familiar with the maintenance of electronic devices, leave anything which involves tools and dismantling parts of the machine to those paid to know such things. Should an accident occur as a result of your untrained experimentation inside a machine, it will be no-one's fault but your own.

Certain preventative measures can be taken to minimize the breakdowns which happen in school. Teachers need to be persuaded to exit from programs properly. It is not uncommon for teachers to pull the plug on the micro while the programme is still running; they then complain of continual disc errors, for which they will probably blame you.

Care of discs in general can save you a lot of problems. Of course, accidents will happen, but if you can find ways to minimize them, it will make your life easier. You will need to find out what sort

> Some coordinators have trained one or two children from each class to help preserve discs from the most common abuses. Their main job is to ensure that discs are removed from drives before computers are switched off. Discs do not like to be left on top of radiators, put close to the monitor, bent, written upon or wet. Children are your best allies in a crusade against discs damage.

of arrangements have been made to repair broken computers, upgrade to higher specifications, install chips and to give advice on the running of programs. Your school may have a contract with a local firm or an arrangement with the LEA. You can make this as smooth as possible by supplying teachers with the appropriate forms to report problems and occasionally checking yourself to see if all the computers are in working order. In a few cases teachers reluctant to use IT may not report malfunctions in good time. In such cases it is the children who are being denied their entitlement. Your timely polite and efficient work in this area can minimize disruption to their progress.

Keeping Up with Developments

One area where you may be required to make a judgment is in ensuring that the aspects of the national curriculum are covered by the scheme of work agreed by the staff. IT has a unique position in the national curriculum. IT is specifically mentioned in the access statement at the beginning of the orders for each subject, except PE. For example, 'Pupils should be given opportunities, where appropriate, to develop their IT capability in their study of music.' It is worth noting then that it needs to be the responsibility of every coordinator to promote the use of computers – not yours alone.

You will, of course, need to be thoroughly familiar with the national curriculum program of study for Key Stage 2 and the level descriptors 2 to 5 in order to advise staff. In summary, the programme of study (PoS) builds on that to be achieved in Key Stage 1 particularly, pupils should be taught to extend the range of IT tools that they use for communication, investigation and control, should become discerning in their use of IT, should select information, sources and media for their suitability for purpose and, assess the value of IT in working practices.

> SCAA (1994) published details of the consultation with parents and employers as part of the review of the national curriculum. 'Parents and employers think children of all ages should be taught Information Technology. They feel they primarily should learn how to use computers, and the main types of software (word processing, databases and spreadsheets).'

Acting as a Resource for Your Colleagues

If you are to be able to act as a resource for your staff you in turn will need to develop contacts and sources of help. Personal contacts and sources of information are built up slowly through attending courses and building relationships with those in equivalent positions to yourself. However, for newcomers, some general help is at hand. A local network of IT coordinators may exist already and can be of help in sorting out local problems with common software and finding out about good quality INSET.

The most crucial part of your role is that in which you motivate, cajole and persuade staff to work together in IT just as in any other area of the curriculum. Your best indicator of performance as a coordinator will be the extent to which you achieve objectives in this area. There are a number of formal and informal ways to induce staff to cooperate. *Whole-school INSET days* can allow staff to have time to discuss the way IT is being used and have access to new machines and a variety of software. Visiting speakers bring a new perspective on the value of activities and frequently say things that you may not be able to say. Problems may be discussed which were not previously aired, issues may arise involving different areas of the school, and unthought of cooperation may result.

INSET days can be used as opportunity for new beginnings and therefore must be properly thought out to maximize their effectiveness. Any guest speaker will need to be properly briefed on the current activities of the school. Some suggestions for the best use of INSET time can be found in earlier chapters. *Incidental INSET* can arise from time-to-time in which you have the opportunity to show individual teachers features of a machine or software. These opportunities occasionally arise in the solution of everyday problems, but they may also come from a deliberate tactic on your behalf to be in the right place at the right time. Some coordinators have been successful by setting up a computer in the staffroom at lunchtime once a fortnight. Such occasions could consist of a demonstration by you of a piece of software or just an opportunity for individual staff, at their leisure, to try out something with you close at hand to help.

Whichever methods of training have been used in the past, they have not been as effective as many would like in persuading teachers to use IT to support children's learning across the curriculum (Morrison, 1988; Harrison, 1994). It could be that the steps teachers have been asked to take are just too big and they have been asked to take them far too quickly. Jane Devereux (1991) suggests that for some children 'the use of other, more familiar technologies might provide a safer, smaller step for those children a little daunted by the computer itself.' She goes on to show ways in which IT other than computers can be used to support primary science. Perhaps such simpler steps might commend themselves to some coordinators trying to help teachers who are overfaced by technical complexities.

It has been argued that another problem of INSET has been the deficit model it has used. The deficit model says to teachers, 'You lack certain technical knowledge and skills. Come on this course and I will show you how to connect up this system; configure this machine; run this program.' Such training has largely been characterized by telling participants which button to press and when and how to operate accessories. It has not called upon the professional experience of teachers, nor used their motivation to help children learn, which is their first calling. Because of this it has been less effective than it might have been.

An alternative model which is beginning to be seen as more successful, however, concentrates on building the need for IT, and presents it as a solution to teachers' own problems. Thus, as well as some technical help and training, the core of the effort should be in helping teachers to understand how IT can support children's learning in various areas of the curriculum. Thus *attending topic planning meetings* to suggest the appropriate use of computers as the teachers' needs arise, looking at forecasts of teachers' work and showing ways in which the use of computers can help them to achieve *their own ends* is likely to be more effective and longer lasting than any amount of technical instruction.

Whether or not you feel confident enough to work in such a way these further ideas may commend themselves to you as your career develops. You could arrange for staff to visit schools in the district with a brief not to centre on the technical wizardry of the resident teachers but to see if their use of IT proffers any solutions to the visiting teachers' problems, such as individualizing work for certain children, handling information in pie charts and graphs, empathizing with children of the past, helping children understand the movements of the planets, creating perfectly lettered 3-D titles to show off children's work.

You could obtain on-approval software for teachers to try out in their own classrooms and ask them to write a few words on whether it helped with their classwork. You will display infant computer work in the juniors and vice versa to demonstrate its value in different areas of the school.

Thus it is in utilizing teachers' desires to serve their children to the best of their ability that the source of motivation may lie.

Research facts

Using IT makes teachers take a fresh look at how they teach and the ways in which students learn.

Giving teachers easy access to computers encourages and improves the use of IT in the curriculum.

IT gives children the power to try out different ideas.

IT is particularly successful in holding the attention of pupils with emotional and behavioural difficulties.

The Inspector Calls

When schools are being inspected by OFSTED, the team member with responsibility for information technology will almost certainly want to talk with you. This is nothing to be afraid of. Inspectors will be making judgments throughout their visit, and indeed before it via the documentation the head will have supplied, about the standards achieved, the quality of learning and the quality of teaching with IT (and of course, other subjects and aspects). What they will want to do is to check their facts with you, understand the progress the school is making towards its goals and refine the judgments made through observations. This is your chance to show the inspector the plans you are making, if appropriate, and the range of resources and their management. NCET and NAACE (the National Association of Advisers for Computers in Education) have produced a pack to support the inspection of IT in schools. It is important that coordinators study this material for in this way they will begin to develop the understanding of how to look at their own school through fresh eyes. For example, the quality of the management and administration is amplified thus:

Where IT is well managed, there will be a whole-school policy which details practice and informs decisions. The policy will have been developed with the involvement of all staff. . . and will have the support of governors. It will deal with a range of issues from curriculum delivery and asset management. Operation of the policy will be regularly monitored and the policy itself periodically reviewed. The school will have a negotiated plan for the development of IT embracing both the extension of its use and the consequent requirements for staff (training), resources and accommodation.

Where IT is not well managed staff will be unclear about their contribution to the development of children's IT capability. Equipment remains unserviceable for long periods. Purchasing decisions taken independently or on the spur of the moment lead to hardware or software environment which lacks coherence with both itself and the curriculum. Negative attitudes will be prevalent amongst the staff.

As was set out in Chapter 1, many of these features are out of your hands – the givens – but you can, little-by-little, effect some of the above; by good classroom practice in IT, a growing awareness of the possible and good intentions, you can effect for the good the provision of IT for children in your school and those yet to arrive.

References

CROSS, A. and BIRCH, A. (1994) *Portable Computers, portable learning: a practical evaluation project in a primary education context* paper given to 7# 10STE Symposium, part 1 pp. 156–169.

DEVEREUX, J. (1991) 'Using IT, other than computers, to support primary science', in *Primary Science Review*, 20 Dec.

Research facts in boxes in this chapter are reported in full in the NCET booklet – Seen IT in the UK.

HARRISON, M. (1994) 'Teachers, computers and the curriculum', HARRISION, M. (ed.) *Beyond the Core Curriculum*, Plymouth Northcote House.

MORRISON, A. (1988) *Information Technology in Primary Schools: A Research Review for the Scottish Education Department*, ESRC.

NCET/NAACE (1993) *Inspecting IT – Support materials*, Coventry, NCET.

NCET (1993) *Seen IT in the UK*, Coventry, NCET.

NCET (1994) *Portable Computers in Action*, Coventry, NCET.

SCAA (1994) *The Review of the National Curriculum: A Report on the 1994 Consultation* London, SCAA.

Chapter 8

Religious Education in Key Stage 2

Gwen Mattock

Setting the Scene

The aims of the primary curriculum in maintained schools, as set out in the first section of the Education Reform Act 1988, are to provide a balanced and broadly based curriculum that promotes the spiritual, moral, mental and physical development of pupils at the school and of society; and, prepares such pupils for the opportunities, responsibilities and experiences of adult life. These aims are to be realized through the core and foundation subjects of the national curriculum and by religious education and other aspects of the basic curriculum. Religious education (RE) must be provided on a regular basis in every maintained school in addition to a daily act of worship.

Significant statements were made in the 1944 Education Act concerning religious teaching in such schools. These might be summarized briefly as:

- religious instruction must be given in every county school;
- it must be non-denominational. (Nothing was said about Christianity *vis-à-vis* other faiths since the tacit assumption was that all teaching would be Christian and largely Bible-based);
- teachers have the right to withdraw from the teaching of religious instruction;
- parents have the right to withdraw their children from religious instruction;
- all religious instruction must be in accordance with a locally agreed syllabus.

At the time when the 1944 Act was passed children in the great majority of schools in England were from at least nominally Christian backgrounds and the syllabuses in use at that time were predominantly biblical in content with the addition of sections on saints and famous Christians – missionaries, explorers, etc. Aims and objectives of some of those syllabuses made unequivocally Christian statements.

As numbers of other faith communities began to establish themselves and grow, and new syllabuses were produced, certain changes of emphasis were seen, some in terms of the professional purposes of religious teaching and some in terms of content. Piaget's influence and the work of Ronald Goldman (1964; 1965) and others in the 1960s and 1970s contributed to a reduction of biblical content and more emphasis on the emotional development of children. This could be achieved by encouraging children to think about themselves and their relationships, by participation in celebrating festivals, by the use of non-religious stories to introduce religious concepts. This was often designated the implicit approach to religious teaching and used most with what we would now know as Key Stage 1 children as a foundation for more overtly religious content in Key Stage 2. In common with much of the primary curriculum, a thematic approach was frequently used as the basis for the syllabus and since the 1944 Act did not forbid this, teaching about the other major faiths gradually found a place in many of them.

The 1988 Education Reform Act confirmed all of the elements outlined above whilst making some of them more specific. A significant change was the title – from Religious Instruction to Religious Education. This should have removed any kind of concern that teachers might be expected to teach religion rather than teach about religion – emphasizing that no particular faith or denomination should be promoted in maintained schools. Syllabuses were, however, allowed to include teaching about denominations.

The 1988 Act was also more specific about the content of RE syllabuses. All syllabuses produced after 1988 were to 'reflect the fact that the religious traditions in Great Britain are in the main Christian while taking account of the teaching and practices of the other principal religions represented in Great Britain' (1988 Act, Section 11).

The Act also required each LEA to set up a Standing Advisory Council for Religious Education (SACRE). This body would consist of representatives of four groups:

- such Christian and other religious groups as will represent the local community;
- the Church of England;
- the LEA;
- teachers' associations.

The function of the SACRE is to advise the LEA on matters to do with RE and collective worship. It has the power to require an LEA to review and amend its agreed syllabus; it is the SACRE which hears requests from schools for a determination that fulfillment of the requirements of the Act in terms of collective worship is not appropriate for a particular school or for specific groups of children within a school. Some LEAs refer any parental complaints about RE or school worship to the SACRE. Each SACRE has to publish an annual public report outlining their work.

Recent Updates

The 1993 Education Act made further stipulations about RE; these may be found in DFE Circular 1/94 Religious Education and Collective Worship, a copy of which should be in every school. The Introduction to the Circular re-emphasizes the statements from the 1988 Act quoted at the beginning of this chapter indicating that RE has an important part to play in spiritual, moral and cultural development and underlines the government's aim to improve the quality of provision for all pupils. It indicates that further discussion of this area may be found in *Spiritual and Moral Development: A Discussion Paper*, 1993 (NCC).

It is stated that the legislation is designed 'in RE to ensure that pupils gain both a thorough knowledge of Christianity reflecting the Christian heritage of this country, and knowledge of the other principal religions represented in Great Britain' (Introduction, para. 7). The Circular, which provides guidance, but is not an authoritative legal interpretation of the Education Acts, (Introduction, para. 10) also suggests that RE has a role to play in enabling pupils to develop their own sets of values and to respect those of others.

Many of the additions to the 1988 Act have to do with requirements for grant maintained schools in terms of RE and worship. In brief, grant maintained schools follow the set of requirements which applied before they obtained grant maintained status. There are also provisions for their representation on SACREs and syllabus conferences (see below). The details of these provisions may be found in the Circular. The 1993 Act also requires LEAs who have not produced a new agreed syllabus since 1988 to set up a writing conference by 1 April 1995. Such a conference must be made up of groups identical with those named for the SACRE, in proportions as far as possible representing the balance of faiths/denominations within the area served by the LEA.

What Should We Teach?

It is apparent from the above that, in RE, the locally agreed syllabus holds an important place. One of the major differences between an agreed syllabus and national curriculum documents is that whereas the national curriculum is nationally determined with programmes of study, level descriptors and assessment requirements, RE is tailored to the needs of a local population. Once an LEA has drawn up and secured approval for an RE syllabus, it becomes the document from which all religious education in its maintained schools should be drawn, via a school policy and syllabus. The agreed syllabus must, and school syllabuses should;

- ensure that in total content and at each Key Stage, teaching on Christianity should receive the largest proportion of the time available;

- ensure that all the principal religions of Great Britain are represented within the total content;
- identify which of the religions other than Christianity should be taught at each Key Stage; (Not all need be taught at each Key Stage or in equal depth. The local situation may determine sequence and balance. The standing conference responsible for writing the syllabus is required by Circular 1/94 (para. 35) to consider how best to minimize the number of pupils who might be withdrawn from RE by their parents.)
- provide sufficient detail of what is to be taught to fulfill the points above. This detail must form part of the syllabus and not simply be provided in an accompanying non-mandatory handbook (DFE Circular 1/94, paras. 31–9.)

The LEA, through the syllabus conference may, if it chooses, provide programmes of study, level descriptors and assessment guidelines. Consequently the agreed syllabus will provide the basis for RE in maintained schools, but in order for teachers to feel that they are at ease with it and have some sense of ownership of what needs to be done in classrooms each school should develop its own policy statement and syllabus.

This has the advantage of enabling individual schools:

- to put particular emphasis on appropriate aspects of the syllabus in line with their own constituency;
- to ensure continuity and progression where topics are returned to at different points of the children's time in primary school;
- to identify points where cross-curricular approaches will be of particular value;
- to ensure that adequate time will be available for RE. The Dearing Report on National Curriculum Assessment (SCAA, 1993) recommends 45 hours a year at Key Stage 2. This is over and above the time given to collective worship and assemblies;
- to outline any common approaches to assessment;
- to provide statements for the school brochure as required by the 1993 Education Act;
- to include information about: the ethos of the school which underpins pupils' spiritual, moral, cultural and social development.

A Basis for Teaching

When religious teaching was seen as instruction, the content was almost entirely knowledge-based. As indicated earlier, the Bible and the lives of famous Christians provided the content and storytelling and writing or memorization of key passages comprised the major methods of teaching.

The research of Goldman (1964; 1965) Loukes (1965) and Madge (1965) indicated that this was not a successful approach, even in terms of retaining knowledge, so the syllabuses from the late 1960s onwards began to concern themselves with a more holistic approach to learning in RE. Along with other areas of curriculum, concern began to be expressed for the kinds of concepts that children acquired. In terms of RE it was recognized that many children tended to see Christianity as *long ago and far away* without any relevance to their own lives. In order to alter the emphasis, the newer syllabuses began to concern themselves with the lifestyles of Christian communities around the world – celebration of festivals, rites of passage, ethics, buildings, patterns of worship, sacred writings and traditions. These approaches were also used in the teaching of other faiths.

Without promotion of any particular religion, the intended outcome of this work was that children would understand that the pattern of life for many people, locally and across the world, was based on religious belief and practice. However, it was also possible that change of content would simply provide a different type of knowledge. There needed to be a change in the underlying approach to RE and this developed into a concern not only for knowledge but also for concepts, experience, skills and attitudes. Many of the syllabuses produced over the last ten years use these terms as a focus for the work to be done under specific programmes of study or Key Stages. For example, see those of Devon, Essex and Berkshire County Councils.

Supportive Structures

As indicated above an increasing number of LEAs are producing syllabuses which begin by considering the teaching approach rather than the subject content. These often focus on or around terms such as skills, concepts, experience and attitudes as well as knowledge.

Skills are tools which enable children to use their knowledge and experience to construct and develop concepts. Appropriate concepts enable children to make sense of the area of study and to draw conclusions. The formation of positive attitudes to self and others is essential if children are to be able to appreciate their own place in society and to respect the values of others – all aspirations expressed in the Circular.

> As a new RE coordinator you should:
> Search out and become familiar with Circular 1/94.
> Find out about your local SACRE, obtain and read its reports.
> Look at your Agreed syllabus. Has it been written or revised since 1988?
> If not, does the SACRE plan to do this?
> Does it contain enough detail to allow you to fulfill the legal requirements?
> Try to find out whether or not it is actually used.

As we consider in more detail what we mean by these terms, it becomes apparent that there is a considerable area of overlap between RE, other subject areas and the wider world of the child. If we take as an example the theme of *Loving and Caring*, we find that the major religious faiths all have things to say. Before children can be expected to understand what these terms mean in the setting of a religious faith they need to develop some understanding and experience of what is meant by them in a broader setting. So one group of concepts, which we might call general concepts, built up through human experience of relationships and interactions, as givers and receivers – with family, friends and pets, in school and in other social groups – becomes significant. Clearly these concepts begin to form in early childhood, long before children reach Key Stage 2, but if a good foundation has been laid, the child will be more easily able to construct more explicitly religious concepts about the meaning of, for instance, 'Love your neighbour as yourself' or the Muslim teaching on almsgiving.

In the same way the skills necessary for effective learning about religion are also important in other areas of the curriculum. Good interpersonal skills, along with the development of empathy, are needed if children are to be able to learn from and respect one another.

Language skills are closely linked with these; listening and talking enables children to express beliefs or emotions and to raise questions in open and sensitive ways. Use of appropriate technical religious language and vocabulary becomes appropriate at Key Stage 2 as does the necessity to understand the significance of symbol and myth and the ability to use it themselves. Of great importance also are the development of skills related to appreciation and expression through drama, music, dance and the visual arts, all of which play an important part in religious experience and expression. Skills of logical thought and analysis are also necessary, linked with, for instance, examination of sacred writings.

The attitudes to be encouraged for effective RE include those of mutual care and concern, openness to and respect for the ideas, beliefs and lifestyles of others and curiosity about and sensitivity to the natural world. Experience is a vital part of RE, developed both through the general concepts referred to above and by use of the strategies outlined below.

Knowledge/information will provide a lot of the content of religious education, but as indicated earlier, there must be more than a mere collection of pieces of information. Within the school syllabus and schemes of work arising from it there must always be the underpinning issues of what concepts and attitudes are to be concentrated upon at any given time and then which skills need to be introduced or refined in order to fulfill those intentions.

Strategies

If the need for a conceptual framework for any scheme of work in RE (as opposed to the collection of a ragbag of information) has been recognized and implemented, there still remains the task of deciding how to present the concepts in ways most likely to be assimilated – in other words – what strategies should be used?

As the RE coordinator:
Look at some of the RE in your class/school.
Analyse it in terms of concepts, attitudes, experience, skills.
Where are there links with other subject areas?
Think about ways in which you might produce a school policy and syllabus or analyse your current documents in this way.

Artefacts

After gaining the attention of a group of children, capturing and retaining their interest is the next vital stage in ensuring that learning will take place. One of the most attractive ways of doing this in RE is by the use of artefacts. By this I mean objects rather than pictures, except perhaps an icon, since objects appeal to tactile as well as visual responses. There are various ways of introducing artefacts, and it is essential to emphasize that whatever is being used must be treated with respect and handled carefully. It is an article of importance to members of that faith group. It is also essential to ensure that the objects chosen are acceptable for this purpose in the view of that faith group. For example, you would not choose to use a copy of the Q'ran, because there are particular requirements about how it is handled and where it is kept, but it would be acceptable to use a string of prayer beads or a prayer carpet. Children could be asked to:

- see what they could tell you about the object;
- decide what they think it is used for and why;
- make a list of things they want to know about it.

Depending on the age/ability of the children and the resources available the object could be identified and knowledge expanded by

- teacher input;
- input from a member, adult or child, from the faith group;
- use of reference books/information sheets;
- use of video material.

This could then be further extended by some kind of factual written and/or illustrated account; by imagining that the object belonged to you and writing a story about it; by creating a dramatic scene around it. The nature of the artefact would determine which of these could be appropriate.

Picture/Poster Work

This is most suited to work in groups of various sizes. The posters produced by Pictorial Charts Educational Trust may be used along with questions or a problem solving challenge to provide information, stimulate a broader enquiry and enable children to demonstrate an ability to analyse what they see and read.

Pictures or posters without any text, such as some of those produced by CEM could be used to stimulate open-ended enquiry. 'What do you think is going on here?' 'Why do you think that?' 'Does this picture remind you of any other work you've done or things you've seen?' Or a more imaginative approach: 'Imagine that you are *x* in the picture and describe how you feel.' 'In your group become the people in the picture and have a conversation about . . .'

Looking at pictures is also a good way to introduce an exploration of myth and symbolism in religion.

- Why are some Hindu deities shown as having six hands?
- Are there special reasons why the Buddha is sometimes shown sitting, sometimes lying on his side and with different hand positions and facial expressions – or is it just the choice of the artist or sculptor?
- Find as many pictures of Jesus as possible – prints of Old Masters as well as modern illustration. Consider the varieties of physique, dress, expressions portrayed and consider possible reasons.
- A version of this can also be done with Christmas cards of the nativity scenes. It is particularly valuable to include some of the modern portrayals from Africa, South America, etc. These are frequently produced by the Aid Agencies. Why do people see the story so differently and is there a right way?

The other side of this coin is to ask the children, perhaps in pairs or small groups to design a poster to 'create a feeling about . . .' or 'tell the story of . . .' or 'tell what happens at . . .' or 'what do you think it was like at . . .'

It is important that where factual information is being researched the resources provided are accurate and that discussions are held with children, especially at the older end of Key Stage 2, to draw out from them why they need to be as accurate as possible in their drawing and writing when they are describing a historical or ongoing activity. This may often be underlined by the children's work being used as a teaching resource for another group or class.

Story/Drama/Music

These are all ways of actively involving children in RE. Few children fail to respond to a good story well told or read, and story is an important element in most world faiths, either as a vehicle for recounting its history or presenting its teaching.

It is important to be sure that the stories used are from sources which have been approved by the faith concerned, so that the details and emphases are a true reflection of the teaching or happening. Some addresses of faith groups are included at the end of this chapter; others are often included in the supporting materials linked to an agreed syllabus or may be obtained from faith groups themselves, from the local SACRE or advisory teachers. Whereas for Key Stage 1 children the story will very often be presented simply as a story, for Key Stage 2 children, the significance of myth and symbolic language in religion should be introduced and some story material begun to be seen as a way of conveying a religious truth. Older Key Stage 2 children may also enjoy comparing and contrasting different versions of stories, such as the stories of the birth of Jesus in the gospels of Matthew and Luke and considering why Mark and John have no similar narratives.

Children retelling stories is another way for them to feel their way into situations and characters. This is closely linked with drama which could be a further development. Drama is particularly valuable in helping children to express their own feelings and empathize with those of others. Both of these are important skills for RE. The celebration of Passover would be one instance where role play and story could come together to contribute to children's understanding of an important Jewish festival.

Music is an important part of the worship of some religions and Key Stage 2 children could enjoy looking at some of the different kinds of music produced, for example, the way in which Handel produced *The Messiah* and also to explore something like *Joseph and the Amazing Technicolour Dreamcoat*. The use of singing or chanting and the use, or non-use, of musical instruments in worship is another area for exploration as is the kind of music used in the school for collective worship. A different way of using music is as a stimulus for role play or a background to encourage reflection or meditation. In addition to listening, children should be encouraged to create their own music for these kinds of situations.

Audio and Visual Materials

These are invaluable in RE because they are another way of helping children to enter into situations and experiences without imposing any demands for personal commitment or involvement. Materials are now available from various sources including the BBC, Independent Television and Christian Education Movement (CEM). As with this kind of material in any subject area, there needs to be preparation and follow-up.

Visitors and Visits

Visits to a variety of places of worship provide an opportunity which few children would otherwise have and from which they will gain not only in gathering information but by experiencing the, feel, of the place. As with any other visit it would need to have been arranged carefully, with teachers making preliminary visits (this might be a valuable in-service session for everyone) and discussing with the person concerned what the children will hear about and be able to see and do. Will they be able to move around independently or will they remain together in one place? Checking up on any requirements for appropriate dress, such as removal of shoes or bringing a head covering should be part of these discussions so that children know what is expected of them. Some teachers like to supply worksheets while others want children to look, listen, touch (where appropriate) and remember. Whichever approach is used it is important to give children a little time to absorb the atmosphere and pursue their own thoughts. It may be possible for the person who will talk to the children to visit them in the classroom first. This would help to indicate at what level the children are working. Such mutual hospitality creates the beginning of a positive relationship as well as being a useful bridge for the children as they visit a new place. It will give the teacher a further opportunity to talk about the practicalities of the visit – what degree of detail the children will understand and how long they will be able to listen.

Inviting members of different faiths into school to demonstrate or talk about various aspects of their faith or practice is a way of enabling children to

---

As the RE coordinator
- Build up a collection of resources. To do this you will need:
  - a budget to buy things you cannot obtain in other ways;
  - facilities for storage;
  - to raise the awareness and trade on the goodwill of colleagues, governors, family and friends to collect for you.
- Begin collections of artefacts. At first these will probably be categorized simply by faith – the Judaism Box – but as the collection grows it may be re-defined as the Jewish Worship Box, the Passover Box, etc.
- Collect pictures and posters. The colour supplements from national newspapers are useful as well as the publications mentioned above. Travel agents or airline companies will sometimes donate large posters.
- Collect stories story tapes and appropriate music of the major faiths in the school library or the RE resource area.
- Build up contacts with faith groups so that visits and visitors can be built into the RE programme. Use those contacts if available to provide background to the celebration of festivals.
- Identify in-service needs and set up appropriate sessions. Further suggestions may be found in *Beyond the Core Curriculum*, ch. 11, Mattock, 1994.

---

hear firsthand things that they might otherwise only read in books or hear from their teacher. Again, it needs preparation. It very often works best if done in a class setting rather than with a much larger age group and in a planned question and answer session. If the children have prepared the questions and the visitor knows in advance what they will be, but responds to them when the children ask them, there are various benefits. The children feel ownership and involvement, the responses will probably not be so long that attention will be lost and the teacher, having organized the arrangement of the questions, will be able to ensure that there is some kind of sequence to the session. It is also easier for most people to make themselves heard in a classroom than in a much larger space like a school hall. If no one objects the session might also be tape recorded so that details can be reviewed afterwards. If a school has limited contacts with members of faith groups the local SACRE may be able to suggest possible speakers. Patterns of visits and visitors could be built into the school RE syllabus so that they are evenly distributed through both Key Stages.

Celebrations

Taking the celebration of a festival as a school or class theme is another way of helping children to enter, in a limited way, into the experience of what it means to be a member of a particular faith. For this to have real value a considerable amount of attention needs to be given to planning and clear decisions must be made about which subject areas will be incorporated into the celebration and the amount of time which will be devoted to it. A number of the approaches to RE outlined above will probably contribute either to preparation or celebration. Particular resources may be obtainable through parents or advisory teachers. The local SACRE may be able to suggest suitable contacts within the faith community. Many LEAs produce booklets for use in multicultural education which contain ideas and activities for festivals, and increasingly, publisher's lists include such materials.

SHAP (registered educational charity) produces an annual calendar of religious festivals which would be a useful addition to a staff library or RE resource area. Since, as indicated above, quite a lot of time will be needed, it would be appropriate to consider which festival(s) would be celebrated in major ways each year, possibly changing the emphasis over a period of time. This does not mean that all others would be ignored but that mention would be more low key. Choices will usually be determined by the ethnic or cultural backgrounds of children in the school.

Assessment

Although there are no nationally prescribed programmes of study or level descriptors in RE, syllabus conferences may draw up materials for local use.

These, together with outlines of assessment patterns, appear in some of the more recent syllabuses. It is certainly important that teachers keep records of pupils' progress in RE, although formal patterns of testing may not be appropriate.

Individual schools should follow the guidelines given in the local syllabus if these exist. If there are none, or they are very open it would appear sensible to link assessment patterns in RE, as far as possible, with those followed in foundation areas within the school. If school syllabuses are being produced or updated, setting out programmes of study based on the principles of concepts, experience, attitudes and skills, then ways of assessing progress in each area should be built into the programme of study. For the most part this will be a continuing formative process based on observation of children's responses and developing awareness and sensitivity – a more holistic approach than simply a catalogue of 'facts known about . . .'. Ways of asking children to record their work will vary according to the nature of the study.

> RE coordinators should:
> Consider the area of recording and assessment with the staff and come to a common mind on what is being assessed and why; evolve a pattern of recording which will demonstrate this and indicate continuity and progression.

It should be possible to identify lines of continuity from the agreed syllabus to the children's work via the school syllabus and teachers' records of work done. As well as providing information for official visitors this is a way of checking on continuity and progression. There are very useful detailed considerations of these areas in *Attainment in RE – A Handbook for Teachers*, 1989 and *Assessing, Recording and Reporting RE*, 1991, both from the Midlands Regional RE Centre.

Postscript

Now you have some ideas to start you on your task, but you still need to consider how you can share your thoughts, and it is hoped, enthusiasm, with colleagues on the staff most of whom will have been teaching for much longer than you! You must also recognize that running a class will take a lot of your time and attention, especially for the first year or two in the profession. So, you need to make some impact without endangering your efficiency within your own class. Here are some ways:

- When you are asked to take the responsibility for RE, negotiate some time allowance. This will enable you to work alongside a colleague on a joint project or to go to the occasional day course.

- See if there is space on a staffroom notice board to display information about RE or to identify topics to be raised at staff meetings or in-service sessions.
- Encourage your school to subscribe to one of the RE periodicals such as the CEM Primary Pack. These have ideas for the whole primary age group on a range of topics and will become a useful staffroom resource.
- Don't be afraid to ask for help from colleagues, advisory teachers, parents, governors or members of the local SACRE.
- Do an audit of your schools' practice in RE against what an OFSTED inspection would be looking for. Use this to set your agenda.
- If there is no school syllabus for RE this should be a fairly early priority, but you will need to get to know the school a little before launching into this. Decisions about what you do must be agreed not imposed. This will take longer but will have more chance of being used. Remember that it must be based on your local agreed syllabus.
- In-service sessions need to be carefully planned to include time for staff to absorb and discuss the content they have been offered. There should be a visible goal, for example, finding out more about the background and activities for a festival to be celebrated as a school project. There will also be less tangible but very significant benefits in terms of a general widening of horizons and growth in confidence.
- As a general rule-of-thumb steady development is more effective than an occasional major onslaught. There are many other subjects competing for time and attention from teachers. You may find it useful to plan your work in conjunction with other coordinators so that there is an even spread of demand in terms of staff meetings.

References

BERKSHIRE DEPARTMENT OF EDUCATION (1990) *Religious Heritage and Personal Quest*, Reading, Berkshire County Council.

HMSO/DFE Circular 1/94 (1994) *Religious Education and Collective Worship*, London, DFE.

DES (1988) *Education Reform Act 1988*, HMSO.

DFE (1993) *Education Act 1993*, HMSO.

DFE (1994) Religious Education and Collective Worship, London, DFE Publications Centre.

DEVON COUNTY COUNCIL (1992) *Promoting Quality. Religious Education in the Basic Curriculum*, Exeter, Devon County Council.

ESSEX LEA (1992) *Recognizing Attainment in RE*, Chelmsford, Essex County Council.

GOLDMAN, R.J. (1964) *Religious Understanding from Childhood to Adolescence*, London, Routledge and Kegan Paul.

GOLDMAN, R.J. (1965) *Readiness for Religion*, London, Routledge and Kegan Paul.

LOUKES, H. (1965) *New Ground in Christian Education*, London, SCM.

MADGE, V. (1965) *Children in Search of Meaning*, London, SCM.

MATTOCK, G. (1994) 'Religious education: A new era', in HARRISON, M. (ed.) *Beyond the Core Curriculum*, Plymouth, Northcote House.

NCC (1993) *Spiritual and Moral Development; A Discussion Paper*, York, NCC.

REGIONAL RE CENTRE (MIDLANDS) WESTHILL COLLEGE (1989) *Attainment in RE*, Birmingham, Westhill.

RUDGE, J. (1991) *Assessing, Recording and Reporting RE*, Regional RE Centre (Midlands) Westhill College.

Addresses and Resource References

Articles of Faith. Bury Business Centre, Key St. Bury, BL6.
Artefacts of all major faiths. Catalogue available.

Berkshire syllabus, Department of Education, Shire Hall, Shinfield Park, Reading, Berks. RG2 9XE.

Bible Society, Stonehill Green, Westlea, Swindon, SN5 7DG.
Materials related to the study of the Bible.

British Council of Churches, Inter-Church House, 35–41, Lower Marsh, London, SE1 7RL.
Packs of materials for primary schools available.

The Buddhist Society, 58, Eccleston Square, London, SW1V 1PH.

Christian Education Movement, Royal Buildings, Victoria St. Derby, DE1 1GW (CEM) Publishes theme booklets, posters, video material, the magazine *RE Today* and material on school worship and assemblies. A resources list is available. These materials deal with a variety of world faiths.

Devon County Council, Education Department, Topsham Rd., Exeter, EX2 4QG.

Essex County Council, Education Department, Curriculum and Assessment Section, PO Box 47, Chelmsford, Essex. CM1 1LD.

Islamic Foundation Publications, Unit 9, The Old Dunlop Factory, 62, Evington Valley Rd., Leicester, LE5 5LJ.
Materials for schools.

Jewish Education Bureau, 8, Westcombe Avenue, Leeds, LS8 2BS.
Books and artefacts.

Pictorial Charts Education Trust, 27, Kirchen Rd, London W13 0UD. Publishes a large variety of sets of posters on many aspects of world faiths. A list is available on request.

The Regional RE Centre (Midlands), Westhill College, Selly Oak, Birmingham, B29 6LL.

SHAP publications may be obtained from; Alan Brown, The National Society's RE Centre, 36, Causten St. London, SW1P 4AU.

The National Society RE Centre also has a wide selection of books and materials for RE.

Sikh Education Council, 10, Featherstone Rd., Southall, Middlesex, UB2 5AA.

Chapter 9

Providing a Sense of Direction in Key Stage 2

Bill Boyle

Scene Setting

Geography stands in limbo through a revised Order which has substantially reduced the extent of the subject in the first two Key Stages. This diminution is in both required curriculum content and assessment arrangements. The reductions have been welcomed widely from within the teaching profession on the grounds of prescription and overload. However, it is to be hoped that the gains made in establishing a sense of the subject's identity in the primary years due to the national curriculum requirements since 1991 are not lost along with the redundant statements of attainment (SoA).

The teaching of geography in the primary years before the national curriculum was roundly condemned by HMI. 'Overall standards of work in geography were very disappointing' being strong language for an HMI report, as it detailed the 'tendency for geography to lose its distinctive contribution' (HMI, 1989). A generalized description of any geography teaching that took place in the primary sector pre–1991 would undoubtedly utilize the term *topic* for its method of delivery. Even under national curriculum change was slow, despite the knowledge that, until Dearing, external assessment was around the corner. A national primary survey conducted by the Centre for Formative Assessment Studies (CFAS) University of Manchester between autumn 1991 and summer 1992 revealed that over half the teachers sampled (55 per cent of n = 120 teachers) reported *no* work on any geography theme in the autumn term, with a further 32 per cent teaching between 1–3 hours over the same period. By the summer of 1992, a calendar year into national curriculum, the percentage reporting nil involvement had at least reduced to 47 per cent with a significant 6 per cent reporting teaching geography for more than 10 hours a term (see Table 9.1).

Coordinators who are beginning to review the work in their school might like to start by auditing time spent in teaching geography over a year and in each term. How is geography taught? Is it single subject or topic or project delivered and, if the latter, how are the planned geography elements distinguished?

Table 9.1: *Reported time spent on geography in one year (1991–2)*

	Autumn term 1991		Spring term 1992		Summer term 1992	
	n	per cent	n	per cent	n	per cent
No response	14	–	14	–	14	–
None	58	55	55	52	50	47
1–3 hours	34	32	32	30	31	29
4–6 hours	10	9	12	11	14	13
7–9 hours	3	5	5	5		
> 10 hours	4	4	4	4	6	6

Although the figures are early indicators of tensions between time allocation for core and foundation subjects, at least they show a measurable time increase. Similar data have not as yet been collated for 1993, but a further rise could surely be expected – stimulated by the availability in schools of non-mandatory assessment materials (SEAC). For although these were targetted at the end of Key Stage 1 the dearth of teaching as revealed meant that the Level 2 and 3 materials included would represent the major structured source of geographical thinking for children across Years 2, 3 and possibly 4.

However, before a full programme of geography national curriculum teaching and assessment could run its course (a Y1 child in 1991 was due to complete the Y6 programme of study in 1997), change was decreed politically expedient. The stentorian cries for change, some arising from within the geography hierarchy, were difficult to resist. Roger Carter's address to *Times Educational Supplement* readers was typical of the calls for revision of an order seen as assessment driven and too prescriptive.

> Currently we lead the field in the number of statements of attainment (183 in all). I suspect that it is the existing assessment requirements rather than the content which has contributed most to the perception of overload. Teachers have been urged into chasing statements, many of which are tied to bits of content . . . It will be hugely comforting to move away from such complexities (Carter, 1994).

For different reasons similar concerns were being expressed at classroom level, these myriad SoA were atomizing the curriculum ran the wisdom of the time! The danger of leaning from the specific SoA-driven to the generalized – in the proposed *best fit* level description model – is already obvious. Carter presciently continues, 'The danger here is [the descriptions] will assume such a high level of generality that they will offer scant support to less confident teachers in planning learning routes and sequences and interpreting achievement in them.' (p. 2)

Revisions to the Order

To primary class teachers, the major observable changes to the order are the reduction in the number of attainment targets from five to one, to 'emphasise the inter-relatedness of the various elements of geographical knowledge, understanding and skills' (SCAA, 1994, p. iv) and the replacement of SoA by level descriptions. The intention behind the introduction of the latter is to provide a 'summary of performance' and to allow teachers a reflective opportunity to judge which level best describes a pupil's attainment without the burden of recording and aggregating SoA related assessment.

At Key Stage 2 reduction in content has been achieved by removing two of the five studies of places and reducing the number of themes to be studied from eleven to four, while maintaining a balance between physical, human and environmental geography. Pupils at Key Stage 2 are therefore required to carry out studies of three places (teaching focused at the extent of a locality) and four themes in addition to applying a 'wider range of geographical skills' (SCAA, 1994, p. iv) and expanding their framework of locational knowledge.

Look at your school's present scheme of work to check compliance with this minimum requirement and to establish necessary planning amendments. Which aspects need reinforcing or introducing into plans? Which optional elements can also be planned in?

Geography in the Key Stage

Without wasting undue space in replicating requirements for the new order which are already widely disseminated it is worth reflecting on two issues of concern to the subject coordinator. These are progression within the subject and the subject's place within the overall planning of the primary curriculum in Key Stage 2.

Progression

The rationale for the provision of progression across the Key Stages in the revised, SoA-less Order is that it has been secured in terms of breadth of studies, depth of studies and complexity of concepts, 'an increase in the range of spatial scales of what is studied and a continuing development of a widening range of increasingly complex skills' (SCAA, 1994, p. iv). To achieve these praiseworthy aims at the primary stage much depends on quality of teachers' knowledge and skills. The comment of Keith Lloyd HMI, that 'the lack of subject knowledge, skills and understanding of geography among those who have to teach it, particularly at Key Stage 2, continues to limit progress', (Lloyd, 1994, pp. 7–9) would indicate that any consistent match of

Table 9.2: A revised set of strands for Key Stage 2

AT		Strands in Order		Relevant strands at KS2
1	1 2	map work field work	1	recognize the local area in visual and verbal representation
2	3 4 5 6	knowledge of places distinctive features of places similarities/differences between places relationships between themed issues in places	2 3	knowledge of places relationship between land and people
3	7 8 9 10 11	weather and climate rivers, river basins seas and oceans landforms animals, plants and soil	4	weather, water and landforms
4	12 13 14	population and settlements communication and movement economic activities	5 6 7	settlements journeys work
5	15 16 17	use and misuse of natural resources quality and vulnerability of different environments possibilities for protecting and managing environments	8 9	description of land as a resource judgment of land as a resource

teaching quality and progression of children would need to be a long-term aim for a new coordinator.

For the primary class teacher progression and development of children's understanding of geography and its parallel curriculum planning and tracking were at least more specific using strands within the original geography order. An approach to the streamlining of these was outlined by CFAS (1991, pp. 5–6) as shown in Table 9.2 above. This, it was hoped, would provide useful curriculum and assessment guidance for a subject in which primary teachers freely admitted their insecurity. Any taught experience is necessarily limited in value if the teacher does not recognize where it leads. A framework for geographical progression is therefore clearly required. Do the level descriptions provide that framework? Do statements such as 'through the Key Stage pupils will increasingly broaden and deepen their knowledge and understanding of places and themes . . . offer explanations for the characteristics of places . . . develop and use appropriate geographical skills,' (SCAA, 1994, p. 4) offer much in the way of structured assistance?

The strands within the original attainment targets were meant to provide that framework. Teachers could be encouraged to organize their curriculum in strands. However, it is a big step from one level to the next in a strand, and revising orders will not alter that! It may be a step that a child is not ready to make. For many children a side-step will be more useful, using their current understanding (in one strand) to help them come to terms with another. This used to be called the spiral curriculum. Children may well make better progress by consolidating their understanding at one level across several strands, before revisiting a strand and making the jump to the next level. Therefore, the strands are a way of recognizing the organization of the curriculum and evaluating the completeness of coverage offered by geographical experiences delivered, for example, within the vehicle of topic work.

Organizing the curriculum by strands offers a sense of direction. Strands should be flexible, readily embedded in the broad themes in use in primary planning practice with its associated rolling programmes, such as routes and journeys, planet earth, and shopping. Teachers are familiar in working with themes such as these but welcome the guidance on interpretation offered by the strands embedded within them. The 'strands within themes' approach was seen as useful curriculum and assessment guidance. (TES, 1992) Put this in the context of HMI comments such as 'Many schools still need help and advice with (geography) curriculum design, particularly at Key Stage 2' (Keith Lloyd, 1994) and there is an obvious need to deconstruct the skills, theme and place requirements of the new order to provide these pathways for planning and progression.

The acquired experience of the last three years points in this direction as does the absence of specialist teaching in the subject. Reference HMI again,

> Variations in the quality of planning are still too wide. Many teachers need more support with the planning of lessons or units of work, as well as a better understanding of the Programmes of Study. The influence of effective coordinators in these important areas has been clearly demonstrated but many schools do not have access to this kind of advice (Lloyd, 1994).

Planning

In the absence of this difficult-to-quantify ideal of *effective coordination*, what is the current situation? What weaknesses in planning do HMI pinpoint? What is the status of geography as a subject at Key Stage 2? It is now clear that the abstruseness of the structure of the 1991 Order confounded non-specialist primary teachers' attempts at effective planning of the subject (OFSTED, 1993). Their strategies of planning for the teaching of geography in the contexts of cross-curricular themes or rolling programmes further bedevil the picture in the primary stage leading to the inevitable fragmentary selection of content at the expense of continuity and progression. 'The question of balance between the ATs has not been properly addressed' (Lloyd, 1994). Weakness in planning has led to undue concentration on one or two Attainment Targets in isolation from the rest, particularly the geographical skills aspect of AT1 (OFSTED, 1993). This presumably has been rendered a non-issue by replacing the five ATs with one catch-all titled *Geography* which will magically 'avoid fragmentation and an artificial divide between knowledge, understanding and skills' (DFE, 1994).

Too much emphasis on 'mapwork, the local area and studying weather, together with a general neglect of most aspects of human and environmental geography and the study of unfamiliar places' (Lloyd, 1994) were also highlighted. The new order at Key Stage 2 inexplicably offers the following required diet to assuage these concerns!

- 3 *locality* focused place studies, one of which is the same local area (of the school) studied at Key Stage 1, although 'in more depth' [how quantifiable to the non-specialist is depth?] while another is specified as within the United Kingdom;
- 4 of the 6 skills requirements for the Key Stage focus on *mapwork*;
- *weather* is one of the four required themes, retained from the original order despite the demotion of landforms, population and economic activities to a third Key Stage conception.

However, the reduced curriculum provided by the revised order should clearly be regarded solely as a core entitlement which allows the coordinator to suggest and prompt for the inclusion of non-statutory content reflecting individual interests, concerns and specialisms, alongside local issues.

Key Coordination Issues

Focus on *collaborative planning*: the majority of primary schools, for a variety of external and internal reasons, are now used to the notion of collaborative whole school or Key Stage planning. The age of isolated learning cells and autonomous teachers has disappeared – one national curriculum victory at least. The role of the coordinator here is to negotiate and agree with teachers a progressive structure through the key stage. If children work on topics rather than single subjects, it is essential that the geography components are clearly specified at the planning stage.

Progression through the Key Stage should be clearly signalled in the planning of units of study. I see no way this can be achieved other than by developing routes or strands for teaching and learning objectives, making judicious use of the original SoA as no clear lines of progression are provided in the final revised Order. Even the experts seem to agree that 'less confident teachers' need support 'in planning learning routes and sequences and interpreting achievement in them' (Carter, 1994, p. 1).

'The best guidelines indicated how differentiation could be achieved in each unit of work' (Lloyd, 1994). *Differentiation* is easily thrown away in an overview statement but the initiation, monitoring and updating of differentiated work programmes to match pupils' needs and progress them will tax the skills and time allocation of even the most effective coordinator.

Assessment is largely ignored in the draft proposals because it carried the bulk of the blame for over-prescription as we have discussed, but an effective means of interpreting achievement will need developing. This will surely have to be centrally controlled for standardization of indicators of perform-ance to be achieved, to provide a baseline for Teacher Assessment, possibly a reverse centre-periphery model, with the best of the myriad LEA devised materials being scrutinized, amended and issued by SCAA/DFE. A first step for coordinators is to review models of assessment of children's geographical understanding and achievement being used in the school. This audit may reveal a measure of consistency or the need for such.

The school coordinator should plan a series of meetings, almost in-school agreement trials, to negotiate standardized agreement for the indicators of performance required for each level description. The experience of the last three years won't be wasted here as the former SoA with their correlation to school portfolios of evidence can be recognized easily within each level description.

Level descriptions are clearly here to stay (at least for five years!). In the absence of national guidance, the coordinator will need to help colleagues make sense of differentiation in levels of achievement in the context of such phrases as 'widening range of scales' and 'growing understanding of similar-ities and differences in places'.

Places and Themes

The coordinator's role at planning sessions will be crucial in encouraging and enabling less-specialist colleagues to set their work on the four themes as realistically as possible in the contexts of actual places. Clearly, availability of and access to a range of locality extent (small-scale studies) resources will be a major issue in the success or failure of this intention. How does the co-ordinator persuade colleagues to search for resources on small-scale locations at home and abroad within a subject that has been so clearly marginalized even within its foundation status?

Subject Identity

If the coordinator retains this for geography, in view of the above, in the primary curriculum, that will be success in itself. Good luck!

References

CARTER, R. (1994) 'Full of risk and promise', *TES*, April, p. 1.
CHRISTIE, T., BOYLE, B. and DAVIES, P. (1992) *Final Report, KS1 Geography Non-statutory SAT Development*, Manchester, CFAS, University of Manchester.

CHRISTIE, T., BOYLE, B. and DAVIES, P. (1991) *Development of Standard Assessment Tasks to Assess Geography at Key Stage One*, Manchester, CFAS, University of Manchester.

CHRISTIE, T., BOYLE, B. and DAVIES, P. (1992) 'Left Stranded', *TES* November, p. 1.

HMI (1989) *Aspects of Primary Education: The Teaching and Learning of History and Geography*, London, DES.

LLOYD, K (1994) 'Place and practice in the current state of geography in the primary curriculum', *Primary Geographer*, **17**, p. 3.

OFSTED (1993) *Geography Key Stages 1, 2 and 3 – Second Year 1992–3*, London, OFSTED.

SCAA (1994) *Draft Proposals: Geography in the National Curriculum*, London, SCAA.

DFE (1995) Geography in the National Curriculum, London, DFE.

Recommended Reading

BOYLE, B. (1991) *Our Local Community*, Oxford, Heinemann Education.

BOYLE, B. and RAY, R. (1992) *Homes and Settlements*, Oxford, Heinemann Education.

BOYLE, T. (1993) *Comparing Places Teacher's Guide*, Oxford, Heinemann Education.

DAY, C., HALL, G., GAMMAGE, P. and COLES, M. (1993) *Leadership and Curriculum in the Primary School*, London, Paul Chapman Publishing Ltd.

MARSDEN, B. and HUGHES, J. (eds) (1994) *Primary School Geography*, London, D. Fulton.

WIEGAND, P. (1992) *Places in the Primary School*, London, Falmer Press.

WIEGAND, P. (1994) *Children and Primary Geography*, London, Cassell.

Chapter 10

Design and Technology at Key Stage 2

Alan Cross

Introduction

Design and technology as a subject has much to offer children in the primary years. The history of design and technology as a subject in its own right is short. Its roots stem from a craft tradition (Eggleston, 1992). The inclusion of design and technology in the UK's national curriculum from 5–16 (the first time in any country) is very significant. This is part of a recent history in which the government has sought to influence the technology curriculum specifically, i.e., Technical and Vocational Education Initiative (TVEI); Educational Support Grant (ESG); Grant for Education Support and Training (GEST); and most recently 20-day courses. Those considering specialization, and those examining the role of design and technology coordinator for the first time may be struck by the size or breadth of the subject and by the range of extent and styles of implementation from classroom-to-classroom, phase-to-phase and school-to-school (DES, 1992a; 1994).

Context

This section will first consider the broader context in which schools operate. In the section entitled strategies you will be asked to consider the curricular context within your school. This will help to form a base of information so that you can proceed from an informed position.

Design and technology is correctly a subject within the national curriculum, however, this status can work against the very cross-curricular nature of the subject. This tension within the subject will be examined later. Design and technology requires more than a passing commitment to cross-curricular teaching. The subject is about problem solving.

The subject uses skills, knowledge and understanding from language, mathematics, science, the arts, the humanities and from different cultures. Children need to be well motivated and engaged, and they need to develop the design and the product within a meaningful context. For example, they must aspire to construct, a bridge or a healthy meal which fulfils a clearly identified need. It is important that criteria are spelt out clearly, ideally by the children themselves so that success can be identified. Children must experience and learn to deal with the effects of constraints like cost, safety and time so that their design and technology products represent increasingly realistic situations.

What is Design and Technology?

The 1994 proposals (SCAA, 1994b) describe design and technology capability as requiring 'pupils to combine their designing and making skills with knowledge and understanding, in order to design and make products'. Definition of this subject often causes problems. It can be defined in terms of its nature – seeking solutions to human problems, in terms of its breadth – that it includes experience of construction materials, of foods, of textiles, and in terms of its process – that recognizable behaviours can be identified within the design and make process which can be seen as elements of the process. How they are linked is an area of some interest. The 1991 statutory orders (DES, 1990) were based on the following process.

Figure 10.1: The design process

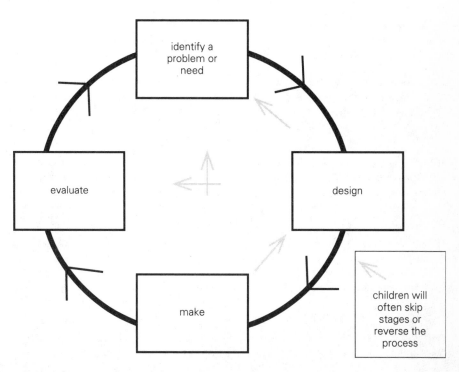

Figure 10.2: Interaction between hand and mind
From the Goldsmith's Project SEAC, 1991

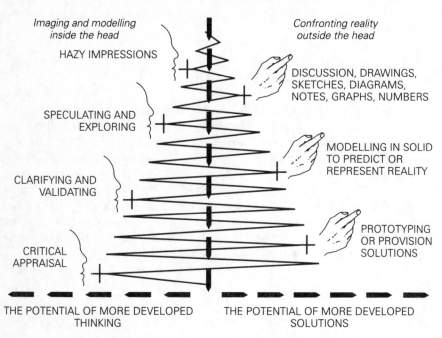

The interaction of hand and mind

Imaging and modelling
inside the head

Confronting reality
outside the head

HAZY IMPRESSIONS

DISCUSSION, DRAWINGS,
SKETCHES, DIAGRAMS,
NOTES, GRAPHS, NUMBERS

SPECULATING AND
EXPLORING

MODELLING IN SOLID
TO PREDICT OR
REPRESENT REALITY

CLARIFYING AND
VALIDATING

PROTOTYPING
OR PROVISION
SOLUTIONS

CRITICAL
APPRAISAL

THE POTENTIAL OF MORE DEVELOPED
THINKING

THE POTENTIAL OF MORE DEVELOPED
SOLUTIONS

This process is often misunderstood. Children do not always need to start at the stage of identifying needs. It is often fruitful to start with the challenge of evaluation of known artifacts or systems. When they design and make, you will find that children do not necessarily follow this cycle to the letter. They will often skip or miss out a stage. They will sometimes backtrack. This appears natural and productive. In doing so they copy the way many design technologists work. It is therefore important that we use this cycle flexibly and as a guide, not as a straightjacket. Other models of design and technology have been produced. The Goldsmith's project (SEAC, 1991) emphasized the interaction between hand and mind. These models are useful to teachers who can use them to plan teaching and to monitor work in the area of design and technology.

During the primary phase of education, children have traditionally used simple tools and a limited range of materials. Emphasis throughout the last twenty years has been to broaden and deepen that experience (DES, 1987). However this has been against a background of low confidence on the part of primary teachers (Wragg, *et al.*, 1989; Lever, 1990; Webb, 1993) and poor resourcing and accommodation (DES, 1992a). Initiatives mentioned earlier have sought to make good this shortfall but there remains much to do. A series of changes to the National Curriculum orders (NCC, 1992, etc) sought to make delivery of the subject more manageable. While successful in some areas, this constant change has detrimentally affected the status of the subject. As teachers have implemented the subject, issues like assessment, recording and progression have required attention (OFSTED, 1993). All of this means that there is much to do. Primary schools require leadership within design and technology. The coordinator should therefore be in a strong position to affect school policy and practice.

Considering the Role of Coordinator at Key Stage 2

Should the coordinator be specialist or generalist? This question is at the heart of present discussion about curriculum overload particularly at Key Stage 2 (Alexander, Rose and Woodhead, 1992; OFSTED, 1993). This is an important question for schools to consider. First, what is school policy? What are the roles of other coordinators in school? Has the school had a design and technology coordinator before? Does the school development plan include development of the role of coordinators? Does it include design and technology? The essential questions for design and technology at Key Stage 2 are to do with breadth across such a wide field and the relation of this Key Stage to other Key Stages (1 and 3). To what extent can teachers have expertise over such a wide field? To what extent can the design and technology coordinator assist, support, lead? Is this role best filled by a generalist teacher acting as a coordinator? As a consultant? As a specialist teacher? Are there differences between years 3/4 and 5/6? The solution will, in most schools, be a compromise which should be discussed and written down to promote clarity about the nature and purpose of the role. Specialist teaching requires very careful preparation so that individual children remain the focus rather than the subject. Advantages of specialist teaching are traded against the detailed knowledge of the child held by the child's own teacher and possibilities for interaction with other curriculum areas. A teacher's specialist knowledge might be shared amongst colleagues in a series of staff development sessions. A particularly useful emphasis of that sharing might be progression. This, of course, ignores the fact that primary education generally lacks the specialist design and technologists.

A number of key elements should guide your work as a coordinator of design and technology.

- Access: All primary children should have full access to design and technology, this is more than merely providing it.
- Communication: All those involved (children, colleagues, parents) should have opportunities to understand and contribute to the subject.
- Explicit: Policy should be clear for all staff, the place of design and

technology should be clear to children, colleagues and parents, children's design and technology activities should be clear in the intended outcomes.

- Challenging: Implementing the subject well in school will present teachers and colleagues with a challenge, children should be challenged by their work in the subject.
- Active participation: Colleagues and children should be involved at every level in their design and technology (this means more than doing design and technology) and at times parents ought to be involved as action is the most concrete demonstration of the value of the subject.

Design and Technology at Key Stage 2

What is it that typifies design and technology at Key Stage 2? This must be answered in the general context of education at Key Stage 2. The junior years might be seen to suffer somewhat from tensions which pull teachers towards secondary forms of schooling and others which recognise a necessity to build from the infant years. We might see the junior years as those which move the child from infancy to adolescence. These years are vital, formative years. Throughout Key Stage 2 children are maturing and their socialization is becoming more sophisticated. Their knowledge, skills and attitudes develop considerably. Concentration spans tend to lengthen, abstract ideas can be dealt with by more children. In design and technology we should to expect increased capability to:

- work alone and in teams;
- move from the known to the unknown;
- be critical;
- deal with more and different variables and aspects of the design process at the same time;
- be self-motivated, seek solutions and evaluate.

Important indicators (not necessarily the only indicators) of the above are:

- the child's ability to make informed choices in design and technology – choosing tools, materials techniques, whether to work alone or in a team, etc.;
- once techniques and materials have been chosen to aspire to the highest appropriate level of quality;
- the child's capability to determine the quality of the outcome judged against the criteria of the task. The meal may look delicious but perhaps we were asked to make a healthy meal! The bridge may be strong but are pedestrians safe? What would be the cost of construction?
- the child's capability to use an increasing range of skills and techniques in increasingly sophisticated ways.

One important step for teachers of Key Stage 2 is to know what happens at Key Stage 1 in your school as a foundation for the junior years. Also important is clarity about what capability you would like to see in children embarking on the next phase of education (Key Stage 3). As a profession we have some shared understanding about where we want children to go in terms of literacy and numeracy. We are less clear about such objectives in design and technology. Objectives ought to include capability in some areas with an overall awareness of the place of technology in society; such technological literacy should allow the individual to exercise personal rights in a democracy.

Strategies

This and the following section on evaluation are enmeshed, as evaluation must be a major strategy for managing any subject. Emphasis on evaluation is appropriate, as design and technology itself is very much about evaluation of products. First, however, we will deal with strategies by which change and development might occur and then move to evaluation.

Using a Design and Technology Approach

Elsewhere (Cross, 1994) I have suggested a design–and–technology approach to coordinating the subject. The school has needs; in collaboration with staff you can design a plan to fulfil them. You must be clear about what you wish to do, carry it out, and move to the stage of evaluation and subsequent determination of further development.

The Role of the Coordinator

Leadership is important for each curriculum area, particularly for one such as design and technology (DES, 1990), which has seen so much change and which continues to develop. The coordinator has a number of tasks detailed below, but it is important to develop the right attitude yourself, amongst colleagues and ultimately in the children. You must convey a professional optimism and enthusiasm while recognizing the realities of the classroom. You will require personal capabilities of perseverance, communication, foresight, leadership, clarity, willingness to share, empathy, flexibility and some humour. You must show that you are credible as a teacher and as a design and technology coordinator. You must begin early to discuss your role with the head.

Clarify the Role

You will require a job description. This should be negotiated with the headteacher. You ought to discuss the needs of the school and how your role might best fit these needs. Make it clear to what extent you are expected to be an organizer, a coordinator, a generalist, a specialist, a consultant. A job description for design technology at Key Stage 2 might include:

- a statement of intent;
- a reference to how the role fits in to school policy and management;
- a list of areas of responsibility;
- an action plan including short-term and long-term goals.

The third area, listing responsibility areas, will be a little daunting at first, so tackle it one or two items at a time. They might include: review of policy; reporting to staff, head and governors; development of continuity; progression; differentiation; access; assessment; design and technology for all; record keeping and reporting to parents; ordering and managing resources; liaison with outside bodies including teachers of Key Stage 1 and 3. Selecting one or two to deal with in the short term, and one or two to deal with longer term (in collaboration with the head) will be more respected than attempting to do everything at once. A word of caution before you embark on ambitious development. It is important to understand the position you and the school are in now. Take some time to conduct some action research, build up as clear a picture as possible about what is happening now. You will need to constantly seek and develop sources of assistance for you and your colleagues. These will include a resource bank of teacher material, local courses, LEA support, universities, subject associations (DATA, ASE), books, local SEMERC and SATRO (Science and Technology Regional Organization) organizations (see the list of useful addresses at the end of this chapter), local primary schools and high schools.

Involving the Headteacher

While the head may give you 100 per cent moral support, headteachers understandably have their energies dissipated. The head should help you to clarify and develop your job description and provide some guidance on the timing of and development of policy. You should develop a list of priorities, the head could be consulted as you seek to prioritize these with specific reference to the school development plan. Importantly, the head is in a position to provide resources, including time for you to work with colleagues and suggest how to perform other aspects of the role. New coordinators find it essential to review what colleagues do when teaching design and technology in the classroom. You will require the head's backing to gain access to teachers' documentation and planning and other classrooms. Keep the head informed of progress. If your headteacher sees direct benefit from backing you, he or she is more likely to find other ways to help you. An annual meeting with, or short report to the head will help in keeping the subject on the head's list of priorities and will help the head to help you. Such an approach may form part of the school's teacher appraisal or curriculum monitoring system.

Working Alongside Colleagues

This has been identified by DES (1992a) and others as a crucial way in which the coordinator can be influential. Classroom release is expensive and your class is deprived of its teacher. However, if you are going to support colleagues, you need to know what is going on in their rooms and they need to see that you are interested in the classroom you must, however, avoid any threat to their professionalism. If you are young, newly qualified, or both, you will naturally be apprehensive. The best tactic is to be honest and use your apprehension as a leveller so that your colleagues feel more at ease with you (they may feel threatened by you). It is important to discuss with the teachers exactly what is happening and to negotiate the agenda with them. Is it for you to teach the children or to help the teachers develop? Try to allow the teachers to determine the starting point. Beware of doing demonstration lessons, teachers can be dismissive of someone (who may be young into the bargain) coming in and making it look easy. Offer to provide advice and support and perhaps in the longer term when you are feeling more confident to do some team-teaching. Constantly move the emphasis towards them and facilitate their own success. It is often useful to focus attention on classroom management and aspects of good practice. If the teacher feels threatened, move the focus on to the children. Make sure that any session in the classroom is not seen as the end of it. Arrange to meet again and help the teacher establish an objective which can be achieved without your presence in the classroom.

Build Your Personal Professional and Subject Knowledge

This can be done by:

- attending courses;
- visiting local schools;
- reading;
- improving your own classroom practice;
- working alongside colleagues;
- making contact with outsiders and by joining subject associations.

Conducting an Audit

This ought to be done periodically but will be especially important in the early stages. As a newly qualified teacher you can do this informally by observing and more formally through the head. Can you get a feel for how much and what sort of design and technology goes on? Is it always under that heading? What is the school's approach to the National Curriculum? How is it used? How independently do children work in design and technology? What range of skills is displayed? Is there evidence of progression? What range of materials are used? Have their been any inspections? Were any recommendations made for design and technology? Were any of these phase specific? What accommodation is available? What resources and materials are available? Do all children get equality of access? How are children with special needs catered for? To what extent does IT contribute to design and technology? Is assessment and record keeping used to inform teaching? Have there been links with feeder schools? Keep in mind present provision and how these parameters will change as the subject develops. These questions will be answered by visiting other classrooms during and outside the school day, talking to children and colleagues, looking at plans and records, examining all school documentation, looking at displays and assemblies and involving colleagues formally and informally in review of the subject. Some things will be obvious, others less so. Such an audit will assist you to set out objectives for your work. If you have difficulty gaining access around the school or are new to the role it is always a good idea to try out such ideas in your own classroom first. Thus, you can say that you are not asking colleagues to do something that you have not done yourself. You will also find pitfalls prior to going public!

Long and Short-Term Goals

You cannot change everything at once. An action plan might consist of short-term goals, such as tidy the resource shelves, order new teachers books, visit every classroom, and longer-term ones, such as develop the school policy and/or scheme, establish annual review with the head, make progress in catering for special needs. This does not mean putting things off, rather it is realism, recognition that some things will require time and care. It is a good idea to try to complete one short-term goal each half-term, so that you are seen to be making progress and so that you feel the achievement of success. These goals should be reviewed by yourself two or three times a year. The head should be informed and involved at least annually. An action plan will help you clarify in what order to do these things, to determine any prerequisites for progress and to evaluate your success.

Policy and Planning

It is most important to engage with your colleagues in a dialogue to further develop the teaching of design and technology in your school. They may find the subject daunting but most can find an area within it where they have some knowledge. With encouragement and support they will begin to feel positive. As stated earlier, a design-and-technology approach may be helpful in this role. As you identify the school's needs you might then develop criteria: that training occur within a given period; that goals for that training be established; that the training be delivered within a budget. You might then design a solution, construct a plan, evaluate it, revise it, implement it and finally evaluate its success. One important objective will be to develop and implement a policy for design and technology. These vary from school-to-school, some prefer a short statement of policy and then more detail in a scheme, file or booklet which enlarges on the items in the statement. The policy should include: the school's aims in respect of the subject and/or a short definition of the subject; some mention of how the subject fits into the whole curriculum; a guide about breadth including time allocation; notes on the school's agreed forms of teaching and classroom management; clarity that design and technology requires children to be active; practical advice about resources; advice about carrying out and using assessment; schemes in use; safety and hygiene; use of parents or other classroom assistants; recording and reporting; special needs; access and entitlement for all; progression and continuity and the procedures for monitoring and review. You will not be able to do all of this at once, hence the earlier emphasis on an overall statement which is progressively developed.

The National Curriculum

Having undergone change in the National Curriculum and accepting that change is possible in the future (five years from Dearing, (SCAA, 1993)) it may be sensible to construct a policy document which states your school's understanding of design and technology, which refers to the National Curriculum, but which does not rely on any one version of the National Curriculum. It will be important to plan design and technology into the school's plans for the Key Stage. Within Key Stage 2 you have four years to ensure coverage. For these purposes you might divide this into two sets of two years, with collaboration to ensure coverage. The programme of study is divided into sections (see Figure 10.3) so that staff may agree that for example, in Year 3, during term 2, that the topic is 'Out and About'; various elements of the programme of study (PoS) are covered. An alternative is to give teachers more freedom but rely on record keeping to convey clearly to the next teacher what has been covered. Both systems require some form of monitoring as neither is a guarantee that work is being completed, that things are not being missed and that work is of a high enough standard.

The attainment targets (AT 1 Designing and AT 2 Making (SCAA, 1994b)) also require consideration. Each may occur simultaneously during design and technology activity. As a school you may decide that during a design and make assignment (which may occur over several sessions) colleagues will

Figure 10.3:   A group record based on the programme of study from SCAA, 1994b

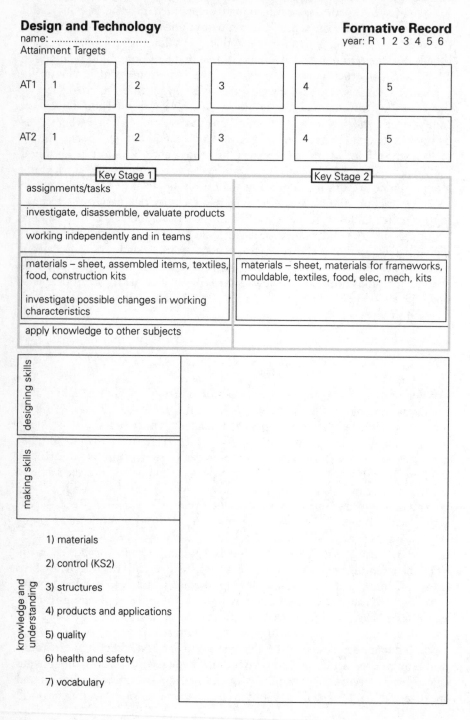

Design and Technology
name: ....
Attainment Targets

Formative Record
year: R 1 2 3 4 5 6

AT1 | 1 | 2 | 3 | 4 | 5 |

AT2 | 1 | 2 | 3 | 4 | 5 |

Key Stage 1

| | Key Stage 2 |

assignments/tasks

investigate, disassemble, evaluate products

working independently and in teams

materials – sheet, assembled items, textiles, food, construction kits

investigate possible changes in working characteristics

materials – sheet, materials for frameworks, mouldable, textiles, food, elec, mech, kits

apply knowledge to other subjects

designing skills

making skills

knowledge and understanding

1) materials

2) control (KS2)

3) structures

4) products and applications

5) quality

6) health and safety

7) vocabulary

provide at least one major focus on design, another on making and a third and fourth drawing these together. Each would also stress elements from the programme of study relating to knowledge and understanding, materials and skills, etc.

How Much Design and Technology?

This has been a problem as some teachers have tried in the past to include design and technology in each topic. Proposals to change the National Curriculum have contained first design and make tasks (DfE, 1992b) and then replaced by design and make assignments (SCAA, 1994a). These are a device to encourage us to limit time and to focus attention at specific times. While not emphasized in the most recent documents (SCAA, 1994b and DfE, 1995), the spirit of concentrating design and technology time around teacher-specified activities is an important lesson.

The Dearing Report (SCAA, 1993) has suggested that each foundation subject is studied for 45 hours at Key Stage 2. How this advice is interpreted is a matter for each school.

There are important questions about the desirability of and meaning of time allocations. Teachers in the primary years have found difficulty balancing the various demands of the curriculum and so such guidance and more particularly school policy may give greater potential for continuity. Suffice to say that design and technology may have to fight for time amongst other subjects, time allocations may not provide enough time, but in some circumstances they may guarantee that at least some time is devoted to the subject. There is something to be said for regularly returning to design and technology and much to be gained from prolonged activity – whole days or half-days. 45 hours per year could be divided equally amongst six half-terms giving 7.5 hours each half-term. Alternatively four design and technology projects in a year would each receive 11.25 hours. Some flexibility might be achieved if schools positively recognize the cross-curricular nature of the subject and reflect this in any such allocations. You may not be in a position to influence time allocations, however it may become an issue, so you need to be conversant with the arguments and prepared to make a case for design and technology.

Cross-curricular Working

I have suggested that while design and technology is a subject, it is in many ways like a cross-curricular dimension (Cross, 1994). Design and technology work must have a context so that children can design and make meaningful products.

Figure 10.4: A cross-curricular broad based theme (e.g., my body and the senses)

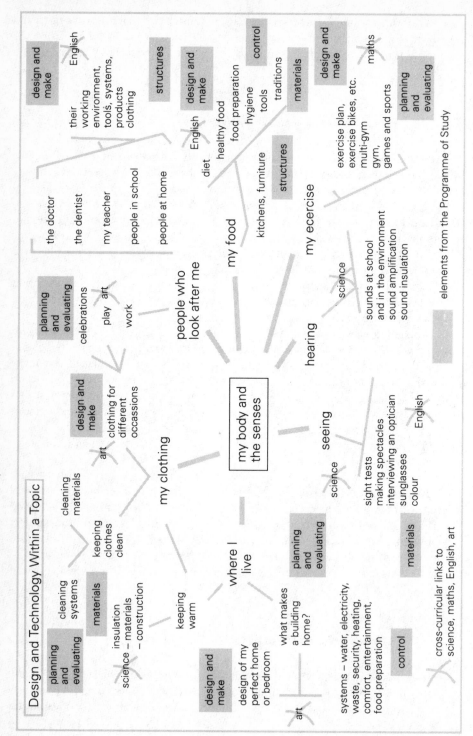

Design and Technology Within a Topic

my body and the senses

people who look after me
- the doctor
- the dentist
- my teacher
- people in school
- people at home

my food
- English
- diet
- healthy food
- food preparation
- hygiene
- tools
- traditions

my ecercise
- exercise plan, exercise bikes, etc.
- multi-gym
- gym, games and sports

hearing
- science
- sounds at school and in the environment
- sound amplification
- sound insulation

seeing
- science
- sight tests
- making spectacles
- interviewing an optician
- sunglasses
- colour
- English

my clothing
- celebrations
- play
- art
- work
- clothing for different occassions
- cleaning materials
- keeping clothes clean

where I live
- keeping warm
- what makes a building home?
- design of my perfect home or bedroom
- insulation
- science – materials – construction
- systems – water, electricity, waste, security, heating, comfort, entertainment, food preparation
- cross-curricular links to science, maths, English, art

design and make
- their working environment, tools, systems, products
- clothing
- English

structures

design and make

control

materials

design and make
- maths

planning and evaluating

structures
- kitchens, furniture

planning and evaluating

planning and evaluating

materials

control

elements from the Programme of Study

Assessment and Record Keeping

As coordinator you will need information about how individual children are progressing and about how the school is achieving this in order to evaluate the school's provision of the subject. There is much to be gained from involving the children in their own assessment and record keeping; after all, an important part of design and technology is evaluation. Children enjoy evaluating their work, and they often find it challenging. You will need to be involved to support and validate their self assessment. To do this the teacher will have to observe children working, listen to children, talk to children and observe the children's products. A good approach is to determine a close focus – can the child select and use a range of tools? and a wider focus – how does this fit into the child's overall capability?

For colleagues wishing to start some assessment of design and technology a good start would be to focus attention on one attainment target, examine the level descriptors from Levels 2 and 3 and ask colleagues to collect evidence from two, three or four children which they feel might relate to these levels. These would then be examined by a group of staff, terms might require definition, compromise would be required, but some consensus must be agreed about the range of capability represented by Level 3, etc. An exemplar file might be made using a collection of material. Short comments here from the teacher and/or from the child will assist to provide a context as would photographs.

Children can contribute to this process through the use of planning sheets as in Figure 10.5.

Continuity and Progression

Progression in learning was highlighted by Alexander, Rose and Woodhead (1992). In design and technology teachers can tackle this in quite simple ways by encouraging similar approaches to designing in the lower juniors and later development with older juniors or having particular tools available in the lower juniors and perhaps a wider range available later on. As you become more confident as a school you might like to look at all the areas in Figure 10.6.

Classroom Management

This often proves to be a most important issue in design and technology. Children need space, attention, flexibility and choice; it is possible to do this in whole class sessions and in forms of group work. Much depends on the activity, the children's maturity, their capability to co-operate, the responsibility you are giving them, the extent of co-operation required and the style of your teaching. As coordinator you will be expected to assist colleagues as

Figure 10.5a: *Children's planning sheets*

Design and Technology My Planning Sheet

| I am going to make a . . . | The materials will be . . . | I will use these tools . . . |

It will look like this . . .

they examine their classroom management. As an NQT you need to recognize the importance of classroom management to the subject, and where appropriate, engage colleagues in a review of their own strategies.

Resources

Much of the work of the coordinator relates to the management of resources. Published schemes for design and technology might be considered, particularly if the staff feel that they need support. A general library of teachers' material is essential and should be established as a matter of urgency (some suggestions are given at the end of this chapter). Basic resources, including materials and equipment, must be dealt with and may require an initial outlay with commitment to the future in the funding of consumable. It will be necessary to have a small stock permanently available to each class including basic tools, materials and perhaps a small selection of books. Elsewhere, a

Figure 10.5b: *Children's planning sheets*

My Design and Technology

I will make a	I will use these materials

I will use these tools

When I finished it looked like this

central resource will house larger stocks of tools, single more expensive items, for example, food technology and textiles technology (this may be a resource shared with the art stock). Trolleys or trucks can contribute to provision; they can be very expensive but cannot, in themselves, solve the resourcing problem.

Information Technology

The relationship between IT and design and technology has developed recently as the new order (SCAA, 1994b) separates design and technology and information technology. Design and technology gains from the inclusion of IT as does any subject. Children can receive design briefs produced on the computer, they can keep notes on a computer and subsequently desktop publish reports at any stage of the design and make process. Graphics packages such as (KIDPICS – Apple; !Draw – Archimedes) enable children to represent their ideas and draw plans onto the computer. Database work is not normally

Figure 10.6: Areas on which to focus for progression

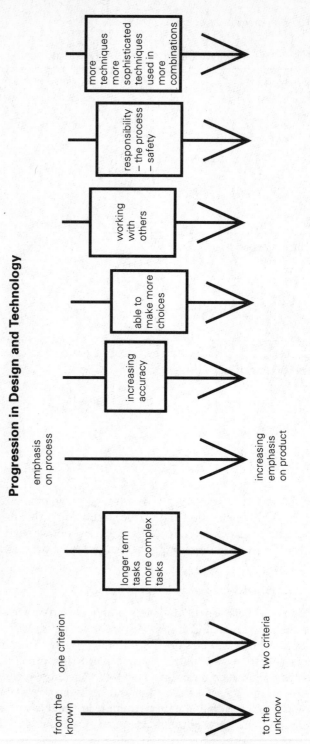

Progression in Design and Technology

from the known → to the unknown

one criterion → two criteria

longer term tasks / more complex tasks

emphasis on process → increasing emphasis on product

increasing accuracy

able to make more choices

working with others

responsibility
– the process
– safety

more techniques / more sophisticated techniques used in more combinations associated with design and technology but there is much to be gained in simple classification of materials, holding information on a database or perhaps using a spreadsheet to deal with the calorific contents of food. Control is a growing area where children use a simple interface or buffer box to link the computer to a model, or use Logo to control a floor or screen turtle. Simple robots exist which contain their own keyboard and computer, i.e., Roamer, Pip and Computer Robot. These are relatively inexpensive and provide an excellent base from which to start and to extend other IT work. IT work should not be perceived as only that requiring a computer. Children might seek prices by phone or fax, they might get a weather forecast from Teletext. They might record their work on a simple tape recorder. The importance of the applications and effects of IT in everyday life, working life and society (SCAA, 1994b) is often overlooked, this can be dealt with well within design and technology.

Evaluation

In no sense does evaluation come last. This chapter began with evaluation of the school's context. It has been suggested that you take a wider view of design and technology in other situations and from the viewpoints of others. The point has also been made that design and technology requires evaluation and that it is only right that these skills are developed. Why should a co-ordinator evaluate? To determine the school's effectiveness delivering design and technology? To judge the progress and effect of reforms you may implement? Your attention should be on the effectiveness of policy, assessment, record keeping, access for all, etc. You can then provide feedback to the senior management team and governors about the effectiveness of their overall planning and provision. Evaluation must have elements which are systematic, others which are flexible. It should be reflective, based on a wide evidence base. It should be clear in its intention – to raise standards in design and technology. Bentley and Watts (1994) provide useful advice on a step-by-step approach to evaluation through a form of action research. This would usefully feed into the school's monitoring procedures.

Monitoring the School's Performance

This is a senior management responsibility, however, most heads will wish to involve subject coordinators. NQTs will need to grow into the role. This aspect may be included at a later date when you are more established in the school. The head and outsiders will expect you to: be aware of any shortcomings in provision of the subject; determine likely causes for such shortcomings and in collaboration with the head determine action to correct the situation – this is likely to involve some or all the staff; be able to describe the subject's situation at present in detail; be able to produce evidence which supports your view; be knowledgeable about the subject's history in school and the plans for its future.

Conclusion

A sign of the professional development of NQTs is a growing awareness of the whole school. One's classroom might remain the centre of one's attention but responsibility for a curricular area like design and technology should give you opportunity to grow professionally. It is not possible to do it on one's own. You must involve colleagues. You must build up a network of people to whom you can turn for help and advice. It will be necessary to focus on subject knowledge and understanding and teaching styles. You will need to gain knowledge about your school resources and those which might be useful in the future. You may very well have curricular responsibility in another area. Use this personal involvement to show how the two subjects complement one another. Learn as much as you can about the way the school's management affects the subject and how colleagues deal with it. Build your experience and capability with different forms of classroom organization, planning, assessment and record keeping. As you develop the role, you should be looking at every aspect of school life and management as opportunities to promote achievement in design and technology. You should be seeking to maintain a professional dialogue with the subject itself as well as with colleagues in school.

Useful Addresses

ASE (Association of Science Education) College Love, Hatfield, Herts, AL10 9AA. Tel 01707–267411; fax 01707–266532.

COMMOTION LTD, Unit 11, Tannery Rd., Tonbridge, Kent, TN9 1RF. Tel: 0732–773399; fax 0732–773390.

DATA (Design and Technology Association), 16 Wellesbourne House, Walton Road, Wellesbourne, Warwickshire, CV35 9JB. Tel: 0789–470007; fax 0789–841955.

ECONOMATICS (Education) Ltd, Epic House, 18–20 Darnell Road, Attercliffe, Sheffield, S9 5AA. Tel: 0742–561122; fax 01142–439306.

HERON EDUCATIONAL LTD, Unit 3, Carrwood House, Carrwood Road, Chesterfield, Derbyshire, S41 9QB. Tel: 0246–453354; fax 0246–260876.

JPR ELECTRONICS, Unit M. Kingsway Industrial Estate, Kingsway, Luton, Bedfordshire, LU1 1LP. Tel: 0582–410055; fax 0582–458674.

NATIONAL ASSOCIATION OF TEACHERS OF HOME ECONOMICS AND TECHNOLOGY, Hamilton House, Mabledon Place, London, WC1 9BJ.

SEMERC (Northwest) Filton Hill CDC, Rosary Rd., Oldham, OL8 2QE Tel: 0106–274469.

SURPLUS BUYING AGENCY, Southfield CPD Centre, Gleadless Road, Sheffield, S12 2QB. Tel: 0742–646186.

TECHNOLOGY TEACHING SYSTEMS, Unit 4, Holmewood Fields Business Park, Park Road, Holmewood, Chesterfield, S42 5UY. Tel: 0246–850085; fax 0246–855557.

Trylon Ltd, Thrift Street, Wollaston, Northamptonshire, N29 7QJ. Tel: 01933–664275; fax 01933–664–960.

References

ALEXANDER, R., ROSE, J. and WOODHEAD, C. (1992) *Curriculum Organisation and Classroom Practice in Primary Schools*, London: DES.

BENTLEY, D. and WATTS, M. (1994) *Primary Science Teaching*, Buckingham: Open University Press.

CROSS, A. (1994) *Design and Technology 5–11*, London: Hodder and Stoughton.

CROSS, A. and CROSS, S. (1993) 'Organising a professional development day for your colleagues', in HARRISON, M. (1993) *Beyond the Core Curriculum*, Plymouth: Northcote House.

DEPARTMENT FOR EDUCATION (1994) *Technology Key Stages 1, 2 and 3: A Report by HM Inspectorate on the Third Year, 1992–93*, London: HMSO.

DEPARTMENT FOR EDUCATION (1995) *Design and Technology in the National Curriculum*, London: HMSO.

DEPARTMENT OF EDUCATION AND SCIENCE (1987) *CDT from 5 to 16. Curriculum Matters 9*, London: HMSO.

DEPARTMENT OF EDUCATION AND SCIENCE (1990) *Technology in the National Curriculum*, London: HMSO.

DEPARTMENT OF EDUCATION AND SCIENCE (1992a) *Technology Key Stages 1, 2 and 3: A Report by HM Inspectorate on the First Year, 1990–91*, London: HMSO.

DEPARTMENT OF EDUCATION AND SCIENCE (1992b) *Technology in the National Curriculum for ages 5 to 16: Proposals of the Secretary of State*, London: HMSO.

EGGLESTON, J. (1992) *Teaching Design and Technology*, Buckingham: Open University Press.

LAYTON, D. (1991) *Aspects of National Curriculum Design and Technology*, York: NCC.

LEVER, C. (1990) *National Curriculum Design and Technology for Key Stages 1, 2 and 3*, Stoke-on-Trent: Trentham Books.

NATIONAL CURRICULUM COUNCIL (1992) *National Curriculum Technology: The Case for Revising the Order*, York: NCC.

OFSTED (1993) *Primary Matters: Discussion on Teaching and Learning in Primary Schools*, London: OFSTED.

SCHOOL'S EXAMINATION AND ASSESSMENT COUNCIL (1991) *The Assessment of Performance in Design and Technology (The Goldsmith's Project)*, London: HMSO.

SCAA (1993) *The National Curriculum and its Assessment: Final Report (The Dearing Report)*, London: Department of Education and Science (1992).

SCHOOLS CURRICULUM AND ASSESSMENT AUTHORITY (1994a) *Design and Technology in the National Curriculum: Draft Proposals*, London: HMSO.

SCHOOLS CURRICULUM AND ASSESSMENT AUTHORITY (1994b) *The National Curriculum Orders – Second Draft*, London: SCAA.

SMITHERS, A. AND ROBINSON, P. (1992) *Technology in the National Curriculum – Getting it Right*, London: The Engineering Council.

WRAGG E., BENNETT, N. and CARRE, C.G. (1989) 'Primary teachers and the national curriculum', Research Papers in *Education* **4** (3) pp. 17–45.

WEBB, R. (1993) *Eating the Elephant Bit by Bit*, London: AMMA.

Chapter 11

The History Coordinator in Key Stage 2

Julie Davies

Introduction

This chapter tackles the history coordinator's central concerns: how to develop an interest in history teaching through discussion and debate; the methodology for effective teaching and learning of history; and how to resource effectively to support the attainment target and programme of study. As a relatively inexperienced professional taking over the role of history coordinator it will be useful to reflect on the change in the quality and quantity of history teaching your colleagues will have experienced in primary schools over the last five years.

The national curriculum made history teaching mandatory in a profession which had little experience of teaching it and meagre resources at its disposal. HMI surveys of 1978 and 1989 found little evidence of history being taught, and where it was being taught, they judged it to be less than adequate in 80 per cent of infant classes and 66 per cent of junior classes seen. This probably means that you, as the history coordinator, will be working with many people who may, until four years ago, have never considered history to be an essential ingredient in their curriculum provision, except as a bolted-on fragment to a topic whose central thrust will have been some other area. The latest OFSTED report, however, notes that history in primary schools now has a 'significant and accepted place'. Their two annual reports so far issued paint a picture of steady development. In 1992–3 standards in history were satisfactory or better in 80 per cent of Key Stage 1 lessons and 70 per cent of Key Stage 2 lessons seen. The inspectors praised the teaching of the skills of sequencing and chronological understanding and the confidence of children in handling sources. Your job, then, would appear to be significantly easier now than if you had taken it over four years ago. History seems to have won an accepted place in the primary curriculum and its teaching appears to be steadily improving. To continue this upward momentum requires a clear picture of where your school is, in history curriculum development terms, so that realistic goals can be set for the future benefit of children's historical knowledge and understanding.

This chapter aims to help you define the key tasks of the curriculum coordinator for history and offer you a range of practical activities which will assist you in your new role.

Where to Begin

You will need to develop in teachers both an understanding of the nature of history and a pedagogy to sustain quality history teaching and learning in the primary school. This means spending time with staff discussing such fundamental questions as:

- Why should history be taught?
- How should it be taught?
- In which order should the study units be taught?

All these different perceptions will need to be thoroughly discussed with staff in the light of your understanding of history as a process of interpretation as well as a knowledge of facts.

Why Should it be Taught?

The simple answer to the above question is – because it is a statutory requirement. However, you will only get vigorous worthwhile teaching from teachers who believe that what they are doing is right for their children's all round development. Getting teachers to acknowledge that history has an important place in the primary

> A strong sense of *why* history is being taught should pervade all curriculum planning, influencing the selection of content and methods of teaching.
> 1.4 History Non-Statutory Guidance

curriculum will make your job, of enhancing their skills and confidence to do it, considerably easier. Teachers who have not taught history in any focused sense before, the vast majority in primary schools before 1989, will feel vulnerable and guarded when confronted with the national curriculum history requirements because these call into question their previous teaching emphases. If you acknowledge this and proceed carefully as you work to enthuse your colleagues about the history curriculum, you are more likely to gain some success and see them begin to develop as effective teachers of history to young children.

'Why teach history?' is a most useful exercise if it clarifies ideas and opinions and will affect practice quite radically. As history coordinator you need to make available some of the INSET time you have for history to discuss the purposes of school history with your colleagues. You could use those listed in the non-statutory guidance as a start. It is always helpful to begin with the teachers' own views, however, before producing the *official line*.

The purposes of school history are listed as follows in the Non-Statutory Guidance:

1.2 There are two main aims of school history:
- to help pupils develop a sense of identity through learning about the development of Britain, Europe and the world;
- to introduce pupils to what is involved in understanding and interpreting the past.

1.3 Other purposes follow:
- to arouse interest in the past;
- to contribute to pupils' knowledge and understanding of other countries and cultures;
- to understand the present in the light of the past;
- to enrich other areas of the curriculum;
- to train the mind by disciplined study;
- to prepare pupils for adult life.

Each purpose is worthy of discussion with your staff. If this is done, the purposes will not remain theoretical statements of good intent, but become translated into achievable objectives with classes of children specifically in mind. Think about the first aim as an example.

How can you, as coordinator, help children develop a sense of identity through learning about Britain, Europe and the World?

Does it feed your children's sense of identity to be told about the Romans, Greeks, Egyptians, Victorians or Tudors? Of course not. This can only be achieved by finding effective links between the child's experience now with that of people in the past. In this way we will nurture their sense of identity. It is by engaging in these sorts of discussions that teachers will be able to see that simple transmission of historical facts is not what the primary history teacher is about. This point must be emphasized because the way that history is arranged in study units can give considerable prominence to the content. This, in turn, could lead to the spurious belief that history is a transferable package of agreed knowledge from teacher to taught.

Key Stage 2 Programme of Study

The history to which Key Stage 2 children are entitled is easily spelled out. The difficulty is how to teach it effectively. Pupils should be taught six Study Units:

1. Romans, Anglo Saxons and Vikings in Britain
2. Life in Tudor Times

3a. Victorian Britain
or
3b. Britain since 1930
4. Ancient Greece
5. Local History
6. A past non-European society chosen from the following list:
   • Ancient Egypt
   • Mesopotamia
   • the Indus Valley
   • the Maya
   • Benin
   • the Aztecs

Across the Key Stage pupils should be given opportunities to study:

• aspects of the past in outline and in depth;
• aspects of the histories of England, Ireland, Scotland and Wales; where appropriate, the history of Britain should be set in its European and world context;
• history from a variety of perspectives – political; economic, techno-logical and scientific; social, religious; cultural and aesthetic.

Key elements which are closely related to and should be developed through the study units are itemized as follows:

• Chronology;
• range and depth of historical knowledge and understanding;
• interpretation of history;
• historical enquiry;
• organization and communication.

There is a great deal of work for you to do with the staff if history is going to be taught in a holistic way rather than in a fragmentary fashion where units are taught discretely and the key elements are taught and practised without any historical context. Staff development meetings concentrating on the programme of study will give you a platform for developing history as a study of the evidence that has survived about the past. To begin in a practical way, the distribution of the units across the four years needs to be done. When the staff have discussed and agreed on this they will already have a feeling of relief that they have a heavy but manageable chunk of history to do rather than think of the whole programme of study.

However, so that teachers do not retreat into their classroom and do their own thing with the Vikings, for example, there needs to be considerable discussion about the rest of the programme of study. The teachers have to teach in outline as well as in depth. It is much simpler to teach in depth than in outline, for when the latter is done without sufficient knowledge and understanding, children can be subjected to the teacher's broad generalizations which may be stereotyped views based on insufficient research. Teaching things in outline requires the ability to select and organize what is significant – the key areas and ideas. It requires some specialist understanding to know what is important. The emphasis in one key element of the ability of pupils to make links and connections between events and developments needs to be used by you to encourage the staff to see units not as isolated elements but as interconnected, through time, in all sorts of ways. By working through each of the key elements in relation to the units and across the units you should give children the chance of seeing history as the seamless robe of the past that it is.

When the staff have allocated the various study units to the year groups and planned to integrate the key elements, where appropriate, within them, there follows the next phase of planning at class level. Here you can be of immediate and practical value to each member of staff through helping them with the resourcing and designing of their unit. You do not need to know a great deal of factual history to be of help here. The teachers will need to know a reasonable amount about their period, but you will be valuable through the prompts you give them. The cross-curricular themes also need addressing. Cross-curricular themes include:

- economic and industrial understanding;
- health education;
- education for citizenship;
- environmental education;
- careers education guidance.

Within the history unit planning there should be reference to some, if not all, of these. Similarly, the political, economic, social and cultural aspects of the age need highlighting and defining.

INSET Activities

To alert teachers to the central importance of continued debate about *what* history, it will be useful to carry out a couple of short INSET activities.

Who is Important in History?

Put up a piece of string across the room and ask the teachers to write on slips of paper two or three names of people who lived in the past to whom they would like to talk and question. Then give them paper clips to attach these papers onto the string time-line in chronological sequence. You should identify which end of string is the present and which one distant past.

First, this exercise nearly always illustrates the glaring omissions in the history teaching experienced by the participants when they were children. Historical men predominate, of course, with the addition of the inevitable Florence Nightingale and Boadicea. Children are never mentioned. History is portrayed, when viewed from these lines, as the story of rich, powerful men in Britain or Europe. It is useful when this exercise has been completed to look again at the purposes of school history, one of which is to help pupils develop a sense of identity. Discuss with teachers whether their feelings of identity are heightened or marginalized by looking at the lines. Second, through mapping the people recalled by the staff onto the study units, it will be shown which periods are less or more familiar to them.

The Statements Game

Teachers will have many ideas about the nature of history. These may be explored by the use of statements like these which may be used to provoke debate.

- History is a series of events to be learned in chronological order.
- History is about enquiry into the past, identifying, interpreting and selecting evidence which appears to be relevant.
- History tells us how modern man is superior to the cave man.
- History is concerned with understanding, seeing the past from the inside, from another's position, empathetically.
- History is argument without end.
- History is concerned not with the conveying of accepted facts but with the making of informed judgments, and to the displaying of the evidence on which those judgments are made.
- History can introduce children to some understanding of what is meant by *real* and *true* in human affairs.

How Should History be Taught?

The School Curriculum and Assessment Authority (SCAA) has emphasized that teachers are free to teach how they wish as long as they teach the content prescribed. For history, of course, the *how* is more complicated. It is not simply about what proportion of time to give to whole class, group or individual teaching. It is about the quandary of whether to teach history as content or process. Of course, both content and process are indispensable features of history; it is getting the balance right that is so important. As coordinator you will want to have worked through your own understandings. It is important for the staff to come to grips with their view of what history is as this will affect their practice.

The question of what history is can be answered only when you, as history coordinator, are clear in your mind as to the answer. History is two things: the past, and the study of the past. If you believe the former is an agreed, unchangeable body of knowledge then the way you study it will be different from the way you will study it if you consider history to be constantly in need of reinterpretation. Again, discussion with colleagues about this is important if you are going to clarify how history should be taught. History as process involves us in an examination of sources and in making interpretations in a critical appraising way in order to generate theories about their validity and reliability. In other words history methodology is characterized by scrupulous respect for evidence and disciplined use of the imagination. Encouraging teachers to view children as budding historians will certainly help channel their energies towards providing first hand sources on which the children can practise these skills.

History can be an exciting activity-based subject which involves children in a process. If our main aim is to get children enthused and interested in finding out about the past then they will need to spend time considering how historical investigations might proceed. Teachers may find it useful to discuss the modes of investigation and draw up a list as an aide memoire to their planning which might include investigating by: problem solving, going out, measuring, raising questions, making connections, thinking, talking, reading, interrogating, observing, listening, hypothesizing, thinking, interpreting. Communicating what they have found out is an equally important part of the historical investigation equation. Teachers know that there are many ways through which to communicate such as dance, drama, music, writing, charts and tables, graphs, IT, maps and plans, model making, art work, debate, discussion.

The History-Biased Topic

While there seems to be a move towards subject specific teaching at Key Stage 2, it is unlikely to be the answer to how to fit the content of the nine subject areas into the time available. The way forward seems to be for focused and carefully planned subject-biased topic work. Here your job will be to give history the highest possible profile when its turn comes for special attention.

The Place of Topic Work in the National Curriculum

The integrated approach, at its best, is fundamental to good primary practice and the requirements of the national curriculum.

Children need to learn how:

- to seek information from many sources and to judge its validity;
- to organize facts and form generalizations based on facts;

- to carry on a discussion based on facts and to make generalizations or conclusions;
- to plan, to carry out plans and to evaluate the work and the planning;
- to accept responsibility as part of living;
- to develop a set of values for judging right and wrong actions.

The Teacher's Role

There is a need for you to work with staff so that they use their discussion and questioning time effectively with the children. The aim, in history, is to enable children to understand, explain and make intelligible what they have learned. Teachers are supremely able at developing oral language through discussion but they need to be aware of the need to encourage children's historical skills and concepts and to develop a critical approach to historical evidence when history is the focus of the session. For example, children may be looking at a building and noting such things as the number and type of windows, the materials used in its construction and in making a count of the people using it. This is fine as an information gathering exercise. To get the children thinking historically, however, the teacher has to get them to ask such questions as:

- How old is the building (*Time*)?
- Has it changed in any way since it was built (*Continuity/Change*)?
- Why have the changes occurred (*Cause/Consequence*)?
- Can you put the changes in chronological order (*Sequence*)?
- Is the building like the others near it (*Similarity/Difference*)?
- Why has it survived?
- What evidence have you to support your conclusions?
- Is the evidence sufficient?

The historical process can be summarized as pupils comprehending a historical issue, posing questions and ideas about it, locating sources of evidence, using, interpreting and evaluating the material, recalling, analysing and synthesizing the findings and communicating the information and explanation in an economical, relevant and lucid way.

Whole School Planning: the History Curriculum

If teachers have gone through some of the processes outlined above, with you as the enabler and catalyst, the job of developing a whole school approach to the history curriculum will be very much easier. They will be more sure about what they perceive to be the particular contribution history has to make to children's cognitive and affective development. In addition, their views of what history is to them will clarify other aims and objectives for teaching primary history. In all probability, there will already be a scheme of work for history. Your first job will be to see whether it is translated into reality in the classroom. Using it as a starting point for further development is necessary. That it cannot remain unaltered is clear from the radical review history has undergone since the Dearing Report. Below are some key points to be made about the necessity of a whole-school plan if teachers are not already sold on it.

Why Whole-School Planning?

To ensure:

- continuity within Key Stage 2 and between Key Stage 1 and Key Stage 2;
- progression in content, concepts, skills and attitudes from Year 1 to Year 6;
- balance between the various types of history: social, political, cultural and aesthetic, religious, economic, technological and scientific;
- balance between local, national and world history;
- balance between ancient and modern history;
- balance between the history of men, women and children, rich and poor, powerful and powerless.

In addition,

- to decide the timing of the core units at Key Stage 2;
- to prioritize the collection of resources to support these decisions;
- to target some aspects of INSET provision as essential if the school is to move forward in its history provision.

Agreement about all these aspects is vital so that the child moving through the primary school has the opportunity of sampling the richness and variety of history.

Alongside this preoccupation with whole-school planning should run another important consideration which should be regarded as an INSET activity for you to use with the staff to develop their history teaching skills.

Planning the History Curriculum

While the history curriculum is set out in the study units there are still choices to be made within the units about depth, content and emphasis and these need to have been carefully considered. Obviously, when choosing the past non-European society, having an expert on the staff on the Indus Valley or Mesopotamia would influence your choice. Given that in the typical school no-one will profess to know anything about any of the topics in supplementary Study Unit 6, which should your colleagues select?

Consideration needs to centre on the programme of study and how it can be taught.

> Pupils should be taught about important episodes and developments in Britain's past, from Roman to modern times, about ancient civil-isations and the history of other parts of the world. They should be helped to develop a chronological framework by making links across the different Study Units. They should have opportunities to invest-igate local history and to learn about the past from a range of sources of information. The Study Units and Key Elements, outlined below should be taught together. (National Curriculum Orders, 1994, p. 4)

The directive is quite clear. Whichever unit is chosen, therefore, there must be opportunities for children to behave like historians: to handle evidence, draw tentative conclusions about it and understand how there may be different interpretations of what they are studying. If the evidence to which they have access is only textbook-based then that may be one reason for *not* choosing that particular period to study. Study Unit 5: Local History is very much more complex than the local environmental study that was so common in primary practice in the past. It also involves staff in selecting one of three options. Whichever is chosen, there is a need to keep the historical nature of the study to the fore, even though other areas of the curriculum, such as geography, art and design and technology naturally occur. It would be helpful to the staff member given this unit for you, through discussion and knowledge of the local area, to help her make an informed choice.

Assessment

History is a non-core foundation subject, which means it is not subject to nationally administered standardized summative tests at the end of each Key Stage. However, there is a statutory duty for schools to report to parents annually on their children's progress in all areas of the curriculum. It is of course also good practice for records of children's development to be passed on to the next teacher so that continuity and progression can be built in the following year.

Level Descriptions of Assessment

Teachers must read carefully the introduction to the proposals where it is made clear that it is the POS which should guide the planning, teaching and day-to-day assessment of pupils work. The essential function of the level descriptions is to assist in the making of summary judgements about pupils' achievement as a basis for reporting at the end of a Key Stage. (History Draft Proposal, 1994, p. i.)

Essentially, they serve a summative purpose. The whole purpose of the new descriptions is to look at pupil performance as a whole and consider which level provides the best fit. The introduction to the new proposals is clear on this issue. 'Teachers will be able to balance one element against another using professional judgment rather than counting numbers of statements of attainment mastered and using a mechanical rule.' (History Draft Proposal, 1994, p. i.) The introduction of level descriptions will reinforce earlier messages that there is no need for elaborate tick lists as a basis for assessment!

National curriculum assessment is a whole school issue. Teachers of Years 2 and 6 must carry out their end of Key Stage teacher assessments and will rely on the records that have been built up through the Key Stage in a format which is consistent and manageable. It is not essential to keep vast quantities of work as evidence; only a few selected samples of pupils' work need be retained.

What is needed above all is a sense of proportion and a combination of professional judgement and common sense, in the use of available time. (SEAC Moderator's Handbook, 1991/92)

Because the programmes of study describe the content and the level descriptions describe the cognitive skills the children should have acquired through its study, there is no way they can remain divorced at the planning stage. You may need to remind your colleagues of this so that while they are planning they will also be looking at how the outcomes can be assessed. While this may be difficult for staff to grasp initially, some joint planning sessions with you, either at the whole staff, or individual teacher level should set them on the right path. One of the key ways to develop staff assessment abilities is to discuss, at length, if necessary, what the level descriptions actually mean.

Clarifying this area is essential, because the staff will then have a common definition in mind when they make their assessments of children's progress. Once they have got into the habit of looking for the assessment opportunities at the planning stage they will realize the need for good quality resources which will help them in their teaching and assessment of children.

This brings us on to the next big area of preoccupation for the history coordinator: what resources are needed to help implement the national curriculum?

Resources

Given that history was rarely taught in primary schools until four years ago, it is not surprising that resources for it were meagre and consisted of an over-reliance on textbooks or TV programmes. The targeting of resources on history is therefore necessary. The OFSTED 1992/93 report provides a figure of £2.50 per pupil – a small increase over the previous year. You can use data such as this to compare your school's spending on history resources with the national or local average. It will add bite to your claims for more resources if your school spends little on history.

However, OFSTED has praised the use by primary schools of history resources outside the classroom. Teachers have used their locality, living history sites and local communities imaginatively. The national curriculum has emphasized the process side of history and demands that children be allowed to learn about the past from a wide range of historical sources, including: artifacts, pictures and photographs, music, adults talking about their past, documents and printed sources, buildings and sites and computer-based material.

Two problems immediately spring to mind.

Where Do You Get These Sources From?

If you remember that one of your main purposes in teaching history to children is to give them a sense of personal identity then you will look for sources within the community that the school serves. Artifacts – the correct term for objects looked at historically – are plentiful in every house and garden. Think of the change there has been in irons over the last fifteen years (even if you cannot get any older than that). Children will bring in pieces of clothing, books and various household utensils which can be handled in a historical way to discuss change and continuity, causation and time. Similarly, pictures and photographs are readily available to be used. A letter requesting artefacts from home for a particular topic will result in pupils bringing in a bewildering array of objects. Some schools still have access to loan collections which can be utilized when appropriate. Collections of ration books, household objects, photographs and the like add to the view. The older members of the community are treasure troves of memories and opinions and welcome being interviewed about any of their experiences. The use of older people in the community, local experts such as archaeologists; local archivists and museum curators is by no means an isolated matter. Local crafts people and musicians, retired policemen, teachers, plumbers, etc., add to the variety of historical sources that can be effectively tapped within communities. Local buildings are near at hand, familiar yet interesting to budding historians. Written sources do not have to be marriage or birth certificates. They can be local newspaper accounts of famous local events or sporting stories, they can be postcards and letters from different periods, or the school log, old advertisements, recipe books or catalogues.

Having started collections based on the community you serve there is also the need to develop resources for the other study units. Indeed, as I have mentioned, lack of some material should lead you to choosing something else to study or to look for another aspect within a study unit upon which to concentrate. One of the reasons why the Egyptians are very popular in the town in which I work is probably related to the superb permanent display of Egyptology at the University of Manchester Museum. You will be able, no doubt, to find similar types of exhibitions in your area. It is, of course, useful to network with other history coordinators in your area in order to build up a resource pack of places of interest to visit.

Providing each unit with source material can be an arduous undertaking. This is partly, though not exclusively, your job. Through staff discussion, there will have been a share out of units according to age groups. From this will have come the need for each teacher to research and make provision for their particular units. You have a role here, not to do all the running around necessary to collect materials, but to support and direct teachers' energies towards fruitful areas where their enthusiasm and confidence can grow. Practically, of course, there will be some need to give teachers time so that they can visit archives or sites in preparation for their planning.

History from the Victorians onwards is relatively easy to deal with in the manner I have described. But how do you do it for the Vikings or Tudors? If you can find no way of giving children access to first-hand investigative experiences, you will not be able to assess them completely on the level descriptions so you might as well encourage teachers to give a brief talk about these phenomena and move on to more useful aspects. For example, the Vikings are only one aspect of a large study unit. If your school is based near Roman or Anglo-Saxon settlement remains then it is sensible to focus work on these. Similarly, if you are close to Tudor buildings then beginning a topic there will lend point to your ultimate aim of discussing aspects of the Tudor Age.

What Do You Do with the Resources When You Have Collected Them?

In a sense, of course, you will have had specific aims in mind to focus your collections so you and the staff will be committed to teaching and assessing history already, through first hand experiences using primary or secondary sources wherever possible. Having said that, there is still a good deal of INSET to be done to ensure that teachers use the resources in a historically accurate way to develop children's historical understanding. Too often, the activity can end up as a useful oral language session or an inspiring art and design experience rather than a session which extends children's historical concepts. To keep a check on how resources are used and the effectiveness of this, it helps to have clarified, through staff meetings, the purpose of any materials introduced into the classroom for the teaching and learning of history. Below I have listed the key types of materials with references for you to follow up on their uses in the classroom. It is essential that the process of coming to one's own understandings about the merits or demerits of particular resources is gone through with the staff rather than they be given a list and told to get on with it.

Resources and References

Below is a very brief section on resources with what I consider to be key publications where appropriate. Each section could be expanded into a chapter if there was room. You could profitably work on these headings and build up a resource file of how to use the various types of evidence I have listed and add references to materials and schemes which you find particularly helpful.

A great deal of help can be obtained from the Historical Association across all the units.

The Historical Association,
59A Kennington Park Road,
London, SE11 4JH.

Artifacts, Portraits and Pictures

Durbin, G., Morris, S. and Wilkinson, S. (1990) *A Teachers' Guide to Learning from Objects*, London, English Heritage Education Service.
    In addition, and useful for INSET purposes, English Heritage produce a Slide Pack, *Using Portraits*, which takes you through twelve slides with careful notes so that your observation skills are enhanced.
Morris, S. (1990) *A Teachers' Guide to Using Portraits*, London, English Heritage Education Service.

Stories and Narrative

Cox, K. and Hughes, P. *Early Years History: An Approach Through Story*, Liverpool Institute of Higher Education, Stand Park Road, Liverpool, L16 9JD.
Farmer, A. (1990) 'Story-telling in history', *Teaching History*, January.
HMI (1985) *History in the Primary and Secondary Years*, London, DES.
HMI (1989) *Aspects of Primary Education. The Teaching and Learning of History and Geography*, London, DES.
Little, V. and John, T. (1988) 'Historical fiction in the classroom', *Teaching of History*, **59**, London, The Historical Association.

Sets of books are also available from:

Madeline LINDLEY, *Early Years History: An Approach through Story*. 79 Acorn Centre, Barry Street, Oldham, OL1 3NE.

Stories for Time book box from Badger Publishing Limited, Unit One, Parsons Green Estate, Boulton Road, Stevenage. Herts, SG1 4QG.

Oral History

PURKIS, S. (1987) *Thanks for the Memory*, London, Collins Educational.

Buildings

For further information on this primary source see the English Heritage series of videos and accompanying booklets for various historic sites. In addition, they produce a series of videos which show how a historian needs to be like a detective in looking for clues and evidence in order to reach conclusions about buildings and objects. These can be fruitfully discussed in staff development time. Information for these and all English Heritage material can be obtained from:

English Heritage Education Service,
Key Sign House,
429, Oxford Street,
London. W1R 2HD
Telephone: 071–973–3442/3

Written Sources

There is a rich variety of documentary material available such as school log books, census returns, parish records, letters, inventories and government reports, marriage and birth certificates and wills. In addition, newspapers, directories, advertisements, posters and other printed matter provide useful material on which to work.

Original documentation will probably be precious and available only to look at carefully and not to work from. Photocopies of these are a good substitute for they provide children with a chance to study the layout, language and writing of the original without fear of damage. You should collect as wide a variety of these materials as possible, but it is essential to catalogue them and to ensure that staff know their whereabouts and that they have decided how best they may be used.

One aspect of documentary evidence needs exploring with the staff. A piece of writing from Victorian times will be difficult for children to decipher, while a piece from the Anglo-Saxon period will be impenetrable. Should this be translated into present day script? The answer depends on what you want the children to get from it. *Essentially, the medium is as important as the message so should not be tampered with lightly*. The very act of carefully looking at and deciphering text is an important and necessary skill for all historians and one children should be inducted into as soon as possible.

Reference

One pack of documents which makes the past accessible to children has been produced by Charlotte Mason College and Cumbria Archive Service and is called *Could do Better. Children at School 1870–1925*.

Living History

This involves children in a dramatic reconstruction of an event in the past. It is useful to inform staff of what is available within reasonable travelling distance in terms of 'In Role' Days so that these can be planned within a topic rather than become a bolt-on after thought. The costs involved make it essential that there is maximum follow-up, so that the children get the most out of the experience and the governors and parents feel the money has been well spent.

Information Technology

Its first and most significant contribution to the history curriculum lies in the data bases that can be created to deal with the material generated from studies involving the local community such as census returns or school rolls. The second area where IT can enhance the history curriculum is through the series of computer-aided learning programs becoming readily available from publishers, but you must be discriminating in the choice of programs which will fully support good teaching.

TV and Published History Schemes

One important piece of information which you need to disseminate to staff regularly until they have absorbed it is that *HMI found that where there was poor primary history practice there was also over-reliance on* TV *programmes and published schemes*. Teachers must come to an understanding that schemes can be useful if used selectively but are not the complete answer to history teaching. There is good material on the market, of course, but there is also a lot that is not suitable for teaching history as effectively as a resource bank built specifically to meet the needs of a particular set of children tackling a particular study unit.

Equal Opportunities and Multicultural Education

National curriculum history requires that children be taught about the cultural and ethnic diversity of past societies and the experiences of men and women. Therefore each time a study unit is planned these two requirements should be carefully addressed. We have all been exposed to history teaching supported by text books which have largely ignored the part played by women and minority ethnic groups in the development of our society. We must be aware of this bias in our own knowledge so that we do not pass it on by default to our children. Your school will no doubt have an equal opportunities and multicultural education set of guidelines. It would seem sensible to use the principles involved in setting up those as a basis for planning your history units. Below are two references I have found useful as a starting point for staff discussion.

Reference

COLLICOTT, S. (1991) A Woman's Place in Junior Education, May.
COLLICOTT, S. (1986) *Connections*, Haringey Local-National-World Links, published by: Haringey Community Information Service in association with the Multicultural Curriculum Support Group, Central Library, Wood Green, High Road, London, N22.

Concluding Remarks

Your commitment to history teaching and learning of quality is vital. It is hoped that you will not be the unwilling conscript who has drawn the short straw of history; you will be the enthusiastic volunteer who will enervate his or her colleagues through love of the subject.

There seems no better way of developing staff confidence in teaching history than for you to pilot various methods and materials and to share your findings with them, in the first instance, before encouraging them to share their own successes with the rest of the staff. Staff development exercises which involve looking not just at how to use a resource but also how to plan for progression in its use is another way in which you can ensure children get a broadly balanced history curriculum. Ultimately, though, as I have said, your personal enthusiasm for history will be a crucial factor in the staff's commitment to its place in the primary curriculum.

Chapter 12

Coordinating the Art Curriculum at Key Stage 2

Judith Piotrowski

This chapter will explore the context in which Key Stage 2 Art coordinators are operating, consider the challenges they are facing and provide some possible pathways for development.

Primary schools have been positive in their response to national curriculum art. A large scale study into the readiness of primary schools to teach national curriculum art (Clement, 1993) revealed that nearly two-thirds of schools were 'positive and welcoming', almost a quarter were 'cautious but considered' and only the remainder were 'negative or hostile' in their response to the original Statutory Orders for Art (p. 5). This is an encouraging context in which to be coordinating art. More specifically the OFSTED Report (1993) identifies that 'there was a strong link between the effectiveness of the subject coordinator and the overall standards of work in Art', para. 26. While this could easily be a direct quote from the Oracle at Delphi, for the purposes of this chapter we shall pursue only positive interpretations of OFSTED's perceived link and explore the implications. The national curriculum document that you are responsible for implementing has a useful structure and draws together many aspects of good practice. There are two attainment targets namely AT1 Investigation and Making and AT2 Knowledge and Understanding. Each AT has strands which are significant aspects of, or ways of, working in the ATs. These appear under the heading '7. Pupils should be given opportunities to . . .' in the revised orders. There are useful programmes of study and, finally, end of Key Stage descriptors for assessment purposes. The non-statutory guidance is particularly useful in most areas although much more was needed on assessment. As already stated national curriculum art is filled with explicit and implicit good practice but lacks a cohesive rationale or indeed a set of aims for art education in the primary curriculum. You will find it useful to allocate part of any time you are given for art INSET to a discussion of the aims of art education with your colleagues. The following (taken from Piotrowski, 1994) may make a useful starting point:

The aims of art education are for children to:

- develop the skills of art, namely drawing, use of colour, painting, printing, modelling, the use of textiles and textures;
- develop visual literacy and appreciation;
- appreciate the work of other artists from a variety of cultures and styles;
- become able to verbalize personal responses to art – to know and use effectively the language of art: line, colour, tone, shape, pattern, form and texture; and,
- to have the opportunity for personal expression and creative endeavour.

Challenges: Children's Development in Art

As coordinator for art you are very probably responsible for both Key Stages, if you are coordinating Key Stage 2 specifically you still need to be aware of the children's development through Key Stage 1. The primary school will typically have a whole school policy to art covering both Key Stages, the quality of art education in a Key Stage 2 school will be improved by liaison with your Key Stage 1 feeder(s). Ray (1995) provides an excellent insight into coordinating art at Key Stage 1. It will be very useful to you and your colleagues to consider children's development in art in the primary years and to hence highlight significant issues for Key Stage 2. This is considered in depth by Kellogg (1970), Lowenfeld and Brittain (1982) and more recently Barnes (1987) and Morgan (1988). Briefly, very young children (one year plus) begin to make marks on paper (or any appealing surface) using dots and dashes which gradually develop into various forms of scribble. By the age of about four the typical child will have discovered that symbols are a convenient shorthand for drawing. Examples of these symbols include triangles to represent female bodies, up-stretched arms for all and the drawing of a house as a large square with a triangular roof. At this stage children will use symbols even when they do not reflect their individual experience, for example, their mother may rarely wear skirts or dresses but she will be drawn with a triangular body, the child may live in a terraced house but will draw a detached house. Ideally, children will become increasingly analytical in their observations and representations on paper as they move through their primary years. This requires appropriate planning and teaching of skills. Many children reach a crisis of confidence early to mid-Key Stage 2, 8- to 9-years of age, as they become dissatisfied with the work they produce. Early teaching of skills can do much to facilitate children's development in art. Your colleagues may traditionally have been reluctant to teach skills in art or may feel that they lack the expertise. At Key Stage 2 it is vital that skills are taught and techniques developed in order that the children can successfully move from an over reliance on the use of symbols to a more analytical representation of their world.

Useful references for you at this point would include Barnes (1987); Rowe (1987); Morgan (1988); and Sedgewick (1994). You could use the CENSAPE Video 1 *Understanding Progression in Primary Art* to develop these ideas with colleagues. The above all deal in sufficient detail with developing essential skills and are user-friendly for non-specialist colleagues. Full references are at the end of the chapter.

In the following section of the chapter I shall use the headings planning with purpose, resourcing for quality and assessing within a context to cover some of the crucial aspects of art education you will be considering with colleagues at KS2.

Planning with Purpose

The two major approaches to planning for art teaching are often referred to as the *in* and *through* approaches, planning to develop skills in art and planning for art to be taught through other subjects: the separate subject versus thematic planning debate. A detailed consideration of the structure of national curriculum art will probably lead you to the conclusion that much quality art education can usefully be planned to complement existing plans in other subjects, such as history and geography study units, but that colleagues will need to plan for the development of skills in art such as drawing and colour mixing. The greatest difficulty is the possible lack of expertise amongst staff leading to what the Caloustie Gulbenkian Foundation referred to as 'the cycle of constraint'. You will need to introduce and develop resources such as the Folens Primary Art Packs for Key Stage 2 to show colleagues that developing art through a topic, say, the Victorians, is about considering the artefacts and art forms including architecture of the time. Developing art through such a topic is not mere illustration – copying a picture of Queen Victoria from a history text book. The CENSAPE video 2 is very useful to look at for planning and include case studies, for example, Year 6 Victorian Design Project.

In working with your colleagues on planning much of your deliberations will centre around the PoS and the strands. It may well be useful to discuss the strands initially since these are significant aspects of learning in art which run throughout the Key Stages. The PoS will then give colleagues a more detailed picture of what is intended. Also in your early stages of in-service training use the example planning sheets from the non-statutory guidance. These demonstrate very clearly that art work needs to be carefully planned, that what is intended is a quality approach allowing time for gathering resources, making observations and working in different groupings producing a variety of outcomes. The example planning sheets clearly demonstrate to colleagues that producing art work is a developmental process which may typically be planned to take place over several weeks. This is a quite different situation to the class lesson in which every child completes a very prescribed task. You will need to invite colleagues to share strategies for organization and classroom management which facilitate particular activities as you work through the PoS. The PoS are littered with statements that have significant implications for colleagues' planning and organization. For example,

'select and record (images and ideas) from first hand observation' (Key Stage 2 AT1 (a))

and

'record observations and ideas, and collect visual evidence and information, using a sketchbook' AT1(b) Key Stage 2. (p. 5)

The strands state that pupils should be given opportunities to, for example,

- gather resources and materials, using them to stimulate and develop ideas;
- explore and use two- and three-dimensional media, working on a variety of scales;
- review and modify their work as it progresses.

These statements reflect good practice and require that children are provided with opportunities to work accordingly. You may find it useful to use the analogy of drafting and editing in the writing process with quality work in art. Planning for drafting and editing in art means allowing time for gathering images, developing ideas, selecting media and reviewing.

AT2 (Knowledge and Understanding) has caused the greatest difficulty to teachers as is reflected in their considered responses to the Plymouth Report. Equally the OFSTED Report identified that AT2 'is a new departure for schools at Key Stage 1 and 2 and the majority have made a determined effort to improve this aspect of their provision.' A very useful guide to working in AT2 is Knowledge and Understanding one of four texts in the Oliver and Boyd *Primary Art* pack. AT2 can usefully be explored in conjunction with the history and geography coordinators. There are many rich possibilities for enhancing the study units in a way which is mutually beneficial.

Equally helpful for using in INSET time for AT2 is Video 3 from the CENSAPE series. This explores a variety of situations in which schools have developed AT2. A crucial aspect of this planning is developing the natural link between the strands 7(d) 'review and modify their work as it progress' (AT1) and 7(f) 'respond to and evaluate art, including their own and others' work' (AT2). Two key elements for you to develop with colleagues are the language of art and questioning skills. Developing the language of art will give both colleagues and children reference points and routes into reviewing, modifying and assessment. Having the appropriate technical language – line, form, colour, texture, shape, pattern, tone – facilitates communication and the sharing of ideas and experiences. Questioning skills are critical – knowing how to discuss the children's art work, the art work of others and art in the environment is only part of the process of development and enjoyment. Colleagues may well appreciate some discussion of the type of questions to raise with children, for example, about materials, effects achieved, progress, changes. Barnes (1987) deals with discussing and questioning in art education well in *Art for Children 4–9*, Chapter 7.

A final point here regarding planning: share it! Most teachers discuss the experiences planned for the coming half-term/term with their class. Some teachers go further and design a user-friendly A4 planning sheet to give to parents at the end of the previous term and so share their planning with parents. All the research of the 80s into parental involvement shows that the majority are very keen to be actively involved. Involving parents like this should improve the quality of the children's learning, and encourage parents to offer to share any relevant skills and techniques.

Resourcing for Quality

I am including here a list of basic art resources which a typical class would require. Clearly such a list is not exhaustive but the contents may assist you in ordering efficiently. You could give a copy to each of your colleagues for their personal adjustments or use it as a checklist of school wide resources. The list was developed with a group of art coordinators during a recent funded project at the University of Manchester.

Range of pencils – boxed sets to include both range of soft and hard leads and coloured drawing pencils, such as Derwent Drawing Pencils (6) or Faber–Castell Portrait colours.

- craypas
- oil pastels
- fixative spray
- brushes
- printing ink

- chalk pastels
- charcoal
- watercolours
- diffusers (or air-sprayers)
- cut paper–sizes A4/A3/A2
  Quality: cartridge
              sugar
              tracing
  Colours: carefully selected.

- sketch pads – bought or made
- brushes – 0–11 range of sizes, short handled
- long handled brushes
- trays for printing
- polyprint tiles
- scissors – 6 right-handed, 2 left-handed and of good quality

- large 'decorators' brushes
- rollers

- powder paint/liquid paint – primary (red, blue, yellow) plus black and white
- glue stick and pots (collect plastic tablet pots or photo film pots)
- glue – PVA and powder

The links between planning and organization, resourcing and assessment are essential. You can only assess children's progress given a knowledge of the opportunities afforded and the resources available to them. There are some specific resources which require additional comment:

Sketchbooks

One of the specific requirements as regards resources for KS2 is that the children are required to use a sketchbook.

AT1 PoS (b) 'use a sketchbook to record observations and ideas, and collect visual evidence and information for their work.'

The use of sketchbooks is another one of those national curriculum art statements which is full of good practice and implications for organization. In fact many primary schools are introducing sketchbooks at KS1 due to their value in the developmental process of working in art and due to their role as ongoing record of progression. In some ways the label sketchbook is misleading – it can be so much more than a book of sketches. Children can put into their sketchbooks sketches, certainly, but also notes, experimental lines with mark making tools, photographs, references to other artists' work, and related prose or poetry.

A sketchbook described as such is likely to be expensive. Much better to contact an art supplier (see addresses at the end of this section) and specify your requirements. For example, you might order an A4 book of 140 grams cartridge paper with a stapled heavy sugar paper cover, these will be good quality and surprisingly cheap.

Mark-making Tools

Ensure a range which reflects quality not quantity. The children need experience with the different effects achieved with a range of drawing pencils (hard and soft leads), charcoal (willow sticks occasionally and pencils always available), oil pastels, chalk pastels, conté drawing sticks (in rich colours – ivory, sepia, terracotta, venetian red . . .), blendable and water-colour crayons. As with brushes you do not need thirty of each in each classroom but a small permanent selection to which the children have easy access – clearly labelled and organized.

Brushes

Again a restricted range of short and long-handled, a variety of widths from a decorators brush to very fine, round tipped as well as blunt.

Paint

As with most of the resources you will need, Morgan (1988) has a useful section on ordering paint (pp. 53–6). Children will gain a greater insight into the possibilities of paint, colour and texture if they experience mixing their own colours in powder paint. This is well worth the minimal training period needed, children readily become experts capable of training others. That said, liquid paint is very useful for larger scale work and again children will benefit from seeing the different effects they can achieve with standard free flow liquid paint and acrylic.

The important feature of ordering paint, dyes and printing ink is to order essentially the primary colours (red, blue, yellow) and lots of white. While purists would argue for no black at all, I feel that a little black is essential for creating very dark shades and for witches hats!

To refer in detail to Morgan (1988: p. 56) her useful checklist of colours comprises:

blue (bright blue, ultra marine and greeny blue, Prussian); red (scarlet or vermilion and crimson); yellow (lemon and ochre); white and black. Order twice as much yellow and white as other colours, hardly any black and you might want to add viridian (a green) for an even more extensive range.

3–D Work

OFSTED (1993) identified that opportunities for 3–D work were restricted. Colleagues will need appropriate resources for this, while some are relatively expensive others can be gathered from parents. You will need: Modroc; clay (either air drying or firing if you have a kiln); also glazes if you have a kiln.

For working with clay you will need to gather:

- tea towels or similar for rolling onto – (easy to peel off).
- rolling pins
- a variety of cutting tools, such as lollipop sticks, plastic cutlery, blunt knives and forks, pastry cutters.

For modelling with recycled materials you will need a variety of clean discarded containers, tubes, boxes, pots and strong glue. Spray paint (use out of doors) is a useful medium for coverage – store with care!

Paper maché – ask parents to donate newspapers, washing up bowls or even baby baths. If you are making a mask on a plasticine mold remember to use an initial layer of vaseline and alternate newspaper and tissue paper layers, beginning and ending with tissue.

Resources for AT2: Knowledge and Understanding

There are now some extremely helpful materials which are designed to support non-specialist colleagues, for example:

- Oliver and Boyd Primary Art Pack – very useful resource especially the text Knowledge and Understanding for AT2.
- Folens Photopacks – Primary Art Pack Key Stage 2, very useful and includes teachers' notes.
- You may find Ray and Piotrowski (1993) helpful for exploring issues regarding multicultural education. At Key Stage 2 in the programme of study there is the requirement that 'pupils should be introduced to the work of artists . . . in order to develop their appreciation of the richness of our diverse cultural heritage. The selection should include work in a variety of genres and styles from the locality, the past and present, and a variety of cultures, Western and non-Western.' (p. 4)
- Children will also benefit from understanding that artefacts in galleries have typically been commissioned, donated or sold by a certain section of society. It can be argued that much of what one typically sees in permanent collections in galleries is a reflection of the predilection in taste of wealthy European men. Indeed much of the art work accepted as *significant* is that of deceased European males, due to a variety of social factors.

Assessment in a Context

The structure of national curriculum art incorporates end of Key Stage statements. For Key Stage 2 these are AT1: Investigating and Making.

> Pupils record what they have experienced and imagined, expressing ideas and feelings confidently. They represent chosen features of the world around them with increasing accuracy and attention to detail. They select relevant resources and materials and experiment with ideas that are suggested by these. They experiment with, and show increasing control over, a range of materials, tools and techniques. They choose materials and methods and visual elements appropriate to their intentions, making images and artefacts for different purposes. They reflect on and adapt their work, identifying ways in which it can be developed and improved. (p. 9)

This end of Key Stage statement assumes that in planning colleagues have:

- allowed sufficient time for gathering evidence, making observations;
- allowed time for development from experimental to expressive use of materials – children and adults need to revisit new materials and techniques to do this;
- developed ideas and awareness of themes/images with the children;
- given opportunity for the full range of artistic elements (drawing, painting, printing, using colour, textiles, 3–D, architecture);
- organized resources so that children can select appropriate media.

The end of Key Stage 2 statement for AT2: Knowledge and Understanding is:

> Pupils compare images and artefacts, using an art, craft and design vocabulary, and identify similarities and differences in methods and approaches. They begin to recognise how works of art, craft and design are affected by their purpose, including, where appropriate, the intentions of the artist, craftsperson or designer, and the time and place in which they are made. They evaluate their own and others' work in the light of what was intended. (p. 9)

Again it is useful to consider what this assumes for planning and resourcing. Colleagues will have to give children opportunities to:

- develop an art vocabulary – one significant aspect of visual literacy is that the children describe their response to a work of art. The vocabulary will include line, tone, form, shape, colour, tone, texture, pattern. This will require significant exposure to the language and a relevant range of artefacts;
- demonstrate their art vocabulary so that it can be assessed – opportunities to discuss their work with the teacher;
- learn about common images (for example, representation of family groups);
- set images and artefacts within their contexts of time, place and purpose and understand how the image/artefact is affected by its context.

Conclusion

Throughout the chapter I have given references to published resources which will support you and your colleagues in developing art education in your school. These are listed at the end of this chapter. There are other resources and contacts which will support both your curriculum and professional development. Here are a few:

Working with Local Artists in Schools

Many schools have a policy to involve local artists, designers and crafts people. Such people can offer valuable specialist expertise and are usually keen to share it with children and teachers.

Developing Contacts with Local Galleries

Contact your local galleries and find out:

- what specialist areas they cover in their permanent collection;
- what exhibitions are in their programme;
- do they have an education curator?;
- do they have study rooms – you can usually arrange for a tailor-made session led either by the curator or teacher;
- what items are available for schools to borrow?

Professional Associations

NSEAD – National Society for Education in Art and Design. They offer different levels of membership entitling you to the Journal of Art and Design Education, address NSEAD, the Gatehouse, Corsham Court, Corsham, Wiltshire, SN13 0BZ.

NFAE – National Foundation for Arts Education. Membership includes their Arts Education magazine – very good. Address NFAE, The Spendlove Centre, Enstone Road, Charlbury, Oxford, OX7 3PQ.

NFAE have also a wide range of publication including *Planning for the Arts in the Primary School* (1993).

Useful Staffroom Magazine/Journal

Scholastic's *Art and Craft* (Design and Technology).

Builds up over the year into a very useful resource, largely written by teachers for teachers, includes posters – ideal for the staff-room. Address: Art & Craft, Scholastic Publications Limited, Freepost, Westfield Road, Southam, Leamington Spa, Warwickshire, CV33 0BR.

Finally, when you feel you are working hard to develop policy and good practice in your school think about art education from the child's perspective. Laurie Lee (1959) wrote the following in *Cider with Rosie*, long before Key Stage 1 and Key Stage 2 were so defined:

Of his infant days

I myself was a natural infant . . . skilled at cutting out men from paper, chalking suns on the walls, making snakes from clay, idling voluptuously through the milky days . . .

and of the juniors

infant no longer he learned techniques and the intimacy of objects in being set to draw them.

References

BARNES (1987) *Teaching Art to Young Children 4–9*, London, Routledge.

CLEMENT, R. (1993) *The Readiness of Primary Schools to Teach the National Curriculum in Art*, Plymouth, University of Plymouth.

GULBENKIAN FOUNDATION (1985) *The Gulbenkian Report: The Arts in Schools*, London, Calouste GULBENKIAN FOUNDATION.

KELLOGG, R. (1970) *Analysing Children's Art*, San Francisco, CA, National Press.

LEE, L. (1959) *Cider With Rosie*, London, Penguin.

LOWENFELD, V. and BRITTAIN, W. (1982) *Creative and Mental Growth*, New York, Macmillan.

MORGAN, M. (1988) *Art 4–11*, New York, Simon & Schuster.

OFSTED (1993) *Art Key Stages 1, 2 and 3. First Year, 1992–1993*, Report, London, HMSO.

PIOTROWSKI, J. (1994) 'Art for everyone's sake', in HARRISON, M. (ed.) *Beyond the Core Curriculum*, Plymouth, Northcote House.

RAY, R. (1995) 'Not sunflowers again! Coordinating art at Key Stage 1', in DAVIES, J. (ed.) *Developing a Leadership Role within the Key Stage 1 Curriculum*, London, Falmer Press.

RAY, R. and PIOTROWSKI, J. (1993) 'Art and Multicultural Education', in PUMFREY, P. and VERMA, G. (1993) *Cultural Diversity and the Curriculum*, **3**, London, Falmer Press.

ROWE, G. (1987) *Guiding Young Artists: Curriculum Ideas for Teachers*, OUP, Melbourne.

SEDGWICK, D. and F. (1994) *Drawing to Learn*, London, Hodder & Stoughton.

Other Useful Texts:

GENTLE, K. (1992) *Teaching Painting in the Primary School*, London, Cassell.

LANCASTER, J. (1990) *Art in the Primary School*, London, Routledge.

LANCASTER, J. (1990) *Art, Craft and Design in the Primary School*, NSEAD.

MATHIESON, K. (1993) *Children's Art and the Computer*, London, Hodder & Stoughton.

NCC (1990) The Arts 5–16, Oliver & Boyd, London.

Resources Referred to in Text:

OLIVER and BOYD (1992) *Primary Art Pack*.

FOLENS (1992) *Primary Art Key Stage 2 Packs*.
    Titles: *Influential Artists* (also KS1),

      Modern Artists (also KS1),
      Art of Different Cultures (also KS1),
      Art of Ancient Civilizations.
Folens Photopacks (1993)
    Titles: *Ancient Egypt*
           Ancient Greece
           Vikings
           Romans
           Anglo-Saxons
CENSAPE Videos: set of three videos from
    CENSAPE,
    Faculty of Arts and Education,
    University of Plymouth,
    Douglas Avenue,
    Exmouth, EX8 2AT.
SCHOLASTIC (1993) *Understanding Art*, Scholastic.
THAMES and HUDSON (1987) series includes the following titles: *African Art, Art of Mesoamerica, Chinese Art, Indian Art, Islamic Art* and *Japanese Art.*

Suppliers

PISCES, Westwood Studios, West Avenue, Crewe, CW1 3AD. Tel: 01270–216211.
BEROL LIMITED, Old Meadow Road, King's Lynn, Norfolk, PE30 4JR, Tel: 0553–761–221.
JACKSON–CONTRA–BANNED, Unit 2, Gatehouse Enterprise Centre, Albert Street, Lockwood, Huddersfield, HD1 3QD, Tel: 01484 530855.
NES/Arnold, Ludlow Hill Road, West Bridgford, Nottingham, NG2 6HD, Tel: 0115 945 2200.

Chapter 13

Physical Education and Dance: Leading the Way

Patricia Sanderson

That you are sufficiently interested in physical education (PE) and dance teaching to consider taking on the responsibility of curriculum coordinator is an excellent start and the factor that is most likely to help you make a success of an important, as well as a demanding role in the school. Note that you do not need to have great physical expertise in any PE activity, but you must have an enthusiasm for the subject as a whole, based on your conviction that PE can provide unique learning experiences for primary school children. You will also have to be resilient and prepared for a good deal of hard work as initially you may find that your enthusiasm is not shared by your colleagues!

Although PE including dance has been part of the primary school national curriculum ever since the latter's inception, you may find that in practice it has rarely been given a great deal of attention by some teachers. A major cause is likely to be the demands of the eight other subjects with which most teachers have to deal, still the case despite the Dearing reforms, although there may also be a genuine lack of interest in the area, for traditionally, PE has not been taken seriously in the primary school. Too often it is regarded as an unnecessary interruption in the serious business of the school day and little more than playtime. The PE coordinator is therefore frequently in the position of having to start from scratch in generating enthusiasm for teaching PE and raising its status within the school. On the other hand you may find unexpected allies among the staff, such as senior teachers with a background in PE who retain their enthusiasm for the area and are more than willing to give you advice and support.

It is worth considering why PE may be unpopular among teachers so that you can anticipate any reluctance to teach the subject, and be prepared with sympathy as well as encouragement! Some teachers, for instance, will have unhappy memories of their own PE experiences, particularly at secondary school, and you must reassure them that most primary children today love PE because the emphasis is on the involvement of everyone, not just those with a natural aptitude for physical activity. You will also probably find that a major cause of a lack of enthusiasm is the very basic PE course most teachers will have received during their initial teacher training. Surveys such as that of the Physical Education Association (1987) and the Calouste Gulbenkian Foundation (1989) confirm that students are often given barely a cursory acquaintance with any aspect of the subject and it is not uncommon for some to receive no training at all! As a result, you are likely to find that many teachers lack confidence and so avoid teaching PE whenever possible. The latest slimmed down version of the national curriculum requirements will not remove the anxiety that even the most experienced classroom teacher can feel when confronted with the unique organizational and teaching approaches needed for PE.

The PE Curriculum Coordinator therefore faces the challenging prospect of persuading the staff that:

- PE can be fun to teach.
- PE can offer opportunities to develop good teacher – pupil relationships.
- PE is very important for children's all-round development.

How can you help teachers to improve their knowledge, skills and understanding so that these aspirations become a reality? How do you make the implementation of a national curriculum at Key Stage (KS) 2 a less daunting prospect? How can you ensure continuity, progression and consistency through a whole school approach?

At this point you could very well be thinking that this is not a job for you after all! You may feel that your own knowledge, skills and understanding in the six areas of activity at Key Stage 2, gymnastics, games, dance, athletics, swimming, outdoor and adventurous activities, are inadequate. Take heart! No-one could be expected to begin with an all-embracing expertise but there are certain key areas where you should initially focus your attention.

- Begin by concentrating on the three central activities of gymnastics, games and dance. Strengthening your knowledge, skills and understanding in these areas will give you confidence and a firm base from which to proceed. Make this a priority.
- Become thoroughly familiar with the Key Stage 2 Programme of Study and End of Key Stage Statement. You will find that these are now relatively clear, explicit and jargon free. It would also be useful to look at the requirements at Key Stage 1 so that you are aware of the development expected. For example, during that first stage, experience in only gymnastic, dance and games activities are required – although schools may choose to teach swimming.
- Assessment and recording of progress have been greatly simplified but you should nevertheless know what is involved and be able to explain it to others.

- Gain as much experience as possible with the full range of teaching strategies and organizational techniques so that you are confident in your discussions with colleagues.
- Acquire the necessary skills in order to budget and care for equipment and other resources.

The next question could well be where and how you are to acquire such a range of expertise. There are a variety of opportunities which should be readily available to you. For example, relevant INSET courses are offered on a regular basis by LEAs and Institutes of Higher Education, visits to other schools could also be helpful, while familiarizing yourself with teaching resources such as PE handbooks and videotapes would be good general preparation. You will find relevant details at the end of this chapter. There are other skills, however, that you need to acquire and perhaps had not anticipated. You, along with the other curriculum coordinators in your school, are essentially a manager. You will have to work alongside your colleagues persuading and cajoling them into accepting changes that will inevitably be necessary. You have the responsibility of finding ways to increase your colleagues' understanding and improve their practice. This fundamental managerial aspect of the role is often not appreciated, as Alexander, Rose and Woodhead (1992) point out. They suggest that although curriculum coordinators have developed expertise in the provision of resources and the writing of syllabuses, they have been considerably less successful in the major task of *influencing* and *motivating* teachers. Perhaps the term *subject manager* which is preferred by the authors of a recent OFSTED (1994) report, more accurately describes the task in hand and also underlines the importance of seeking the advice and support of senior members of staff.

Your own enthusiasm is an important means of making a positive impact on others but it is not enough. You could also raise awareness of PE by ensuring that eye-catching posters and photographs are a regular feature of corridor walls, but you need to do more. It is essential that you are persuasive and articulate in advocating PE as offering invaluable experiences for children. You must convince the head and the staff of this.

What's so Special about Physical Education?

Teachers will not develop the knowledge, organizational skills and teaching techniques necessary to teach PE well unless they are motivated. After all, they have enough to do already! What arguments can you employ to convince your colleagues that PE should be taken seriously, not merely because it is a requirement of the national curriculum? You will also need to present sound arguments to your headteacher and governors when competing for resources. Sanderson (1994, p. 55) argues that:

> 'PE experiences make valuable contributions to the development of the whole child by offering *integrated* physical, motor skill, cognitive, personal and social, creative and aesthetic education.'

Presenting such a case for PE could be a very useful first step in raising its profile within the school.

Physical Development

This is probably one purpose of PE with which most primary teachers will readily agree. The importance of vigorous exercise for the acquisition and maintenance of overall good health is also stressed in the national curriculum document. Virtually everyone acknowledges that in today's sophisticated society, children do not get enough exercise, and that without PE in school, some children would be almost completely inactive. Ongoing research at Exeter University, which continues to receive widespread publicity through TV programmes, consistently confirms the low levels of fitness nation-wide among children of primary school age and the serious implications this can have for the development of the heart muscle, possibly causing heart disease in later life.

Motor Skill Coordination and Development

The primary school years, and particularly in Key Stage 2, represent a crucially important time for the development of basic physical skills, motor control and coordination, a point which is also stressed in the national curriculum document. Besides, children of this age enjoy the practice and repetition essential for skill development. For many, the self-conscious secondary school stage is too late, as numerous adults know from experience. If a child has difficulty in throwing, catching and hitting a ball, cannot respond to a simple skipping rhythm, is unable to stay afloat in the swimming pool and so on, then the possibility of joining in various play activities becomes increasingly limited. All primary school teachers will recognize that such difficulties can cause great distress to a child and they will certainly want to avoid that happening.

The safety aspect should also be raised, not only in relation to water but also the outdoors where climbing, balance and general motor coordination are important factors. Your teachers will also readily acknowledge that the children with special abilities in the physical domain should be given the same opportunities to fully develop their talents as those who are gifted in other areas.

Personal and Social Development

In the national curriculum document the importance of children learning to co-operate and compete fairly in physical activities is underlined. You should also draw teachers' attention to the potential of PE to contribute to the development of a positive self image, for it is an area of the curriculum where all children can achieve some success and merit genuine praise. However, you need to stress the importance of this for the self esteem of *all* children. Teachers usually recognize it as relevant to those who have difficulties with classwork yet often fail to realize the needs of children who may have no problems in other subjects.

Cognitive Development

Teachers sometimes need to be reminded that PE is a cognitive as well as a physical activity. The national PE curriculum demands that children make decisions, devise solutions to problems, plan, select, observe, judge, reflect, and adapt; PE experiences must make substantial contributions to cognitive development. Physical exercise also has an invigorating effect on the whole being, releasing tensions and so helping learning to occur. There is also research completed in the USA which may interest your teachers, which claims that there is a direct relationship between certain sensori-motor experiences, such as those offered by dance and gymnastics, and cognitive development. Kephart (1960) and Frostig and Maslow (1973), argue that PE should be given a high priority with additional experiences to any statutory requirements as the latter are always likely to be severely curtailed by other curricular demands. There are other less controversial claims, for instance that the physical exploration of certain concepts including those of a spatial nature (left, right, down, up and so on) can help promote understanding of associated verbal and written symbols.

Aesthetic Development

Although the national PE curriculum at Key Stage 2 appears to stress the competitive aspect of PE, along with the need for vigorous exercise and the development of motor skills, this does not exclude the encouragement of an awareness of an aesthetic dimension to physical activity. Indeed it could be argued that the aesthetic is a prime motivator for taking part in PE for it relates to enjoyment, the feelings associated with a good performance, something done well. You could also point out that at Key Stage 2 children are required to evaluate their own and others' performances in a variety of contexts and these are in effect aesthetic evaluations, for the focus is on the quality of the movement. For example, not just *that* a goal is scored but the manner of scoring, in other words *how*.

Creative Development

In virtually every PE lesson children are involved in the creative processes of experimentation, selection and rejection as they devise gymnastic sequences, games and dances. You might also point out to your colleagues that in such activities the whole child is involved, physically, cognitively and emotionally thereby making these creative experiences particularly valuable.

By gradually introducing arguments such as these, teachers will be in a better position to debate the fundamental question, 'Why teach PE?' The answer needs to be more than 'Because we have to – it's part of the national curriculum!' Teachers need to be clear about the overall *aim* of PE, and you need to guide them through discussion to a general agreed statement. For example this could be:

> The overall aim of the PE curriculum is the integrated physical, motor skill, personal and social, aesthetic, and creative development of each child.

All of the aspects of PE at Key Stage 2, that is, games, gymnastics, dance, athletics, swimming, outdoor and adventurous activities, contribute to this integrated development across all these dimensions. However, teachers, headteachers and governors are likely to want to know more specifically the value of each activity. They will be interested in what you have to say about the objectives of PE. For example,

What is the Value of Teaching

Games?

The importance of games experience is stressed in the national curriculum. There is the potential for developing and maintaining cardiovascular health and for promoting positive social attitudes by competing fairly and co-operating with others. Games are an important part of our culture and so it is essential that basic knowledge, skills and understanding are promoted. Games experiences can also contribute to creativity, cognitive development – and an appreciation of the aesthetic aspects of sport, an important antidote to the *win at all costs* approach.

Gymnastics?

Controlled management of the body is developed through creative gymnastic skill experiences. Gymnastic activity improves flexibility, endurance, co-ordination, balance, strength and mobility. Integral to the activity is the aesthetic aspect, how a movement is performed. Distinctive perceptual experiences may also contribute to cognitive growth.

Dance?

This activity offers a wide range of possibilities for both aesthetic and creative growth by means of the expression and communication of feelings and ideas. Thus the range of expressive possibilities is extended for each child beyond that of language and other art symbols. Fitness, coordination and mobility may all be developed, tensions released and basic spatial awareness and rhythmical skills improved. Familiarity with traditional dances contributes to knowledge of different cultures.

Swimming?

We live on an island replete with rivers, canals and lakes; it is therefore essential that each child learns to survive in water, and this is recognized in the national PE curriculum. Involvement in any water sports activity also demands swimming skills. Swimming is an activity which can be enjoyed throughout life regardless of physical or cognitive ability, providing excellent all-round exercise and recreation for all.

Athletics?

This activity contributes to the development of running, throwing, dodging and jumping which are all fundamental games skills, but it is particularly valuable for improving flexibility, suppleness, endurance, muscular strength and cardiovascular health.

Outdoor and adventurous activities?

Children learn to respond safely to challenges presented by different environments, to assess situations and to co-operate with others. Meanwhile perseverance, stamina and endurance are all being developed; a respect for and an aesthetic appreciation of the environment encouraged.

Arguments such as these should help convince your colleagues that PE is worth the personal efforts and a fair share of resources, in order to achieve a whole school approach to the organization and teaching of the subject. As PE coordinator this should be your overall aim.

Meanwhile you should also be trying to find out as much as possible about the general situation concerning PE in your school. Remember that you must be as diplomatic as possible when you gather basic information, using gentle questioning and careful observation – no interrogation of the staff or the head! Your zeal should not make you the world's most unpopular PE coordinator, and besides you need everyone's co-operation if you are to make progress.

Some tasks are relatively straightforward such as discovering the extent, state of repair and suitability of the equipment and general facilities currently available. Others require careful thought and preparation.

Undertaking a Review of the PE Curriculum

The National Curriculum Council (NCC) (1989) stresses the need to be honest and open in any planning and it is true that teachers can get very anxious when they don't know what is going on and don't feel involved. On the other hand you do need to assess the current situation and these broad questions will be helpful to you at an early stage in your planning.

- What does the curriculum consist of at present?
- What are its strengths?
- What are its weaknesses?
- How does it compare with the requirements of the National Curriculum?
- Where are the gaps?
- What action is needed to fill them? (NCC, 1989, p. 4)

It will, of course, take some time to answer these questions satisfactorily. Remember that such knowledge can be gathered in a variety of ways, ranging from casual conversations during break times to more formal meetings arranged for a specific purpose, from being generally alert, to actually observing teachers in action – with their permission of course! Incidentally, the latter is more likely to happen if teachers don't feel threatened in any way.

Your headteacher is a key figure in your quest to raise the profile of PE in the school and you need to seek advice on a number of important issues so that you are fully aware at the outset of the possibilities – and the limitations. Therefore try to find out:

Whether there are already any priorities in terms of curriculum development in PE. The allocation you will have for essential resources and whether it is yours alone to spend.

Availability and status of any existing PE documents.

The support you can expect for the development of your own knowledge, skills and understanding.

The non-contact time which will be available for staff development.

INSET possibilities such as demonstration lessons, team teaching and observing good practice outside the school.

Timetable arrangements to meet national curriculum requirements.

Provision for swimming.

The possibility of residential outdoor activities experience.

Current provision for equality of opportunity in terms of ethnic minorities, special educational needs and gender.

The policy on multicultural education.

Meanwhile by finding out your teachers' opinions on matters relating to PE in the school, you will be building up a clear picture of the best way to proceed. Gradually discover:

Areas where individuals feel most or least confident.

Interest or expertise in any aspect on which you can build.

Aspects which are overemphasized or conversely, neglected.

The level of awareness among teachers of each other's work and children's progress.

The degree of co-operation existing as far as PE is concerned.

Current familiarity or otherwise with the national PE curriculum.

Whether an overall scheme of work exists and is implemented.

If there is a common lesson plan for each activity.

Whether there is consistency in methods of handling and organization of equipment.

How much agreement there is on teaching approaches.

The level of confidence in assessing progress.

Opportunities taken for multicultural education.

To what extent equality of access and opportunity are catered for in terms of gender, ethnic minorities and special educational needs.

By gentle probing you should be able to discover what the teachers consider to be their immediate needs.

You could now encourage the staff to produce a school policy statement on PE. This should not be too difficult after you have spent some time finding out their views and encouraging them to reflect on the purposes of teaching

PE at Key Stage 2. For example, a collective conclusion after due deliberation might be:

> We believe that PE can provide valuable integrated educational experiences.
> We are committed to the provision of a broad, balanced and differentiated PE curriculum which is progressive, stimulating and challenging for pupils of all abilities and backgrounds.

A statement such as this establishes an overall sense of purpose and direction. It is a vital step towards achieving a whole school approach for PE. The national PE document will be the focus of your planning.

The National PE Curriculum

You will find that as a result of The Dearing Report the PE statutory requirements including those at Key Stage 2 are greatly simplified. The PE curriculum is certainly less intimidating than in its previous versions, but you should continue to bear in mind that the teacher has eight other subjects with which to cope, and no doubt several enthusiastic curriculum co-ordinators! Therefore, become fully familiar with Key Stage 2 requirements so that you can convey the main points to the staff, answer any queries and reassure where necessary.

Teachers will need to know that PE at Key Stage 2 is comprised of six activities, games, gymnastics, dance, athletics, outdoor and adventurous activities, and swimming. The emphasis, however, is on games, gymnastics and dance which must be taught throughout the Key Stage whereas the requirement for the three remaining activities is that they are taught 'at some point'.

- There is no separate, stated Attainment Target. The Attainment Target is simply the End of Key Stage Description (EKSD).
- There are general requirements for PE applicable across all four Key Stages. These are confined to one page of three major points concerned with developing healthy lifestyles, positive attitudes and safe practice.
- The Key Stage 2 PoS is comprised of just two pages, is divided into sections relating to each of the six areas of activity, and contains the majority of the content.
- Athletics and outdoor and adventurous activities are introduced at Key Stage 2; these activities are no longer part of the curriculum at Key Stage 1.
- Traditional dances must be included in addition to creative dance.

- All children should be able to swim unaided, completently and safely, for at least twenty-five metres at the end of Key Stage 2.
- Throughout Key Stage 2, children must be thought how to sustain energetic activity over appropriate periods of time and also the short-term effects of exercise on the body.
- The EKSS is just one substantial paragraph and is designed to help teachers judge their pupils' attainment in relation to expectations. There are no statutory assessments for PE.
- Knowledge, skills and understanding in each of the six activities will be developed by means of planning, performing and evaluating. The emphasis, however, is placed on the performance aspect, underlining the importance of strenuous physical activity.
- In PE, as in every other subject of the national curriculum, opportunities must be taken to improve pupils' ability to express themselves clearly in speech.
- Appropriate provision must be made for those pupils who need activities equipment to be adapted, and any other aids in order to participate in PE.

Because the national PE curriculum is now so clear and straightforward, it might be a good idea to ask the headteacher if you could have an hour with the staff when you could illustrate this. By expanding briefly on the main points listed above you could easily convince everyone that teaching PE is well within the capabilities of the generalist primary school teacher. You will, of course, have to stress that you will endeavour to provide the support and help with resources that they might need, but reassuring teachers at an early stage that there has indeed been considerable pruning and clarification should awaken some interest – even enthusiasm – upon which you can build. The reduced prescribed content also offers the opportunity for adaptation to your school's particular circumstances and needs.

On the other hand, you could confirm many teachers' convictions that they 'can't teach PE' if you are not completely familiar with all aspects of the most recent requirements yourself and so make everything appear to be more difficult than it is. You must be able to present everything in an uncomplicated manner without the use of jargon, be prepared to answer questions and offer reassurances. Give some thought particularly to the following:

- the actual content of the Common Requirements, general requirements and Key Stage 2 PoS and how they can be related;
- illustrations of the points in the EKSS with examples from different age groups. Bear in mind that the EKSS can be used as a basis for the reporting of a pupil's attainment;
- the overall requirements of Key Stage 3 and Key Stage 1 so that you can place Key Stage 2 in context. Teachers will want to know where

they are starting from and where they are going to, as well as how the needs of those children with special requirements will be met;

- any genuine links which can be made with the other subjects of the national curriculum.

You will find that the various publications in the Resources section at the end of this chapter will provide you with many of the ideas you need.

Developing a Whole-school Approach to PE

How can you help your colleagues develop a whole-school approach to PE? Your assessments of the current provision for PE, the production of a school policy statement and discussions with staff on the national curriculum requirements will all give you the basis you need to move towards achieving this aim. A whole-school approach embodies the concepts of:

Continuity

Progression

Consistency

You will need to work with your colleagues in developing schemes of work which are based on these principles, so that everyone has a vested interest in the successful delivery of the whole of the PE curriculum.

For the sake of clarity, continuity, progression and consistency are dealt with separately here although they are closely interrelated. In practice you should aim at making more or less simultaneous advances in all three areas. The extent to which you can do this will however depend upon your circumstances.

Achieving Continuity

As the PE curriculum coordinator you must work towards ensuring continuity between classes so that as pupils move from one year to the next there is no unplanned break in PE provision and no unnecessary repetition of previous work. Similarly you will want to achieve a smooth transition from Key Stage 1 and provide a good preparation for the children's entry to Key Stage 3. If you can have some informal contact with the PE coordinators in your school's associated infant and secondary schools then this would obviously be helpful. Any overlap should be deliberately designed to reinforce learning and increase knowledge, skills and understanding.

You will have the overall view and so you must try to relate whole-school planning to individual schemes of work. Teachers may need guidance in devising their own scheme which is in harmony with the general school policy on PE, the national curriculum general requirements, PoS and EKSS, and any existing system of recording progress. The scheme should be as clear and straightforward as possible and incorporate the teachers' own ideas. Sectionalized in a loose-leaf file for easy access it should include the following items:

- The knowledge, skills and experiences appropriate for each age group and each activity. Work from the PoS for Key Stage 2.
- A sample lesson plan for each area, which illustrates organization and development.
- A good range of resources for each aspect of PE. It is very important that there is ready access to suitable ideas, poems and different types of music to ensure different dance experiences; various possible arrangements of gymnastic apparatus; appropriate games activities; instructions and taped music for the teaching of the traditional dances now required by the national curriculum.
- Teaching techniques and class organization for each of the six different PE activities, highlighting the relevant safety procedures in each case. These are the aspects which often give teachers most anxiety.
- Suggestions for topic work after consultation with other curriculum coordinators. The emphasis in the PE national curriculum on promoting healthy lifestyles offers immediate possibilities. Links can be made between some aspect of PE and virtually every subject in the curriculum – athletics and maths, outdoor activities and geography, while dance offers many opportunities including that of exploring aspects of various cultures.
- A simple assessment sheet, comprising a series of short, unambiguous statements and based on the EKSS. From this teachers should be able to easily judge each child's attainment.

    An example of a self appraisal sheet for children could also be included; two or three statements such as: What I enjoy in PE; What I don't enjoy; What I think I'm good at.
- The timetable for each term, showing clearly when swimming, athletics and outdoor activities are likely to occur. Games, gymnastics and dance lessons will probably feature throughout the year.

Achieving Progression

By studying the PoS and the EKSS for Key Stages 1 and 2 you will quickly see the progression that is expected between the ages of 7 and 11. You will have to devise intermediate goals for your colleagues and as your own knowledge and understanding improves you will find this is an increasingly straightforward task.

But how can you ensure that theory turns into practice? You will need to work with your senior teachers on improving teachers' knowledge and understanding of PE; organizational strategies and teaching techniques; and ability to recognize progress.

Knowledge and understanding of PE

No doubt you will have realized from your own experience that subject knowledge underlies everything else. The gradual improvement of teachers' understanding in the various aspects of PE should therefore be a priority. Often a root cause of insecurity is not being entirely sure as to what the basic principles are, particularly those of gymnastics, games and dance. It might be a good idea therefore to begin with summaries, as straightforward and jargon-free as possible, so that teachers are confident in what they are pursuing.

In dance, by extending the use of the body, space and dynamics, a range of expressive movements are developed. Various ideas and feelings can then be expressed in a dance form which may be a single phrase or more complex combinations. Traditional dances are examples of the latter. Different types of poems, words, music, percussive and other sounds are used as sources of ideas, stimulation and accompaniment.

Games teaching is concerned with the acquisition and improvement of the basic skills of throwing, catching, running, jumping, marking, dodging, kicking, dribbling, aiming, hitting, bowling, intercepting, trapping, fielding and developing an understanding of what is meant by playing a game.

Gymnastics is about developing skilled whole body actions both on the floor and on apparatus. Actions such as travelling on different parts of the body, jumping and landing safely, stillness and balance, swinging and hanging are varied by changing dynamics and the use of space. By selecting and linking actions together, gymnastic phrases are formed; these in turn are combined to form increasingly complex skilful sequences.

Organizational strategies and teaching techniques

The lesson plan for games, gymnastics and dance presents a very clear framework and is likely to be of great assistance to your teachers. Furthermore, organizational strategies relating to individual, whole class and group teaching tie in closely with the lesson structure. It is likely that the appropriate employment of the major teaching techniques will have to be stressed, or possibly introduced, as in the past there has often been little teacher intervention during PE lessons. You may need to help them make use of demonstrations, questions, explanations, instructions, comments, suggestions and so on.

Recognizing progress

PE is essentially a practical subject and so teachers need to use skills of observation in order to assess individual levels of attainment and also to recognize obstacles to progress. Such skills will probably need to be developed as it is unlikely that teachers will have been asked to evaluate children's attainment in areas of PE activity before. This is when the simple assessment sheets based on the EKSS will prove very useful, but practice and guidance from you will probably be necessary. You may need to stress that although there are no mandatory assessments for PE, continuous assessment of progress is necessary as an integral part of the teaching process.

Teachers will need to be helped to focus their attention on:

- the child's levels of performances in the different activities;
- the child's compositions, the structure and quality of a game, dance or gymnastic sequence devised.
- the child's spoken and written evaluations, of both personal performances and those of others.

The other types of assessment required of teachers at Key Stage 2 relate to fitness and health and are more straightforward. This part of the curriculum can be easily integrated into classroom work in science and include IT.

The task of the PE coordinator is to find ways of helping teachers to make more or less simultaneous advances in all three areas, that is, knowledge and understanding, organizational strategies and teaching techniques and the ability to recognize progress. You may find it helpful to discuss some of the following suggestions for INSET with your headteacher, senior teachers and other colleagues. By first identifying their priorities and gaining their co-operation, you can proceed with confidence to tackle the hard work and preparation which lie ahead, knowing that you have the approval of everyone concerned.

- Concentrate on one activity at a time, perhaps throughout a term.
- Visit at an early stage to observe work in another school. It could prove to be highly motivating, particularly if there is the opportunity to also to talk to the teachers concerned. Consult a PE expert in a local Institute of Higher Education or your LEA PE adviser so that an appropriate school is chosen. Remember that although only good

practice should be observed, very advanced work can have a negative effect on insecure staff as it seems to be so far out of reach. It is also very important that teachers are clear on the precise purpose and nature of the visit. You will therefore need to have prior discussions with your counterpart in the school concerned.

- Give Demonstration lessons. They are generally very helpful in generating interest and developing confidence. If you do these yourself then you can tailor them more exactly to suit the needs of the teachers concerned. You may also be able to persuade a member of staff who already has some expertise to give others the opportunity to observe a classroom teacher in action in PE. This could be very encouraging as teachers can often identify more easily with a colleague. The value of the experience would be increased still further if followed by a short discussion. Another possibility is to bring in a PE expert from the local college or LEA, but in all instances you must make careful preparations in order to gain maximum benefits from your considerable efforts.

- Try team teaching involving any of the above personnel. In this case you must ensure that the teachers are purposefully involved and not acting merely as child minders. Considerable thought needs to be given as to how the teacher(s) can be given varying degrees of responsibility appropriate to their individual needs.

- Provide videotape recordings as an invaluable INSET resource for the PE coordinator. At the end of this chapter you will find details of those which are available for sale or hire. Videotapes are a versatile teaching aid, for sections can be repeated easily enabling you to illustrate key aspects relating to subject matter, organization, teaching techniques and evidence of progress. You can illustrate a single lesson or give an overview of a PE activity in the primary school. In both cases the videotapes can be used to convey a good deal of information in an efficient and often entertaining manner as well as provoke that all important discussion when issues can be raised and anxieties dealt with.

Before using any videotape make sure that you are fully familiar with its contents, that you have noted the relevant numbers – and that as far as possible you have confidence in the machine!

- There are likely to be courses available locally which are relevant to your teachers' needs. You could also make suggestions to your LEA or local Institute of Higher Education, thereby initiating the kind of course you want rather than just waiting for one to happen. Of course, in both cases you must have the support of your headteacher before embarking on any organizing, persuading and encouraging the staff to take part in any type of INSET during school or personal time.

Achieving Consistency

There are a number of basic important issues on which there must be agreement among the staff if consistency in the implementation of the PE curriculum is to be achieved. You should take into account the national PE curriculum general requirements as well as guidelines from your LEA and professional associations such as the Physical Education Association, as you work towards achieving consensus on the following matters:

- Pupils' clothing, footwear and protection for different activities. The footwear of staff should also be considered;
- rules concerning safe conduct within various PE activities;
- the correct lifting, carrying, placing, fixing, checking and use of all apparatus and equipment;
- the general teaching approach and employment of organizational strategies;
- recording of progress;
- equality of both access and opportunity in all aspects of PE;
- provision for children with special educational needs in PE, including those with impairments, those with exceptional abilities and those from ethnic minority groups.

Many of these issues are associated with safe practice in PE, and you will probably find that your teachers are more than willing to reach agreement on such crucial procedures. Complying with safety procedures is an important part of PE for children as the national curriculum document underlines. Safe conduct also opens up opportunities for teacher and pupils alike, as many of the anxieties which can occur are removed when there are clear and enforceable limits and rules. Thus, the more able children are free to develop within the limits set, while those who are more timid benefit from the security provided.

The School PE Document

The PE document will illustrate the whole-school approach to PE which will always be your overall aim. Thus by bringing together the major components referred to in this chapter, a total picture will be presented to your headteacher and colleagues. The PE document should be user friendly, always available for consultation, and include the following:

- School policy statement;
- PE timetable;
- overall scheme of work;
- sample lesson plans;
- resources available for each activity;
- agreed safety procedures;
- provision for equality of both access and opportunity;
- current information on INSET, facilities and expertise in the local community.

It probably seems an enormous or even impossible task at this stage to compile such a document, but remind yourself that it will be built up gradually and will be the natural result of your discussions and consultations. You will also be able to make good use of the materials listed in the Resources section at the end of this chapter. Once the basic document is in place you can then add, subtract and alter in any way as the need arises.

Meanwhile, make the teaching of PE as easy as possible for the staff:

> Supply sample lesson plans.
> Provide ample resources materials.
> Organize and label boxes of PE equipment.
> Indicate clearly where gymnastic apparatus is to be stored in the hall.
> Make available simple record sheets.

Evaluating your Own Progress as a PE Curriculum Coordinator

Probably the best indicator of your ultimate success as PE Coordinator is when you find that you are scarcely needed! When everything is running smoothly and your main efforts are reduced to updating the school PE document and inducting new members of staff into the system you have created then you will realize that all your hard work has come to fruition. However, between now and that happy day you will want some indications of the positive impact you are beginning to have. You can look for encouraging signs within yourself and also in the changing attitudes of the head, staff, pupils and parents. There will always be setbacks, they happen to everyone whatever their situation; you should learn from any mistakes but not dwell on them. Instead focus on the growing number of signals you will begin to recognize.

In yourself

> Continued enthusiasm for PE and the task in hand.
> Growth in confidence.
> Respect and co-operation from the staff.
> The school PE document is in place *and* actually works.
> Progressively less effort is needed as the job becomes less of a battle.
> Sufficient interest in the various aspects of PE among pupils and staff leads to the establishment of a number of clubs outside school time.
> Requests are received from other teachers, schools or colleges to visit your school.

From the head

> PE automatically appears on the agenda of every staff meeting.
> The subject is given its fair share of resources.
> PE is established as an integral part of the school curriculum.
> You begin to anticipate reasonable support and encouragement for your various ventures.
> The head refers to PE regularly and in positive terms.

Among the staff

> There is evidence of growing interest in PE among members of staff.
> Confidence in teaching various aspects of PE increases.
> No-one avoids teaching the subject.
> PE becomes a topic of conversation at break times and is spoken of in increasingly positive terms.
> Teachers begin to take the initiative more frequently, suggesting lesson material, ideas for INSET, alternative organizational or teaching approaches.
> Withdrawal of a child from PE either as a punishment for a misdemeanour or for additional coaching in another subject is never contemplated.
> Genuine links are made between areas of PE and other curriculum subjects.
> Interest is expressed in PE courses currently available.
> When approached, offers to give demonstration or team-teaching lessons are made more readily.
> New members of staff are given support and encouragement by their colleagues.
> PE is regarded by everyone as an important constituent of the curriculum.

Among pupils

> There is enthusiasm for PE throughout the school.
> Standards of performance, compositions and evaluations in the various areas of PE gradually improve.
> Concentration increases.
> There are no behaviour problems.
> Safe practice is increasingly the norm.
> Pupils are interested in monitoring their own and others' progress in PE, levels of fitness, and so on.
> Pupils want to help each other improve.
> There are clear and obvious differences in the general attainment levels among the age groups.
> Clubs outside school time are requested and then consistently well supported.

Among parents

> PE is regarded as an important and worthwhile curriculum subject.
> Staff and pupils are supported in their efforts.
> Those with expertise offer help with clubs and teams.
> Those without sporting expertise offer moral and other forms of support.
> During Open Days and parent–teacher meetings interest is expressed in the PE programme.

These are the main points. The recognition of any *one* of them should be a cause for celebration; it is very unlikely that all of them will ever be ticked off. Unfortunately, whatever the circumstances you inherit, the job is never going to be as easy as that. However, perseverance and enthusiasm will pay dividends, and you can be sure that as PE curriculum coordinator you will never be bored!

Resources: Written Materials

SANDERSON, P. (1988) 'Physical education and dance' in ROBERTS, T. (ed.) *Encouraging Expression: Arts in the Primary Curriculum*, London, Cassell.
 This chapter gives valuable overviews of PE curriculum content, progression, teaching techniques, organization, safety aspects and special needs.

Two curriculum leader's handbooks published by LEAs are useful particularly for lesson planning and content, lists of suppliers of equipment, curriculum text books, and so on:

HEREFORD AND WORCESTER COUNTY COUNCIL (1991) *The Physical Education Curriculum Leader's Handbook*, Worcester.

JONES, B. (1990) *Curriculum Leadership in Physical Education*, Durham LEA and University of Newcastle-upon-Tyne.

A national curriculum resource pack which provides lots of helpful information and ideas (SEN included) especially in relation to gymnastics teaching and health-related fitness is available from: Persil Funfit, PO Box 360, Warrington, Cheshire WA4 6LB.

You will probably find that your LEA has produced guidelines on various aspects of the PE curriculum. LEA publications which are particularly useful include those of Coventry and Staffordshire. The relevant addresses are:

City of Coventry, Elm Bank Teacher's Centre, Mile Lane, Coventry CV1 2WN.

Staffordshire County Council, PE Section, Education Offices, Tipping Street, Stafford ST16 2DH.

Curriculum journals which are well worth consulting include:

The British Journal of Physical Education and *Primary PE Focus* both published by the Physical Education Association details of which are given below.

Drama and Dance promoted by Leicester Education Committee and available from AB Printers Ltd, 33 Cannock Street, Leicester, LE4 7HR.

Dance Matters published by the National Dance Teachers Association. (See below for address.)

All of these publications include invaluable information for the busy curriculum PE leader relating to current developments, curriculum materials including actual lesson plans and schemes, forthcoming courses and conferences, relevant resources, and so on.

Resources: Audio-Visual Materials and PE Equipment

Videotapes and films on various aspects of the PE curriculum may be bought or hired from:

Ds Information Systems Limited, NAVAL, The Arts Building, Normal College (Top Site), Siliwen Road, Bangor, Gwynned LL57 2DZ.

Concord Video and Film Council, 201 Felixstowe Road, Ipswich IP3 9BJ.

A videotape on teaching dance in the primary school is available on free loan from:

BBC School Radio Cassette Service, Broadcasting House, London W1A 1AA.

Very good tapes of music for dance as well as booklets on dance ideas are produced by:
BBC Educational Publishing, PO Box 234, Wetherby, West Yorkshire LS23 7EU.

Primary school gymnastics is the subject of a videotape produced by Manchester Education Committee in association with:
Continental Sports Products Company, Paddock, Huddersfield HD1 4SD.

Continental Sports Products is also a well-established supplier of PE equipment.

PE and Dance Professional Organizations

If at all possible you or your school should join the national PE Association (PEA) which publishes the two curriculum journals referred to above:
The Physical Education Association, Ling House, Francis House, Francis Street, London SW1 1DG.

You can become a member of the National Dance Teachers Association which publishes *Dance Matters* by writing to:
NDTA Treasurer, 29 Larkspur Avenue, Walsall, Staffordshire WS7 8SR. There may also be a local PE and/or dance association which you could join where you would make contact with other curriculum coordinators, share ideas, receive advice, support and information. The National Associations for PE and Dance should be able to supply the relevant information or you could contact your LEA.
Other organizations which offer very useful advice and information are:
Central Council for Physical Recreation (CCPR), Francis House, Francis Street, London SW1 1DG.
Education Unit, The Arts Council, Piccadilly, London W1.

The latter, along with Regional Arts Associations, deal only with the dance element of PE. You may want to contact them particularly about the Dance Artists in Schools scheme as part of your school's curriculum development.

References

ALEXANDER, R., ROSE, J. and WOODHEAD, C. (1992) *Curriculum Organization and Classroom Practice in Primary Schools*, London, DES.
CALOUSTE GULBENKIAN FOUNDATION (1989) *The Arts in the Primary School*, London.
FROSTIG, M. and MASLOW, P. (1973) *Learning Problems in the Classroom*, New York, Grune and Stratton.
KEPHART, N.C. (1960) *The Slow Learner in the Classroom*, Columbus, OH, Charles Merrill.

NATIONAL CURRICULUM COUNCIL (NCC) (1989) *A Framework for the Primary Curriculum*, York.

NATIONAL CURRICULUM COUNCIL (NCC) (1995) *Physical Education in the National Curriculum*, York.

OFFICE FOR STANDARDS IN EDUCATION (OFSTED) (1994) *Primary Matters*, London.

PHYSICAL EDUCATION ASSOCIATION (1987) *Report of a Commission of Enquiry*, London, Ling House.

SANDERSON, P. (1994) 'Unifying the approach to physical education', in HARRISON, M. (ed.) *Beyond the Core Curriculum*, Plymouth, Northcote House.

Chapter 14

Sounding the Right Note

Anthony Walker

The teaching and learning of music have been generally clothed in a mystique, generating the notion that music is best left for expert musicians to perform, understand and appreciate. However, this chapter aims to show that, once the aura has been removed, music making in the junior years can be as enjoyable and exhilarating for all pupils and teachers as it was during the infant years.

As music coordinator you will be in a leading position of helping children to engage in the interdependent activities of performing, composing and listening with growing skill and fulfilment. Through careful preparation, organization and reflection you will be able to unite a variety of approaches and shared musical accomplishments among staff and children. Yours will be a challenging role in the formulation and provision of music for children across the whole school.

In Harmony with Others

Your musical relationships in school will be diverse and crucial to the success of planning, policies and teaching strategies. These relationships can be seen as follows:

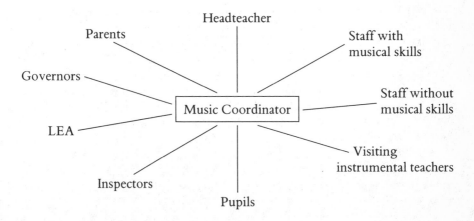

First Meetings with Headteacher and Staff

A basic aim of your work as the music coordinator will be to help colleagues take music with their own classes. Helping staff to build on past experiences, introducing new ideas and investigating hidden capabilities among colleagues (many of whom may be anxious about teaching music) are all part of your role. When talking to your headteacher and colleagues try to be aware that there can be apprehension, diffidence and insecurity in this curricular field. Always make formal and informal approaches and requests in a sensitive and encouraging manner, mindful of musical and professional relationships.

Some Questions to Ask your Headteacher

- What is the current music provision in the school?
- Does documentation already exist in school on the music curriculum? Is it in the school's policy statement?
- What are the head's own priorities regarding the music curriculum?
- Do opportunities already exist for the children to compose, perform and listen to music?
- Do the children experience a balanced blend of music from different styles, cultures and traditions?
- Are music activities occasionally shared with parents, governors, the local community and other schools?
- What timetable arrangements and funding will be needed so that teachers can meet the needs of national curriculum music?
- Are national curriculum, LEA and school guidelines in music available for staff consultation?

A Programme for Music at Key Stage 2

One beneficial result of the national curriculum in music might be that many teachers will feel relieved that general guidelines have been set for the subject. The all too common circumstances in which music featured largely as a flagship for public events (the Christmas carol festivities; end-of-year concert; local schools music festival) and little else, should now be overridden. You will now have the chance to draw up a whole-school music policy and schemes of work both curricular and extra-curricular – according to your school's human and material resources – to fulfil the demands of the national curriculum.

The focus of your music planning should be the Orders for National Curriculum Music. In order to explain the main requirements to your colleagues you should firstly be familiar with them yourself. You may have to attend to the essentials because teachers are already under pressure with details from many other subjects.

Essential Information

Since the published Order for National Curriculum Music (April, 1992) the Dearing Review has reduced the statutory content:

> The overall aim of the changes to the music Order is to clarify the essential skills, knowledge and understanding which should be taught, whilst safeguarding the breadth of the curriculum. (*Music in the National Curriculum: Draft Proposals*, May 1994, p. ii).

There are two attainment targets (ATs) –

AT1: Performing and Composing
AT2: Listening and Appraising

The ATs are shown by means of end of Key Stage descriptions for Music (EKSDs) which point to the nature and span of performance which pupils should exhibit by the end of a Key Stage. It is stressed that requirements from both ATs should be brought together, whenever possible, in order to develop pupils' understanding and enjoyment of music.

Key Stage 2

AT1: Pupils perform accurately and confidently, making expressive use of the musical elements and showing awareness of phrase. They sing songs and rounds that have two parts, and maintain independent instrumental lines with awareness of the other performers. They select and combine appropriate resources, use musical structures, make expressive use of musical elements and achieve a planned effect. They use symbols when performing and communicating musical ideas.

AT2: Pupils respond to music, identifying changes in character and mood, and recognize how musical elements and resources are used to communicate moods and ideas. They evaluate their own work, identifying ways in which it can be improved. They begin to recognize how music is affected by time and place, including, where appropriate, the intentions of the composer(s) and performer(s). They listen with attention to detail and describe and compare music from different traditions, using a musical vocabulary.

There are three parts to the Programme of Study (PoS):

1 Introductory statements defining the range of musical activities and breadth of repertoire for listening and performing.

2 The opportunities that should be given to pupils are:
AT1
- control of sounds made by the voice and instruments;
- performing with others;
- composing;
- communication of musical ideas.

AT2
- listening to, and developing understanding of, music;
- responding to and evaluating music.

3 Definitions of the essential skills, knowledge and understanding to be taught to pupils. Progression and direct relationships across Key Stages have been refined. Non-statutory examples have been greatly reduced.

There are no standard assessment tasks (SATs) in music. The EKSDs are planned to help teachers judge how their pupils' attainment in performing and composing, listening and appraising meets national expectations. Assessment should be continuous and founded on the teacher's observations. (See section on Assessment).

Be Aware and Keep Up-to-date

- Become familiar with the new Orders circulating in schools in January 1995, which will be implemented in August 1995.
- With the above documentation to hand, try to locate gaps in the present music provision in your school.
- Make a careful note of the progression required in the transition from Key Stage 1 to Key Stage 2, building on the children's musical achievements.
- Do not attempt to create a policy/statement/scheme for Key Stage 2 music on your own. All staff should be involved from the start. A successful music curriculum should be a goal for everyone.
- Try writing up some simple statements and criteria for broad areas of music assessment prior to any meetings – use the PoS for music Key Stage 2, any LEA guidelines and existing school documentation, incorporating links between music and other subjects.
- There might already be a school music document from which you can begin. It will have strengths and weaknesses. There may be missing parts such as the use of IT in music. Bear in mind that there are many ways of writing up such a document.

Musical Elements

As well as being aware of current directions in music in schools, establishing cross-curricular links and gradually formulating your own philosophy of music education, you should never lose sight of the elements or concepts that are unique to music. At Key Stage 2 pupils are required to be taught to identify basic elements of music by three means: investigating; distinguishing; internalizing. There are seven basic elements:

- Pitch: gradations of pitch; chords;
- Duration: pulse; metre and rhythm;
- Dynamics: different levels of volume; accents; silence;
- Tempo: gradations of speed;
- Timbre: different qualities of sound;
- Texture: different ways sounds are put together; melody and accompaniment;
- Structure: different ways sounds are organized in simple forms; phrase; repetition; contrast; ostinato (a musical pattern which is repeated many times); melody.

A Sample Music Scheme

Principal features of your work as music coordinator will be to find out about current music provision in your school, discussing, both formally and informally, with staff the national curriculum order and promoting a whole-school approach to music. The following is intended to assist you in the construction of a scheme of work appropriate to Key Stage 2:

Performing and Composing

Singing: Develop control of breathing, sense of phrasing, shape of vowels and clarity of vocal production and diction. Do plenty of unaccompanied singing. Ensure that the children sing a wide variety of songs, including unison, rounds and simple two-part pieces. Sing songs from memory.

Rhythm: Perform musical patterns of growing length/complexity. Create rhythmic ideas and rhythmic accompaniments for voice and instruments. Introduce more advanced music/action songs, body movement and dance to further the child's rhythmic skills and experiences.

Pitch: Using voice sounds, objects from the environment and musical instruments, investigate and perform high/low, repeated notes, steps and skips between notes. Melodic shapes can be explored with hand movements and drawings. Add notes together to form chords.

Composing: Using stimuli of all kinds (words, numbers, a poem, a picture, a story, a dance, a mood, an event, an outing, etc.) improvise musical ideas, both rhythmic and melodic. Explore the many resources of music (voices, instruments and material objects), organizing them into musical structures such as singing conversations, question and answer music, chord sequences of your own (e.g., C chord, F chord, C chord) repeated and contrasted sections, verse and chorus, solo and group. It is essential to allow the children to improve on and practise their compositions, whether created by individuals or groups. Allowing pupils the freedom to work on their own ideas calls for sensitive comments and care in direction. Always ensure that the music is performed, helping the children to communicate their musical ideas to others.

Children's attempts at composing can be effectively linked to listening to music from past centuries, the contemporary setting and other cultures. Such links can inspire and broaden children's listening and music-making in both ATs. Children's music can be stored in several ways. Encourage your colleagues to adopt a variety of means:

- Symbolic notation
- Graphic notation
- Staff notation

- Memory
- Cassette recorder
- Computer

Notation: Extend the children's work on using symbols to record their compositions. Refine and develop ways of writing music down by colours, shapes, words, numbers and diagrams. Graphic scores (using symbols to stand for pitch, duration, dynamics, tone quality, etc.) are useful recording agents. Introduce staff notations gradually, perhaps beginning with a single/two/three line stave and employing tonic sol–fa.

Take care to emphasize that sense of hearing is central to any work in music. Many other cultures rely entirely on an aural heritage. It is easy to fall into the trap of purely notated music, neglecting the development of children's memory, aural sense, impromptu thinking and decision making and powers of improvisation.

Listening and Appraising

The children identify sounds made by a variety of voices and instruments, individually and when heard together. They listen to music from different times, places and cultures, responding to, and discussing, the moods and styles of such music. The pieces, or extracts from pieces, selected for listening should broaden pupils' knowledge, experience and appreciation of our rich musical heritage, including:

- the European classical tradition;
- folk music;
- popular music;
- countries and areas of the British Isles;
- a variety of cultures;
- well-known composers;
- well-known performers.

Children's work in composing and performing can be linked to listening to music from other cultures, past centuries and the present time.

Try to develop an understanding of how music mirrors the time, location and circumstances in which it was written. Help the children to become acquainted with basic music concepts such as rhythm and pitch and to use this knowledge to assist in discussion of their own and others' music in a meaningful way.

Some Questions to Ask your Colleagues

- What is your present provision for music education in school?
- Are you given suggestions/plans to assist your classwork in music?
- In which areas of music do colleagues feel that they have much/little skill, understanding or confidence?
- Are teachers familiar with Key Stage 2 music requirements?
- Do you have an overall scheme of work, and is it used?
- Is there any link up or sharing of information between staff in this curricular area?
- Are teachers utilizing any guidelines from school, LEA, school broadcasting or published schemes in music?
- Are all teachers aware of the school's musical resources? Are there any gaps you consider need filling as a priority? Are present materials and instruments known to all and easily accessible?
- Are pupils' special musical needs identified and met?
- Do teachers ever attend music courses in or out of school? If so, is their developing expertise shared among colleagues?

The main aim of music teaching should be to encourage and assist understanding, sensitivity and enjoyment of music in children through the practical activities of performing, composing and listening. This should be at the heart of your school's policy document. It should give an overall outline to staff, reflecting a whole-school approach to music.

Your School Music Policy

A principal benefit arising in the formulation of a whole-school music policy is that of bringing staff together to discuss, consider and formulate aims and objectives for teaching music in the future. A well-considered, systematic policy will be a cornerstone in your music curriculum.

It will be your responsibility to promote music in your school. Therefore, try to become conversant with current trends and philosophy in music education in addition to national curriculum orders and guidelines. TAKE CARE – you are a new teacher and must be responsive and mindful of working with colleagues of disparate musical accomplishments, many of whom will be highly skilled and experienced classroom practitioners. Ask your colleagues to assist you (for example, in drawing up both an inventory and location of music resources) and respect their views and professional judgment.

When drawing up your school policy document ensure that all staff are involved. The following should help you in the compilation of your music policy document:

Policy ————————— How to Plan ————————— Procedure
schemes of work

- nature and
  value of music
- its contribution to
  education
- nature of learning
  and teaching
- styles of
  teaching
- gender issues
- cultural variety
- special needs

- involvement of all
  the staff
- coordinated across
  the curriculum
- involvement of any
  instrumental
  teachers

Strategy
- NC Key Stage 2
  stipulations
- aims and objectives
- links across the
  whole curriculum
- teaching methods and
  learning programmes
- differentiation
- progression
- use of resources
- assessment procedures

Remember a document is best described as practice into policy rather than the other way about. It can help you to think through the presentation of your practice and give guidance to future development for music education in your school. It should comprise a general statement of your school's agreed intentions in music, adapted to staff, governors, LEA and inspectors. Base it on the philosophy behind the National Curriculum Report for Music which states:

The study of music as a foundation subject should provide for the progressive development of:
- skills in movement, such as motor coordination and dexterity, and in aural imagery, acquired through exploring and organising sound;
- awareness and appreciation of organised sound patterns;
- sensitive, analytical and critical responses to music;
- the capacity to express ideas, thoughts and feelings through music;
- awareness and understanding of traditions, idioms and musical styles from a variety of cultures, times and places; and

- the experience of fulfilment which derives from striving for the highest possible artistic and technical standards. (pp. 3–4)

Music Goals

Together with your colleagues you will need to create space in the curriculum so that these goals can be met by pupils:

- practising and learning a number of songs from various cultures;
- developing skills in both pitched and unpitched instruments;
- creating and notating music;
- becoming musically literate;
- listening to and talking about a wide span of assorted kinds of music.

Suggest that your colleagues should try to develop an awareness of sound in pupils:

A good repertoire of songs, links with other aspects of music-making and the development of musical literacy should be included:

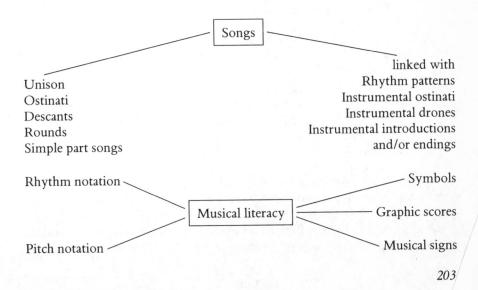

Your scheme of work should join together the requirements of the national curriculum order and your pupils' classroom music experiences. Setting out an intelligible, structured statement of music activities and experiences (related to the policies of the school) should prove to be an essential guide and reference document for your staff. It will prove vital to the progression, continuity and monitoring of your school's music programme.

Conducting Class Music

Ultimately, your headteacher has the responsibility of organizing staff in order to further the whole-school music curriculum. You may find that this obligation is given, in whole or in part, to you as music coordinator. Some schools have organized their teaching so that all staff teach music to their own classes; you will be expected to give assistance, advice and direction.

You must endeavour to encourage the development of musical skills and interests in the staff. Probably by an informal approach, to try to find out which of the staff:

- plays/used to play an instrument;
- sings in a church choir, musical society or operatic association;
- sings/plays in a folk, jazz or pop group;
- plays in an orchestra, band or group;
- can read music;
- has ever written or arranged music;
- attends concerts or listens to music regularly;
- has a knowledge of music from other cultures/traditions, e.g., Afro-Caribbean, Asian, Celtic, Polish, Ukrainian, etc;
- has relatives or friends who might be interested in joining school music events.

It would be useful to plan a friendly, informal meeting early in your first year as music coordinator in order to:

- gather information;
- decide on a plan of future music meetings;
- decide on who will prepare agendas for such meetings;
- ascertain how much time can be allotted to music meetings. When will they take place? lunch-time? after school?

A music workshop is a useful starting-point in finding out musical abilities and experience among the staff, in helping staff confidence when approaching music and in discussing whole-school planning for musical ideas. Conducted with the whole staff, or smaller groups, workshops can be invaluable in sharing knowledge, skills and experience. Look out for any in-service work or peripatetic support within your area. Try to bring the work of any visiting instrumental teachers closely into the developing school music curriculum as soon as possible. Your local university/college/LEA may run courses in school music. Look out for examples of good music planning and practice in nearby schools. It would be wise to establish links with the music department in a local secondary school. Associations concerned with music education can be a particularly gainful source of assistance for school music. (See the end of this chapter for names and addresses of these organizations).

Try to work on these areas in your first year as music coordinator.

Establish a determined, harmonious approach to music in school. Build up a co-operative and sharing whole-staff approach to music.

Take heed of the music suggestions from colleagues.

Observe and listen critically to children's singing, composing and listening activities.

Pay attention to the moods and feelings about music expressed by pupils and teachers.

Reflect on the work in music.

Evaluate – plan ahead – look for a development in skills, knowledge and understanding.

Music Links with Other Statutory Subjects

Here are some lines of action for integrated work.

• The topic or thematic approach: music can play its part in a number of ways, weaving into the topic with songs, stories with music, action games and composing.

• A visit or school outing (to the seaside, an urban farm, an art gallery, a science museum) may stimulate a response such as the creation of simple rhythms or melodies, or a sound recording.

• Music can contribute towards the understanding of another subject, for example the study of an historical period. Care in planning is essential. It is wise to reflect on the musical elements discussed earlier in this chapter, thereby ensuring that the conceptual framework of ideas in music is not disregarded. Examples of links which can serve as starting-points for integrated work in music and other subject areas:

English	• The rhythm of words.
	• Inventing rhythms and chants to words.
	• The words of songs stimulating language development, articulation, control and delivery.
	• Singing songs and thereby developing pronunciation, vocabulary, accentuation, feeling for colour and shape, sense of phrasing.
	• Music contributing to dramatic presentations.

- Setting poems to music.
- Narrative forms and musical structures.

Mathematics
- Counting and number songs.
- Basic counting of simple rhythms, single notes, beats, bars, rests and time.
- Sorting sounds and silences into groups and sets.
- Exploring shapes and patterns in mathematics and music.

Science
- The production, transmission and reception of sound.
- Sounds from the environment – listening, identifying and copying.
- Sounds produced in many ways from many sources.
- The raw materials of music.
- How instruments work: construction and care.
- Sorting and controlling sounds.

History
- Music and its place in the history of people, different eras and countries.
- Music from different centuries/periods of history.
- Music as a stimulus to the study of history – style, instruments and resources.

Geography
- Music from various countries and cultures.
- Music bringing to life a sense of place.
- Differing musical traditions in different continents.
- Recorded music from across the world.
- Contemporary music from other countries.

Art
- Responding to music by creating a picture/collage/design.
- Pictorial/symbolic representation of music by shapes, patterns, structures and textures.
- Responding to a picture by composing music.
- The colour of paint and the timbres of music.

Physical Education
- The shared dimension of time.
- Music as a stimulus for dance.
- Rhythmic movement: fast and slow.
- Exploration of moods and feelings.
- Matching music and movement.
- Free movement and active listening.

Technology
- Using a computer to create, edit or store sounds.
- Writing a music score with IT.
- Designing and making simple musical instruments.
- Investigating instruments.

Religious	• Music's contribution and role in religious ceremonies.
Education	• Hymns and religious songs in corporate acts of worship.

Musical Resources

You will notice that individual schools vary widely in the resources that are available. In some schools music classes take place in the school hall (principally because the school piano is located there) or in a music/drama area. Many teachers, of course, use their own classroom for music sessions. Baskets and trays are essential for the storage and transportation of instruments. One or more trolleys for storing instruments are a great asset; they allow instruments to be moved easily, rapidly and safely to different parts of the school.

You will need to audit the present provision of instruments and list the additional ones necessary to the promotion of a music curriculum that meets the national curriculum order. Some instruments will be essential; others can be purchased later.

Action Now

- Note the instruments that are in working order. Note their type, number, condition and location.
- Set up a repair programme for those in poor condition.
- Identify gaps in provision.
- Sketch out plans for future upkeep (maintenance and tuning of pianos, sets of spare beaters, guitar strings, etc.).

The following should assist you in establishing items of school music equipment:

Basic Classroom Percussion (untuned)

These do not give a definite pitched sound, but add rhythm, variety and colour.

Woodblocks	– including two-tone woodblocks, wooden agogo, claves, temple or tulip block.
Drums	– including tambour, snare drum (various sizes), bongos, tabla drums.
Tambourines	– headless and headed in various sizes.

Maracas	– especially tricoloured ones.
Castanets	– on a handle.
Triangles	– small and large, with holder and metal beater.
Bells	– of various size including Indian bells, sleigh bells, stick jingles, bell trees and cowbell.
Cymbals	– suspended or fitted with knobs, miniature cymbals, finger cymbals.
Guiro	– especially tricoloured fish guiro.
Gong	

Basic Classroom Percussion (tuned)

These give notes of definite pitch and can be used for tunes and chords.

Chime bars	– several full sets.
Xylophone	– start with alto.
Glockenspiel	– start with alto.
Bass resonator bars	

Other Useful Instruments

There are many invaluable, inexpensive and exciting instruments from Eastern and Western cultures. They will add variety and colour to your school music.

Bodhran	– played with a double beater.
Cabasa Afuche	– Latin percussion. Beads spin round a cylinder.
Calabash	– African dried gourd with a loose mesh of woven pieces.
Shekere Kabassa	– as above, but with a mesh of beads/seeds.
Gato Drum	– wooden tone bars of different lengths.
Dholak	– a small two-skin drum, with a different sound from each skin.
Kokoriko	– old Japanese *domino* sound.

Gongbells, Rattles and Thumb Pianos from West Africa.

Ratchet Vibraslap Whistles Wind Chimes Mouth Organ
Flexatone Rainmaker Zither Autoharp Recorders Pipes

Alto/tenor metallophone (diatonic)
Bass xylophone/metallophone (diatonic)
Soprano xylophone/glockenspiel
An assortment of beaters – felt-headed, plastic, rubber and wood. Metal
                  beaters for triangles.
Brushes
Tuning forks (A and C).
Music stands   – full-size adjustable and desk stands.
Cassette player, microphone and plenty of blank tapes.
Modified instruments for children with disabilities.
Guitars   – acoustic and electric.
Piano.
MIDI keyboards with full-size keys, drumpad assigning and multi-track
    sequencing facility.
An overhead projector with screen is very useful for group composing/
    performing activities.

IT in Music

From the time the first musical instrument was made, music technology has existed. Today the impact of electronic equipment, tape and cassette recorders and computers on music in schools is highly significant. At the present day you no longer have to be a performer to be a composer; further, it is not always necessary for you to get players together in order to hear the results of your work.

As coordinator you should aim at eventually being able to provide assistance with audio equipment, recording strategies and computer software. Many teachers at Key Stage 2 will be new to the world of music technology; advice and potential materials can be gained from your school's IT coordinator, primary teaching and micro-journals, LEAs and music education centres.

There are now packages to support the music curriculum, enabling children of all ages and abilities to compose and to learn music theory. A synthesizer as well as conventional instruments can be used to create imaginative, expressive sounds. The computer, a MIDI interface and a keyboard provide a wide range of children with hitherto restricted opportunities. Mid Sussex Softwares, Sherston Software, AB European Marketing, Impac, Acorn Resource Centre and Longman Logotron produce software suited to national curriculum requirements. Details of such products can be found in your local music shop, resource centre or teachers' centre. The monthly journal *The Music Teacher* carries regular articles and information about IT in music.

A recent programme, produced by IMPAC Resources, is particularly useful for teachers who are new to the use of computers in music. Entitled *Music Picturebook*, it helps children to create their own music. Graphic scores, pictures and patterns can be invented, the music being recorded using a MIDI keyboard, microphone or horn (played like a recorder). An accompanying file has topic ideas, worksheets and clear instructions. The Soundbeam Project, launched in 1990, produces *Soundbeam*, which works by sending out an ultrasonic ray which responds to movements including the tiniest gestures. It converts information about movement and distance into MIDI code, sending instructions to electronic instruments. A new expressive medium for the exploration of movement and composing sounds, it is accessible across a wide ability/mobility range.

The Next Movement: Assessment and Progression

The objective assessment of children's achievement in music is an area where most primary teachers have no experience. This is in great contrast to the familiar graded examinations of the national colleges of music, which are among the oldest forms of assessment by public examination. There are no music SATs, but an assessment procedure should be designed that closely relates to the national curriculum. Its main principles should be

- a straightforward, unambiguous scheme that will prove helpful to teachers, parents and pupils;
- assessment should be part of normal classroom procedures such as composing, singing and playing, making reasonable demands on time;
- take into consideration extra-curricular activity or instrumental teaching;
- teachers and pupils should be involved together in the assessments: self-assessment helps pupils to come to an understanding of their strengths and weaknesses;
- design assessment procedures to fit the needs of all your pupils;
- assess pupils' musical skills in a continuous way, taking care that all methods should be valid, reliable and undertaken with sensitivity;
- observe pupils working on their own and as members of a group;
- in addition to judging technical skills, we must never disregard the pupil's features of creativity, imagination and musicianship.

Instead of marks, scores or tick lists, teachers make judgments based on accumulated evidence. The EKSDs will assist you in gauging each pupil's attainment. Some points to note:

- Keep cumulative records on pupils;
- Observe children working in music (e.g., on a song, a composition or a discussion). Try to interact musically with children, assessing the process as well as the product;
- Persuade teachers to share criteria and vocabulary and to moderate each other's judgments;

- We must concern ourselves with the cultivation of musical skills, concepts, attitudes and understanding;
- Try to chart the child's progress in curriculum music over a period of time, noting how it is built into the child's overall development and the class to which he or she belongs.

Good music assessment will not only identify an individual's strengths and weaknesses in, for example, playing a percussion instrument in a group or singing a whole-class song, but also enable you to be analytic and perceptive about your future music planning. Note that in 1996–97, the case for extending the scope of teacher assessments to the foundation subjects is to be reviewed by the Secretary of State.

Coda

Music should not be an extra in school life, solely an accompaniment to speech days and assemblies, or purely a subject for musically gifted children. Schools now have the chance to give opportunities for all children to experience the joys and challenges of a broad music curriculum.

Your pupils' lives will be enriched by music experiences in school. Your committment, leadership and enthusiasm will be crucial factors in promoting the place of music in the primary curriculum.

References and Resources

This is a brief section on resources, including key, up-to-date publications. Basic information on schemes, music and books on music can be obtained from educational publishers, music suppliers and articles and advertisements in music and education journals. Sample music schemes may be seen on approval from publishers, at exhibitions or teachers' centres. It would be wise to search out other schools which already use published schemes; this would provide you with first-hand estimates of their appropriateness. It will be impossible to find a scheme entirely and fully suited to your own school. You will always require extra resources such as songs, cassettes, stories about composers and their music, and music computer software. Ideally these will be based in a central music resource in school under your supervision.

Official Publications

Additional Advice to the Secretary of State for Education and Science on Non-Statutory Statements of Attainment in Art. Music and Physical Education (1992) York, NCC.
Aspects of Primary Education: The Teaching and Learning of Music (1992) London, HMSO.

Music for ages 5 to 14 (1981) DES, London, 1991.
Music from 5 to 16, Curriculum Matters 4 (1985) HMSO, London.
Music in the National Curriculum: Draft Proposals (1994) London, SCAA.
Music in the National Curriculum: Draft Proposals (1995) London, DFE.
National Curriculum Council Consultation Report: Music (1992) York, NCC.
National Curriculum Music Working Group: Interim Report (1990) London, DES.

Books

Glover, J. and Ward, S. (1993) *Teaching Music in the Primary School: A Guide for Primary Teachers*. London, Cassell.
Mills, J. (1993) *Music in the Primary School*, Cambridge, Cambridge University Press.
Plummeridge, C. (1991) *Music Education in Theory and Practice*, London, Falmer Press.
Swanwick, K. (1979) *A Basis for Music Education*, Windsor, NFER-Nelson.
Swanwick, K. (1988) *Music, Mind and Education*, London, Routledge.

Useful Addresses

Associated Board of the Royal Schools of Music,
14, Bedford Square, London, WC1B 3JG.

Association for the Advancement of Teacher Education in Music,
331a Wightman Road, London, N8 0NA.

British Federation of Festivals,
Festivals House, 198 Park Lane, Macclesfield, Cheshire,
SK11 6UD.

British Kodály Academy,
Mary Place, 11 Cotland Acres, Pendleton Park, Redhill, Surrey,
RH1 6LB.
Provides training, courses and published materials, including video, based on the principles of the Hungarian music educator, Zoltán Kodály (1882–1967).

Coomber Electronic Equipment Ltd.,
Croft Walk (Nr. Pitchcroft), Worcester, WR1 3NZ.
Producers of fine quality sound equipment for schools.

Incorporated Society of Musicians,
10 Stratford Place, London, W1N 9AE.

Musician's Union,
National Office, 60/62, Clapham Road, London, SW9 0JJ.
Both associations listed above have a specialist section dealing with music in schools.

Music Advisers' National Association,
Avon House North, St. James Barton, Bristol, BS99 7EB.

Music Education Information and Research Centre,
University of Reading, Bulmershe Court, Woodlands Avenue,

Reading, Berks, RG6 1HY.

Connected to the Centre is the National Primary Music Consultancy Programme exhibiting primary music materials and providing courses in the promotion of classroom skills in musical leadership. It is also the base for the International Society for Music Education, organizing a biennial conference and publishing a journal and occasional papers.

Music for Youth,
4, Blade Mews, Deodar Road, London, SW13 2NN.

Orff Society (UK),
7, Rothsay Avenue, Richmond, Surrey, TW10 5EB.

Runs short courses on the practice of the Bavarian music educator, Carl Orff (1895–1982).

Schools Music Association,
Education Office, Town Hall, Friern Barnet, London, N11 3DL.

Sing for Pleasure,
25, Fryerning Lane, Ingatestone, Essex, CM4 0DD.

Organizes workshops and weekend courses to persuade people, especially the young, to sing.

Trinity College of Music (Music Education Department)
11–13, Mandeville Place, London, W1M 6AQ.

Provides courses on curriculum music. Recent topics have included the organization of wide-ability groups, musicianship and listening skills, documentation, record keeping and assessment.

UK Council for Music Education and Training,
13, Back Lane, South Luffenham, Oakham, Leicestershire, LE15 8NQ.

Notes on Contributors

Bill Boyle managed the University of Manchester teams researching and developing national curriculum assessment tests for geography at Key Stages 1 and 3 (SEAC 1991–93). During 1993–94 he led the development of assessment units for Key Stage 3 geography for the Northern Ireland SEAC and was a member of an advisory panel of assessment experts advising SCAA on the revisions to the geography order. Prior to working in the School of Education, he had nineteen years experience as primary teacher, headteacher and LEA adviser, writing more than fifty primary geography books and television programmes.

Dave Byrne has had twenty years of experience in primary education, including teaching in the UK, North Africa and Australia. Dave was a science coordinator and leader of a LEA advisory team for primary science. He is currently senior lecturer in science education at the North East Wales Institute. Dave writes frequently for education journals and has written a number of books which support teachers and children working in science in the national curriculum.

Alan Cross has taught classes of both infants and juniors. He was deputy headteacher of a Salford primary school and later led a LEA teacher advisory team for primary science and technology. Alan is now a lecturer in education in the School of Education at Manchester University where he leads courses in science and technology for the primary PGCE course. He has led projects dealing with the coordination of technology in schools and regularly leads inservice courses for teachers. At present he is researching the teaching of science and technology. He has written widely in the areas of science and technology, his publications include *Electricity through Stories* (1991) and *Design and Technology 5–11* (1994).

Julie Davies was a primary teacher and headteacher for thirteen years, after graduating in history from Cardiff University. She lectured at Crewe and Alsager College of HE before taking up a lectureship in education in the School of Education at the University of Manchester. She is responsible for teaching primary history to pre-service students and has been the editor of *Primary Historian* the journal of the Primary History Association. In addition, she is the author of several papers on early childhood education and she has a particular interest in teaching children to read. Julie is the editor of volume one in this series.

Mike Harrison, was a primary teacher and headteacher for sixteen years. A scientist, he is currently the Director of the Centre for Primary Education in the School of Education at the University of Manchester, where he has been responsible for science and mathematics in initial training and higher degree courses. He currently acts as leader for he Primary PGCE course and has run a variety of senior and middle-management training courses for the University and many LEAs. He is an OFSTED registered inspector specializing in mathematics, IT and school management. Since managing a project on the training of curriculum coordinators in the foundation subjects in the primary school he edited *Beyond the Core Curriculum*, published by Northcote House, aimed at helping primary teachers to coordinate the non-core foundation areas in the national curriculum. He is a joint author of *Primary School Management*, published by Heinemann Educational in January 1992 and has been appointed series editor for the three books in this series. He is editor of the second volume in this series.

Gwen Mattock taught in primary schools in the south of England for eleven years. Currently the leader of the Post-Graduate Certificate in Education Course at the Manchester Metropolitan University, she has been involved with in-service education for a number of years including a variety of courses on RE for a number of LEAs. She has published a pair of Teachers' Books in the Lutterworth Topic book series and contributed to *Bible Reading Notes for Young People*.

Judith Piotrowski is a lecturer in education at the University of Manchester where she teaches art to initial training students. She is currently coordinating a project looking at the role of coordinators in a number of LEAs. Prior to that she was a primary teacher for eight years and a lecturer at Crewe and Alsager College of HE in Primary Education and Special Needs.

Rita Ray, B.Ed. (Hons.), MA, Ph.D. Poet and Writer-in-School, working in Primary and Special schools. Writer of educational materials. Lecturer in Education, Primary Centre, University of Manchester. Previous experience: Research Associate working on the development of National Curriculum assessment materials for English in England and Wales and Northern Ireland. Reading Advisory Teacher, Salford LEA. Teacher in primary and special (MLD) schools.

Geoffrey R. Roberts formerly Director of the Centre for Primary Education in the University of Manchester, is author of amongst other books and papers *Teaching Children to Read and Write* and *Learning to Teach Reading*. He taught in secondary modern and primary schools and has lectured in Canada, the USA, Australia and Nigeria.

Patricia Sanderson has taught in various schools and colleges in the UK and the USA and at present lectures in the Education Department of Manchester University. Dr Sanderson has published a wide range of book chapters and articles on physical education and dance, and is currently a member of: the Curriculum Committee of the *Physical Education Asociation*, the Editorial Advisory Group of the *British Journal of Physical Education Research Supplement*, and the Editorial Board of the *European Physical Education Review*.

Anthony Walker taught music in schools for nineteen years prior to working in teacher training at De La Salle College of Higher Education, Manchester. Currently he is an honorary tutor in education at the University of Manchester where he teaches music to pre-service students and in-service primary school teachers. He was recently awarded a doctorate for his research in the field of music education. He has run a variety of in-service courses for the DES, the University and schools; in 1992 he was director of the summer course in music for primary teachers at the University of Bethlehem. A member of the former School's Council for Curriculum and Examinations and of several music examining bodies, he is the author of *Walter Carroll, The Children's Composer*, published by Forsyth in 1989.

Index